Books By Tahir Shah

Nasrudin
Travels With Nasrudin
The Misadventures of the Mystifying Nasrudin
The Peregrinations of the Perplexing Nasrudin
The Voyages and Vicissitudes of Nasrudin

Stories
The Arabian Nights Adventures
Scorpion Soup
Tales Told to a Melon
The Afghan Notebook
The Man Who Found Himself
The Caravanserai Stories
The Mysterious Musings of Clementine Fogg

Miscellaneous
The Reason to Write
Zigzag Think
Being Myself

Research
Cultural Research
The Middle East Bedside Book
Three Essays

Anthologies
The Anthologies
The Clockmaker's Box
Tahir Shah Fiction Reader
Tahir Shah Travel Reader

THE
TAHIR SHAH
FICTION READER

TAHIR SHAH

THE
TAHIR SHAH
FICTION READER

TAHIR SHAH

MMXXI

Secretum Mundi Publishing Ltd
Kemp House
City Road
London
EC1V 2NX
United Kingdom

www.secretum-mundi.com
info@secretum-mundi.com

First published by Secretum Mundi Publishing Ltd, 2021
VERSION 12052021

THE TAHIR SHAH FICTION READER

© TAHIR SHAH

Tahir Shah asserts the right to be identified as the Author of the Work
in accordance with the Copyright, Designs and Patents Act 1988.
A CIP catalogue record for this title is available from the British Library.

Visit the author's website at:

Tahirshah.com

ISBN 978-1-912383-77-1

CONTENTS

For the Tate Family

INTRODUCTION

ONCE UPON A time, deep in the forest, there was a little boy who lived in a wooden house built by his father's hands.

His name was Khial, which in Arabic means 'Imagination'.

Very much like other boys of his age, he spent his days down at the river, in the meadows, and on the roof of his family home, gazing up at the tapestry of stars.

On the night Khial was born, a diviner arrived, cloaked in a scarlet robe.

He blessed the babe in arms, and decreed:

'His life will be governed by a single quality, and one quality alone.'

The baby's mother and father exchanged an anxious glance. Neither dared ask what the quality was, for fear it could be inauspicious.

'This boy will have an imagination unlike any other that has ever existed,' the soothsayer said.

The mother seemed agitated.

'An imagination? What good is that?' she sobbed.

'Could he not be strong, brave, or wise?' the boy's father asked.

The diviner stared out of the window, his eyes feasting on the myriad of stars.

'There's nothing in the universe quite so important as an imagination,' he replied. 'So long as it's protected, it will protect him throughout his long and wondrous life.'

In accordance with his horoscope, the baby was named after the quality running through his veins. Raised with love and good sense, he was encouraged to dream big, and to develop his extensive imagination.

At school, the teachers punished Khial, insisting he was an unbridled fantasist. But at home, his parents marvelled at how their little son amused them with stories he'd invented right there and then.

From time to time, they would ask how he could be quite as imaginative as he was. Frowning, Khial would slip them a smile and say:

'It's not that I'm imaginative, but that others are not.'

One night, when their son was tucked up in bed, the parents sat at the fireside. As ever, their thoughts turned to the life and opportunities Khial would enjoy.

'He's a wonder,' the child's mother said, gloating.

'That may be so,' her husband replied, 'but the world out there doesn't need imaginations. It needs muscles, and brains!'

Lying awake in bed, Khial listened to the conversation downstairs. The more he heard of his parents' concerns, the more anxious he became.

'I'm cursed,' he whispered. 'While all the other boys are strong, bright, or both, I have nothing but this nonsensical imagination!'

Next day, the boy's parents were up early, tending to their chores. They were so busy they had forgotten the conversation from the night before.

Taking his place at the table, Khial was sullen.

His mother asked if he was feeling unwell.

'I don't know,' he said.

After breakfast, he padded down to the river, his head slung low.

The zest for life that on other days filled each footstep... was gone.

It was as though all the colour had been drained from the world – vivid hues replaced by shades of grey.

Once at the riverside, Khial scrabbled up into his favourite tree. A great oak, its boughs hung above the rush of water. Sitting there, his stare trained on the ashen world, he cleared his mind and sobbed.

All of a sudden, Khial gasped.

Sitting beside him, dressed in a blinding scarlet robe, was the figure of man.

'Who are you,' the boy asked, 'and how come your robe is the only colour I can see?'

'We've met before,' the ancient said, 'although you are unlikely to remember it.'

'What are you doing here?'

'I've come to give you a word of advice – nothing more, nothing less.'

Khial dabbed a hand to his eyes.

'I don't need advice,' he sobbed.

'On the contrary, I think you do – you see, without realizing it, you've done something that has in turn had an effect.'

'I don't know what you're talking about.'

The diviner smiled from the corner of his mouth.

'Last night, when your parents were arguing,' he said, 'you wished that you didn't have an imagination. And before you could understand what you'd wished for, your imagination drained away.'

Khial swallowed hard, his eyes roaming over the surface of the water and onto the soothsayer's face.

'Will it come back?'

'The only hope is if you appreciate it.'

'But I do! Last night I felt worthless, and now I've woken to find everything pale and grey.'

'Of course it is,' the diviner said. 'A world without imagination is like soup without any nourishment or taste.'

'So, now I appreciate it, how do I get my imagination back?' Khial asked.

The ancient smiled broadly.

'By going in search of it,' he said.

My name may not be Khial – but I am he, and he is me.

Throughout my boyhood, I was pitted against children who were physically strong, intellectual virtuosos, and others who had all sorts of gifts – universally hailed as nothing short of miraculous.

While they amazed each other, and those around them, at being able to lift heavy stones in the woods, or commit epic poems to memory, I sat by myself and slipped into a fantasy world of my own.

Sometimes I felt lonely but, as soon as I imagined, the loneliness melted away. And whenever I was bored, I retreated into the world I'd created for myself.

It was a realm I never spoke about, for fear of others making fun of me.

As years passed, I did my best to use the tool of imagination, in the same way that an inventor or a carpenter might do with their own gifts.

Little by little, I came to understand something pivotal:

Imagination is a muscle that grows in strength only when it's used.

When I started writing books thirty years ago, I started describing the quests I had made in search of adventure and oddity. In hindsight, those travelogues were shaped by a natural wellspring of imagination bubbling up within me.

It was years before I had the confidence to grab hold of the spirit of raw adventure that had guided my travels, and plead with it to guide me into the labyrinth of my own imaginary worlds.

This *Reader* contains an assortment of pieces mined from the books I've written. Although some are more imaginative than others, all share an inner quality that's centrally important to me – a hybrid of imagination and literary invention.

As far as I'm concerned, it's the holy grail of literature.

TAHIR SHAH

Few things fascinate me as much as the way our species allows itself to suspend disbelief in order to be wooed and wowed by a fantastical tale. Turning on a TV, we don't rail in disappointment at a story that's obviously a work of fantasy. Surely, there's a deep-seated reason for this.

My own sense is that the imagination is there to keep us sane, to iron out the kinks, and to heal us. Just as with Khial in the story, the lack of it causes a world of shadows. In the same way, a life brimming with creative and imaginary invention is surely the most intense experience.

I encourage anyone reading this to reach deep within themselves, to believe, and to tap into the lifeblood of imagination that's waiting to be harnessed within them.

The only two rules to follow are these:

(1)   Never doubt yourself.

(2)   Never stop until you're beyond the farthest horizon.

Tahir Shah

The Pastèque Kingdom

IN THE PASTÈQUE Kingdom there was nothing people liked more than melons.

They ate melons for breakfast, for lunch, and for dinner. They celebrated their birthdays with melons, and their weddings, too. All the melons they ate were striped green and black, as they were the only ones that grew in the cold, dark valley in which the kingdom stood.

One day, a young man called Wilbur Melonius fell in love with a girl named Esmeralda, who had eyes as green as the melons she – and everyone else – so adored.

Bending down on one knee, Wilbur asked her to marry him.

Esmeralda thought for a moment, then replied:

'If you love me so much, dear Wilbur, prove your love.'

'How shall I do that?' he asked, blank-faced.

'By finding me something no one has ever known before.'

'What kind of thing, dearest?'

Esmeralda narrowed her eyes, sniffed, and said:

'A delicious new kind of melon.'

'But, dearest…'

'I have spoken,' Esmeralda said. 'If you return with a delicious new kind of melon, I shall marry you… and if you do not return with one, I'll never speak to you again.'

'Return from where, my love?'

'From your adventure.'

With that, Esmeralda strolled back into her house, slamming the door behind her. Wilbur was left wondering where to go and what to do. He'd never been out of the kingdom before, and had no idea how to go about searching for anything, let alone a delicious new kind of melon.

But, being a resourceful young man, he climbed the path to the ruined castle at the top of the cliffs and sought out a wizard who lived there with his cat.

Explaining his predicament, he asked for advice.

'The solution is obvious,' the magician answered. 'Take to the road and don't return until you've found another kind of melon with which to impress Esmeralda.'

'But what if I don't find one?' he moaned.

'You'll have to deal with that if it happens, and not before.'

So, without even bidding his family farewell, Wilbur Melonius climbed down into the valley and set off on the road leading out of town – a road he'd never ventured upon until that very day.

After a few hours of trudging, Wilbur came to the border, where the Pastèque Kingdom ended, and the Land of Blinding Red Carrots began. Without giving it much thought, the young adventurer crossed the no-man's land, and walked on.

In truth, he was anxious at travelling alone in a land that was unfamiliar, but something goaded him on, as though it was his destiny to make the journey in exactly the way he was making it.

From time to time he would pass fields in valleys between the mountains. He saw that, unlike his own kingdom, the farmers were not growing melons, but abundant crops of bright red carrots.

Pausing for the night at a caravanserai, he went in search of food. At a small teahouse on the edge of the encampment, he asked for a watermelon with which to refresh himself.

'We don't have those here,' said the owner. 'All we have are blinding red carrots. There's carrot stew, carrot soup, and carrot dumplings.'

Wilbur gobbled down a bowl of hot carrot soup, thankful for it. But, in the back of his mind, he was already missing the taste of melons.

Next day, he continued, covering half the kingdom at a punishing pace. From time to time he came upon local crofters, all of whom were growing blinding red carrots. Whenever he asked if they ever grew melons, the farmers shook their heads from side to side and pointed to the fields of carrots.

Disheartened, Wilbur strode on, crossing the no-man's land into the next country – the Kingdom of Enormous Aubergines. From the first moment he stepped foot there, he knew deep down that melons would be hard, if not impossible, to find.

Piled up beside the border post were crates of plump aubergines, going for export to a kingdom far away. The fields were lined with impressive aubergine plants, and the caravanserai teahouses were awash with succulent dishes made from the vegetables – roasted aubergines, stuffed aubergines, and baba ghanoush.

After picking his way through a platter of aubergine fritters, Wilbur got chatting to one of the locals.

'I'm searching for a new kind of melon,' he explained. 'Do you know where I might find one?'

The local scratched his head.

'This is the Kingdom of Enormous Aubergines,' he replied, 'so we don't eat melons. But you could try the next kingdom, or the one after that.'

The following morning, Wilbur Melonius set off before dawn, crossing into the Land of Fried Eggs.

The ground here was rocky and, as the name would suggest, the farmers tended to rear chickens for eggs, which were fried for breakfast, lunch, and dinner.

Without bothering to pause, the young adventurer carried on until he reached the next country, the Kingdom of Gleaming Pumpkins.

As soon as he'd crossed the no-man's land and spotted the orderly rows of orange fruit laid out in the fields, Wilbur's heart sank once again. At this rate he'd never find a delicious new kind of melon with which to win his beloved Esmeralda's heart.

He was about to march on to the next kingdom, when something caused him to pause at the edge of a rocky little field.

An aged farmer was moaning to his wife:

'I have no idea what happened,' he said, 'but the seeds I was sold were fakes. Instead of being a wonderful new variety of delicious yellow-skinned pumpkins, they've turned out to be melons.'

The farmer's wife broke down in tears.

'We'll be ruined,' she said. 'For no one in the Kingdom of Gleaming Pumpkins has a taste for melons.'

Having overheard the conversation, Wilbur stepped forward.

'Could I taste one of your melons?' he asked.

'Go ahead,' the farmer answered, 'but don't blame me if you think they taste absolutely foul.'

Taking out his pocket-knife, Wilbur cut one of the melons open. Marvelling at the fine lime-green flesh inside, he took a bite.

It was the most delicious thing he'd ever tasted.

His heart racing, he said:

'I am a poor wayfarer on my travels from far away. As such, I don't have much money. But if you were to trust me, and take this crop of yellow melons back to my kingdom, I promise you'll sell them for a very high price.'

The farmer had never been out of the kingdom before, let alone anywhere beyond. But the prospect of making a fortune excited him.

'If we made money, we could retire!' he whispered.

And so the farmer agreed.

The next day he piled his cart with the yellow melons, then he and Wilbur set off for the Pastèque Kingdom.

They travelled for days on end, from the Kingdom of Gleaming Pumpkins, back through the Land of Fried Eggs, the Kingdom of Enormous Aubergines, and the Land of Blinding Red Carrots.

Eventually, weary and tired, they crossed the no-man's land to the kingdom where Wilbur Melonius was from.

Heading straight for Esmeralda's home, the young adventurer smartened himself up, rapped on the front door, and got down on one knee, a fine yellow melon in his hands.

'My beloved,' he said, 'I have journeyed to the farthest land imaginable, and have brought back a new kind of melon with which to secure your heart.'

Esmeralda raised an eyebrow.

'Well, it certainly looks different to the melons we all know and love,' she said, 'but how does it taste?'

Pulling out his pocket-knife, Wilbur cut a slice and served it.

A moment later, the face of his beloved was glinting with delight.

'This is the most mouth-tingling melon I've ever tasted!' she cried.

'So, will you marry me, dearest Esmeralda?'

'Yes, yes, yes, I will!'

News of the young adventurer's return and his betrothal spread at lightning speed. Everyone had heard of the rare and delicious yellow melons, and wanted to taste one for themselves.

And, very soon, they had.

Within an hour of setting up a stall in the town square, the farmer from the Kingdom of Gleaming Pumpkins had sold out. Thanking Wilbur, he set off for home, a bag of gold tucked into the folds of his robe.

Day and night the people from the Pastèque Kingdom feasted on the amazing new melons. All they did was talk about them, delighting in their beauty and their taste. As the one who'd brought them back from his travels, they were called 'Wilbur melons'.

The farmers tore up their crops of watermelons and sowed the seeds of the new fruit. Very soon, carts of the bright yellow Wilbur melons were being ferried to the market, where they replaced the standard watermelons overnight.

Within a few weeks, the yellow melons had completely replaced the watermelons which, until then, everyone had loved and enjoyed.

By royal decree, the Pastèque Kingdom was renamed 'The Land of Wilbur Melons'. The mere mention of a watermelon singled someone out as old-fashioned and passé. Yellow melons were heralded as the finest and most delectable fruits in the world.

Overnight, special pageants were devised to show them off, and competitions were established in which the very best-shaped Wilbur melons were given awards.

Wilbur and Esmeralda were married, and everyone in the Land of Wilbur Melons rejoiced.

Time passed.

Then, one day, an old crone in the market was heard to say, 'I wish they still sold watermelons, like the ones we used to have.'

At first, the old woman was mocked and shooed away.

But then, someone else said,

'The lovely old watermelons quenched my thirst more than the Wilbur melons.'

And someone else added:

'I miss them too. Eating them reminded me of my childhood.'

'The Wilbur melons give me stomach aches,' someone else said. 'I don't like them any more.'

All of a sudden, people throughout the kingdom were crying out for the old watermelons.

A royal advisor rushed into the throne room.

'Your Majesty!' he yelled. 'There's about to be a public revolt!'

The monarch listened, and was told that, although the yellow melons had not changed in any way, everyone was denouncing them – just as they had denounced the watermelons a few weeks before.

'Tell the farmers to sow their fields with watermelon seeds,' he groaned.

'But what shall we do with all the Wilbur melons that have been grown?'

'Have them taken to the end of the kingdom and thrown over the cliff into the sea.'

Wincing, the chief advisor scratched a thumb to his nose.

'What of the name of our kingdom, sire?'

The monarch groaned a second time.

'Have it changed back to the Pastèque Kingdom,' he said.

14

And so it came to pass that the yellow melons were banished, even though they themselves were not at fault at all. Merely mentioning them by name was decreed illegal. The very same watermelons that everyone had always known and loved were grown once again.

As for Wilbur Melonius, he went on to raise a large family with his beloved Esmeralda.

Many years passed, then one day his eldest son fell in love with a girl with flaxen hair and dimples in her cheeks.

'I'll marry you,' she said, 'if you venture far away and bring a fabled yellow melon for me to taste.'

From: *Tales Told to a Melon*

Indian Movement

AIR INDIA FLIGHT 543 touched down at New Delhi International on time, disgorging a flood of economy travellers into the terminal building.

Once the other passengers had disembarked, a clutch of deportees was chaperoned from the back of the aircraft to immigration. At least three of them were in tears, and two – an elderly couple from Leeds – had tied themselves to their seats, refusing to leave the aircraft.

Sorrowfully, Bitu Jain followed the stream of disgraced returnees to the immigration counter, where the accompanying British officer presented a stack of passports to her Indian counterpart.

Waiting his turn, Bitu was formally interviewed. His fingerprints taken, his passport was stamped and handed over to him.

'You are free to go,' the officer said.

Pacing through to the baggage hall, Bitu found Harry waiting.

'Smells like home,' he said.

'This is scary.'

'What is?'

'Coming to the country I'm from for the first time.'

'The whole world's from India,' Bitu said under his breath. 'But they just don't know it.'

With their luggage in hand, the pair filed out into the sea of people, insects swarming over the floodlights outside.

As soon as they stepped through the automatic glass doors, throngs of taxi drivers and pimps rushed up, offering Harry their services.

'How do they know I'm a foreigner?'

'It's the smell you give off,' Bitu answered.

'That's nuts! I'm not giving off a smell.'

'Oh but you are Harry-bhai. You just don't know it.'

Five minutes later they'd been bustled into a groaning Ambassador taxi, the Sikh driver speeding into town, as though charging a steed into battle.

In a bid to take his mind off charging the spontaneous India trip to his credit card, Harry unwound the window, and pushed his face into the slipstream.

'Can't believe it!' he cried. 'I can't believe I'm here!'

Bitu gave a double thumbs up and wobbled his head.

'It's like I never left,' he said.

The taxi slalomed up to a no-frills hotel in Connaught Place, the gleaming white wheel of buildings built as the centrepiece of the Raj's capital.

They checked in and Bitu sloped straight off to bed.

As though called by a voice whispering to him, Harry hurried out through the doors and onto the street.

Excited to the pit of his stomach, he looked left, right, forward and back, up, down, his nostrils drawing in the scent of India for the first time.

Not the fake India of Manchester's Curry Mile, or the fragments of India you get at English market stalls – but Full Monty India, in dazzling 3D IMAX.

Everything Harry saw was fresh and, at the same time, he already knew it in a back-to-front way… as though he'd seen its reflection ten thousand times.

There were hawkers touting fake Rolexes, beggars selling *beedi* cigarettes, and street stalls offering *paan*, *jalebis* and fresh-squeezed juice. Although it was late, the streets were teeming with people – some moving forward briskly as if in a hurry, while others meandered slowly through the throng. More still paused to eat at one of the makeshift food stalls or to catch one of the many street performances.

At one, a troupe of young children were walking a tightrope slung between a pair of posts. Dressed in sequined costumes, they put on an acrobatic routine while breathing fire, as their older siblings played home-made instruments and begged for donations.

Pushing to the front, Harry was drawn in. He was captivated by the lack of safety, and by the fact there didn't seem to be anyone from the authorities in charge.

The under-age tightrope acrobats paused to spend their takings on rice and *daal*, while the audience sauntered away to the next street corner where another performance was getting underway.

Drifting over with the flow, Harry found himself at the front, a few feet from a slim sinewy figure in a scarlet knee-length cloak. Before him was a high trestle table, on which lay an ordinary wooden box, the size of a child's coffin.

A trumpet sounded in the background, hands clapped fast and hard, and the show began.

Declaring himself the greatest sorcerer in all India, the cloak-clad performer opened the box and pulled out a rabbit by the ears. On proving the creature was very much alive, he whipped a glass medicine bottle from his cloak. Prising open the rabbit's mouth, he poured a few drops of the mystery liquid onto its tongue.

The magician spun round and around three times.

By the time he stopped, the animal was dead.

The audience seemed displeased at the death of an innocent creature. As a wave of susurration coursed through the lines of onlookers, the magician did something unexpected. Unscrewing the top of the medicine bottle once again, he drank the poison, his face contorting.

The crowd gasped.

A drum rolled.

The sorcerer fell to the ground, as lifeless as the rabbit still clutched in his hand.

Again, the audience gasped and, again, the drum rolled.

A king-sized bed sheet was pulled over the casualties.

The magician's child rushed forward, shaking his dead father, begging him to come back to life.

The drum rolled a third time.

A young woman in the crowd began tearing out her hair. Unable to control herself, she begged the deities for a miracle.

A moment of despair passed.

Then the sheet twitched and jerked left and right, and the magician leapt to his feet.

In his hands was the rabbit – dazed but alive once again.

At breakfast next morning Harry sat in silence, replaying the magician's performance in his mind, while his friend sat across from him sipping his tea.

Since childhood he'd been enthralled by illusion, and by the way a stage magician diverts the audience's attention away from what's really going on. For Harry, one of the joys of stage magic was observing another performer's routine, and breaking it down point by point.

At once he saw through the trick:

The rabbit hadn't been poisoned, but rather had been strangled while the magician span round. Faking his own death, he'd substituted a live rabbit, which had been hidden in his cloak.

Bitu cleared his throat and sighed.

'So what is the programme?' he asked.

Harry hadn't heard, or if he had he wasn't interested in answering. His thoughts were still on the sorcerer.

'Harry-bhai!'

'Huh? What?'

'You've only been here two minutes and already you're zoned out.'

'Sorry. I was thinking about something.'

'About the Blackpool Grand?'

'No… I told you, The Great Maharaja Malipasse is dead.'

'So what's the programme?' Bitu repeated.

'To reinvent myself.'

'And get rid of the curse!'

'To reinvent myself and be free of the curse,' Harry said.

'Very good.'

'So… how d'you go about getting rid of a curse in India?'

'Immersion.'

'*Immersion?*'

'*Ha*, yes, immersion. That is right.'

'Immersion in what?'

'In a sacred river.'

'Which sacred river?'

'Ganga and Yamuna.'

'Both of them?'

'*Ha*, yes, both… at the *Sangam*.'

'What's that?'

'Where they meet together. It is extra-special blessed. Just looking at it removes all curses. But immersion in it gives even more blessing,' Bitu said.

'Where is it – the *Sangam*?'

'At Allahabad.'

'Where's that?'

'UP.'

'Uttar Pradesh?'

'*Ha*. We take the express train this afternoon.'

'What then?' Harry asked anxiously.

'Then we see what happens,' Bitu said.

Late in the afternoon, the Poorva Express arrived at the station, iron wheels grinding and sparking against the tracks.

The station was packed to capacity, every available inch of space taken up by people, many with bundles on heads. Following close behind Bitu, Harry found himself breathless at the sheer number of people crammed onto the platform.

'Why are there so many people?!' he yelled.

'Kumbh Mela,' his friend called back.

'What's that?'

'Pilgrimage.'

Even before the train streamed into the station, the pilgrims did their damnedest to clamber aboard. Like a migrating species with no choice, they risked life and limb – the near-suicidal attempts to get inside causing injury and chaos.

Miraculously, Harry and Bitu managed to get on board, although forced to sit in the aisle of an overloaded carriage. Chattering and praying, the other passengers were whipped up with anticipation, as though about to take part in the single most important ceremony of their lives.

The locomotive jerked out from Delhi Station and through the miles of shantytown. Staring out the window, Harry watched the progression of life in horror.

The monumental buildings of the capital were quickly replaced by detritus. Women were scrubbing clothes in the sidings, their little children squatting nearby; rag-pickers and pye-dogs zigzagging through the undergrowth in search of scraps to stave off hunger.

Taking Bitu's advice, Harry had brought no more than a simple cloth bag, with a few knickknacks. Everything else was left at the hotel in the capital. Almost everyone else was travelling as light or even lighter – many of them dressed in single cotton sheets. Those who'd brought bundles along seemed to have packed little more than a few provisions and a rolled-up mattress.

Three hours outside Delhi, a tall blond foreigner pushed his way through into the carriage in which Harry and Bitu were squashed up on the floor. Unmistakably Canadian, he was wearing a backpack on which was sewn a large patch bearing his nation's flag. All kinds of stuff was dangling from the pack, including multiple water bottles, a sleeping bag, and a camping stove. The strap of a camera bag was furled around his wrist, and an iPhone hung around his neck in a transparent pouch. Young and enthusiastic, he'd tapped into the general sense of elation, and was eager to share the experience with anyone who spoke English.

'Crazy, isn't it?!' he called out to Harry, picking up a sense that it was all new to him, too.

'Certainly is,' Harry retorted.

'Where are you guys from?' the Canadian asked.

'England. And you?'

'Toronto. I'm Marney… and you?'

'Harry… and this is Bitu.'

'Heading to the Kumbh?'

'Yeah.'

'First time?'

'Yeah.'

'Me too,' said Marney. 'I'm a Kumbh Mela virgin!'

The train stopped and what seemed like a hundred thousand people clambered on. So many pilgrims were compressed into the carriage that Harry relived the panic of being stuck in a locked coffin when a practice session went wrong.

'I'm not good with crowds,' he mumbled.

'Then I've got a feeling you're gonna find the Kumbh a challenge,' Marney replied.

'Lots of people there, are there?'

The Canadian rolled his eyes as Bitu wobbled his head from side to side.

'They're expecting a hundred million,' Marney said.

Harry looked at the foreigner as though he were stark raving mad.

'Impossible.'

'Nope, it's not.'

'What?!'

Harry shot Bitu a look of terror.

Again, Bitu wobbled his head from side to side.

'Give or take a few million,' he said.

At three o'clock next morning the train screeched into Allahabad Junction, the pilgrims twice as frantic to get off as they had been to get aboard.

Swept forward in a sea of people and scant possessions, Harry and Bitu were carried along by the tidal wave. Weighed down by his luggage, the Canadian was left behind, rooted to the spot.

Amid the pandemonium, hundreds of uniformed police armed with canes were doing what they could to keep the pilgrims in line. Three days earlier one of the station's pedestrian bridges had collapsed, killing dozens of devotees.

Unnerved by the sheer number of people, Harry did his best to calm himself. Half a pace ahead, Bitu led the way as though he knew exactly where he was going.

With no hope of catching an auto-rickshaw, let alone a taxi, they walked the final few miles to the pilgrimage point. As they did so, Harry's head buzzed with questions – the kind formulated by an Occidental mind. Having known Bitu for fifteen years, he knew full well that practical questions would have been met with indecisive answers, or yet more questions.

Once out of the railway station, the two friends reached the open road. Pressed all around them were tens of thousands of pilgrims. As in one of those scenes of mass human exodus that follow a natural disaster, they all had the same vacant expression. It was as though everyone was uncertain what the next minutes, let alone hours, would bring.

Shrouded in white and orange, the pilgrims resembled ghosts, their faces masked with expectation. In this stream of humanity, the old were carried on stretchers; the youngest on shoulders. Some families had tied a rope around themselves so that they didn't get separated in the throng. A number of people were crawling the route on their knees in grave danger of being sucked down in the maelstrom.

Surging forward, the stream of pilgrims began merging with other streams, gushing together from all directions. As the river expanded into a sea and then an ocean, it broke through onto the colossal floodplain of the Kumbh Mela itself.

As the first rays of dawn light broke over the horizon, Harry caught sight of the plateau, edged as it was by the Yamuna and the Ganga. Viewed from a distance it was like something from a Hollywood rendition of a biblical tale – millions and millions of pilgrims filling the vast expanse.

Unnatural, and at the same time utterly natural, the scale defied description. The scene was tinged yellow by dawn, touched by some primordial alchemy.

Profoundly moved by the experience, Harry stopped dead still, the waves of pilgrims lapping past.

'Must keep going,' Bitu called. 'Not far to go now.'

'How often does this gathering take place?'

Bitu urged his friend to start moving again.

'Every twelve years,' he said. 'But every twelve-times-twelve years there's a big Mela… and this is it.'

Throwing his hands up above his head, Harry signalled to his friend.

'What?!'

'Every one hundred and forty-four years,' said Bitu, making the calculation.

'I don't believe it!' Harry bellowed. 'You're telling me the biggest Kumbh Mela in my lifetime happens to be taking place just when we turned up?'

Bitu wobbled his head in agreement.

'Yes, like that.'

'But that's impossible! It can't just happen now – when I needed it to get rid of the curse.'

Bitu Jain frowned at his friend, pulling him to move faster. 'Nothing is impossible in India,' he said.

For three days and nights, Harry followed the routine of every other pilgrim.

At the appointed times he strode down to the isthmus between the Ganga and the Yamuna, venturing there in the wake of the charging naked *naga* holy men. Immersing himself in the water, with literally millions of others around him, he felt as though he were part of something far greater than he'd ever experienced before.

Stripped naked and being cleansed by the hallowed water, the pilgrims seemed oblivious to the commotion around them. As far as they were concerned, they were alone – bound by a sacred bond to the pantheon and ritual of the Hindu faith.

Having immersed himself four times, purifying his soul and dispelling the curse, Harry left Bitu at the ramshackle tent where they were staying, and roamed through the hordes of disciples.

Dozens of pontoon bridges spanned the waterways, each one of them packed with pilgrims. The plateau itself had been laid with great sheets of steel so as to prevent the faithful from being sucked down into the mud.

Skirting around the individual clusters of humanity, hailing from all corners of India, Harry made his way to a lip of higher ground. Every few feet there was a stall selling hot cooked food or such things as flower garlands, clothing, devotional banners, fluorescent pink candy-floss and bottled drinks. In the background constant announcements for lost children blared out over loudspeakers.

Away from the general hullabaloo, Harry reached a far more tranquil area, its expanse dotted with simple white canvas tents. Seated or standing before each was a huddle of figures. In each case, one person was being fussed over or lauded, while devotees streamed up, hoping to be blessed.

Outside one canopy a godman was sitting cross-legged. Seemingly ancient, he was holding his left arm up in the air. The limb was wizened and gnarled; he hadn't allowed it to fall for thirty-three years. At another tent, a holy man was standing on one foot, as he had supposedly done in complete silence since 1971.

Harry was about to retrace his steps to where he and Bitu were staying, when something caught his eye. Against a setting of oddity and wonder, it stuck out not because it was astonishing, but rather on account of its familiarity.

Surrounded by a knot of devotees, a young *sadhu* dressed in a simple lungi and turban was lying outstretched on a bed of nails beside a campfire. To the delight of the pilgrims, he stood up and followed the feat with another.

His palms pressed together under his chin, he mumbled a mantra faster and faster. Then, with the audience pressing forward, he rubbed thumb and forefinger of either hand together, his eyes still closed.

To the amazement of those gathered around, his hands began to stream with oyster-grey smoke.

Lids lifting from his eyes, he said something in Hindi, at which one of the disciples lurched forward, grasped his wrist and felt for his pulse.

Her face rapt in consternation, the pilgrim exclaimed in the negative – there wasn't one. Any normal human without a pulse would be dead – but the *sadhu* was evidently anything but normal.

Intrigued, Harry stepped forward, joining the crowd of devotees. He watched as the *sadhu* picked a dagger from the ground and ran the blade over his thigh. Steel brushing over skin, it left a trail of crimson blood – at which the holy man's minions gasped in anguish and delight.

Wiping away the blood, the ascetic showed that the wound had miraculously healed. Then, without wasting a moment, he held the dagger's blade in the campfire until it glowed orange. Pulling it out, he swigged from a tin cup of sacred water, spat, and touched the red-hot blade to his tongue.

As the disciples cooed and gasped, Harry walked round to the side of the group, and stood a distance behind the *sadhu*. Unobserved, he watched as a variety of other miraculous feats were executed.

First, the godman sprinkled *vibhuti*, holy ash, onto the palms of the audience. Next, he pierced a fold of flesh at his waist with a meat skewer. After that, he prayed and it appeared to rain – a few drops at least.

Having seen enough, Harry zigzagged back towards the filthy tent where Bitu was waiting for him. Although the ground was veiled in thick steel sheets, almost everyone was spattered with mud. But no one seemed to care in the least. Being present at the Kumbh Mela was to be set apart from the tribulations of daily life – and to be blessed in a deep down way.

In a bid to avoid the arterial stream of pilgrims heading towards him, Harry ventured to the plateau's eastern flank and found himself in an area he hadn't visited before.

Fenced off, it was well-drained and exceptionally clean. There was none of the litter or the mess found in the main public zone. Immaculately dressed in pure white robes with white crocheted beanie hats, the pilgrims residing there were spotlessly clean. Unlike everyone else Harry had seen at the Kumbh, they were a vision of order and sterility – each of them with a bottle of cleansing gel hanging around their necks with strings of prayer beads.

The other difference between the white-garbed devotees and all the other pilgrims, was that they weren't Indian, but foreigners. Pacing through the pristine encampment, Harry heard English, French, German, Spanish, and Chinese spoken. As he wondered who they all were and what was going on, someone called his name.

He turned.

The Canadian from the train rushed up.

'Come for the *darshan*?' he asked energetically.

'Huh?'

'The *darshan*. It's about to start.'

'What *darshan*?'

'The one Mother Mee holds every evening. You are here for Mother Mee, aren't you?' Marney uttered severely.

'Um, er… yes… That's right. Yes, I'm here for Mother Mee.'

'Fantastic! I'll show you where it is!'

Harry wanted to ask who Mother Mee was, but feared doing so would single him out as an outsider. So he went along with it and found himself cross-legged on the ground inside a large hexagonal marquee. Everyone else was dressed in spotless white – all of them foreigners, and all with their gaze trained on the dais at the front.

'Any minute now,' Marney whispered in a tense voice.

'Great,' said Harry.

A droning noise of unbridled anticipation began in the front row and moved progressively backwards. Like the sound of an insect colony, it made no sense to anyone unconnected with the group.

A minute or two passed in which a team of technicians hurried about testing the PA system. Amid rapturous applause, Mother Mee stepped into the blinding white light of the stage.

Her delicate bare feet on ivory-white petals, she seemed to float effortlessly from the wings and into the centre of the dais.

Palms pressed together in greeting, the female *sadhu* dipped her head towards the audience in deference. Furled in white robes and crocheted beanie like her multitude of followers, she was blessed with an ear-to-ear grin, and a sense of utter tranquillity.

Harry's gaze followed her, as he observed how the beams of two powerful spotlights glided along with her.

Once seated, the godwoman sat silently in prayer for a few minutes, as though taking her time. Closing their eyes, the pilgrims prayed, clearing their minds in preparation of the sermon that was to come.

Slipping on a wireless headset, Mother Mee thanked the deities, recited a short invocation, and began to address her followers. Although Indian, her accent was imbued with a mid-Atlantic twang, as though she'd spent many years abroad. Speaking slowly, she talked about pure love and pure joy – the kind untainted by the shortcomings of mankind.

For the two and a half hours Mother Mee spoke, the pilgrims listened. Among them, Harry yearned to get up and leave – but doing so would have caused him to stand out. So he sat there, his crossed legs aching and numb, his back sorer than sore.

To his left, Marney the Canadian seemed to glow as if bathed in supreme and unconditional love. His ears drank up the oration, his eyes ingesting the scene of fantastical white.

When it was over, Mother Mee stood up, blew kisses to the audience, and glided off in the same way she'd arrived. Even though she had left, the devotees didn't move. Lost in a state of reflective meditation, they hung on for a long while, before drifting away in ones and twos.

Long after dark, Harry slunk back to the tent, where he found Bitu stretched out on a *charpoy*.

'I've seen wonders,' he said.

'Wonderful girls... or were they wonderful *boys*?!'

'Not girls or boys. Wonderful godmen, and godwomen, too.'

'*Sadhus?*'

Harry nodded.

'I'll take you to see them tomorrow,' he said.

Bitu clicked his tongue, signalling a lack of interest.

'No time for godmen,' he spat. 'They're all tricksters and fakes.'

'Doesn't mean they're not interesting,' Harry replied. 'I saw one out there this afternoon passing off stage magic as real miracles!'

'Told you, they're tricksters and fakes – and they're doing rubbish!'

Harry stared into space, his attention straying.

'It wasn't rubbish,' he countered softly. 'The young guy was performing high-level stuff. Just don't understand where he got the chemicals.'

'*Chemicals?*'

'The ones needed for the tricks.'

Again, Bitu clicked his tongue.

'This is India!' he yelled. 'You can get anything you like!'

'Even insanely dangerous chemicals?'

'Especially insanely dangerous chemicals!' cried Bitu.

The morning after Mother Mee's *darshan*, Harry left Bitu sleeping on his *charpoy* and strolled to the confluence of the two sacred rivers.

Wending his way between the rows of tents, and the streams of pilgrims, he thought how amazing it was that life at the greatest human gathering in history now seemed somehow normal. Harry may have only been in India for a handful of days, but he felt at home there. The layers of life were set apart from the grim, hollow realities of Blackpool.

Down at the shore pilgrims were immersing themselves, each one lost in silent ritual. For most it was the journey of a lifetime, having ventured from distant parts of India. Yet more had come from abroad – from Europe, Africa, the Americas and beyond.

The dark surface of the water was touched by the first strains of yellow light, as though an enchanted cloak had been cast over the scene. At that moment, standing at the river's margin, Harry knew his life would never be quite the same again.

It wasn't a case of conversion – he'd never been a believer, even though his family assumed he was a devout Sikh like the rest of them. The sheer numbers of devotees had touched Harry in a non-spiritual way – as though every one of them was linked to him through raw humanity.

As the sun's golden light swathed the bathers, the water rippled and churned by the activity, Harry watched a family make their way gingerly to the shore.

A thick blue cord was strung around the huddle, keeping the little group safely together. There must have been fifteen of them spanning four or even five generations – from newborn babes in arms to toothless crones. The women's ankles were fettered with heavy silver bands, the kind worn in the remote landscape of Arunachal Pradesh, from where they had come.

Keeping in formation, they slipped into the water, immersing themselves all together.

Awed, Harry gave thanks to the forces of nature for allowing him to have witnessed such an event. Once again he marvelled how the supreme Maha Kumbh Mela – held once every century and a half – was taking place just when he needed it. The coincidence seemed too much – as if it wasn't a coincidence at all.

For a moment, Harry found himself wondering whether he'd been lured to the land of his ancestors by a higher calling. *Nonsense*, he thought to himself, strolling back towards the tent. Thinking like that was the first step on a ladder leading to madness.

Bitu was stretched out on the rope bed, picking his teeth with the end of a *neem* stick.

'Got something for you,' he said as Harry approached.

'What?'

Bitu clicked his tongue, angling the sound towards the space under where he was lying.

'Take it out.'

'Huh?'

'Look under the *charpoy*!'

Harry stooped down and removed a damp cardboard box filled with an assortment of bottles and dented metal tins.

'What's all this?'

'Left by a *sadhu*, that's what.'

'Left where?'

'Here… the tent's owner gave it to me – said it was a hazard to life and limb.'

Perching on the edge of the *charpoy*, Harry looked through the box, reading the labels, his forehead furrowing.

'Sulphuric acid, sulpho-cyanide, ferric chloride… *Jesus*! This is as dangerous as it gets! They're the kind of chemicals Houdini used to do his tricks – it's stuff that's hard to come by in England unless you've got a licence.'

'In India there's no such problem with paperwork,' retorted his friend.

'No need for doctors' prescriptions?'

Bitu-bhai let out a cackle, then coughed.

'Of course not! That's why India's so much fun!'

As the sentence was spoken, the heavens opened and a torrential downpour began. Out on the plain, drenched pilgrims staggered about packing and repacking their belongings.

'Hate rain!' cried Bitu, stretched out on the bed.

'I'm sure it'll end in a minute,' Harry chipped in.

Three hours later there was still no sign of a respite. Racing in from the west, a fresh crop of storm clouds emptied their contents over the Kumbh Mela, along with lightning and hail.

Bored out of his mind, Harry looked through the box again, scribbling notes on a scrap of paper. Grunting from time to time, his spirits seemed buoyed.

Late in the afternoon the storm moved on and the rain stopped as though a leak had been fixed in the sky.

'We'd better think about getting back to Delhi,' said Bitu, sitting up. 'With rain like that the trains'll be delayed.'

Harry looked at his friend and smiled.

'Got an idea,' he said.

Bitu narrowed his eyes.

'No time for nonsense!'

Clapping his hands, Harry dragged his friend up from the *charpoy*, grabbed the cardboard box, and led the way outside.

Ten minutes later, Harry was attired in a *salwar kameez*, a voluminous turban on his head in the same shade of saffron. Having picked up a couple of props, he gave the signal.

'You sure you want to do this?' barked Bitu gruffly.

'Yes! It'll cheer everyone up.'

'But you said Maharaja Malipasse is dead.'

'Then I won't be Malipasse.'

'So who shall I say's about to perform?'

Harry glanced left, then right – taking in the sea of rubbish stirred up by the storm. His eyes stopped on an empty plastic packet of soap powder. Blue and red printed on white, it bore the logo of the OMO brand.

'*Omo-ji*,' said Harry.

'Sounds stupid.'

'What does it matter? I told you, it's just for fun!'

Groaning, Bitu thrust up his arms, announcing that The Great Omo-ji had arrived from a land beyond the horizon.

No one seemed to care – they had far more pressing matters to think about than watching a magic act. Sorting out their drenched belongings was the only thing on their minds.

'They're not interested!' Bitu spat. 'Let's go back inside where it's warm.'

Undeterred, Harry pushed the headdress down tight on his head and began.

For his first trick, he took a hundred-rupee note from his pocket, held it up for all to see, and set fire to it.

But the money didn't burn.

Although it passed off perfectly, the trick was witnessed by a single devotee, and only because he was lame, and was resting for a moment before carrying on.

For his second trick, The Great Omo-ji smashed a coconut on the steel sheet beneath his feet. Erupting in fire, the white meat inside was drenched red as though filled with blood.

The explosion secured Harry three more spectators.

Moving swiftly on, he stopped his pulse, as the magician in Delhi had done. Then, in a pièce de résistance, he flicked open his fist, causing a fireball to billow out from nowhere.

Bemused, the audience sloped away.

'That was fun!' Harry exclaimed with delight. 'Can't say it was a full house, but it was good to perform.'

Bitu was unimpressed – not with the magic, but with his friend.

'That was a waste of time!' he snapped.

That evening Harry and Bitu sat on their *charpoys*, considering what to do next.

'I'll go to Meerut,' said Bitu.

'To your family?'

'*Ha*. They'll wonder where I've been.'

'Where you've been since we landed in Delhi?'

Bitu shook his head melancholically.

'Where I've been for the last thirty-two years,' he said.

'You mean you never told them you were in England?!'

Wobbling his head, Bitu indicated the negative.

'No,' he said after a long pause.

'Why not?!'

'I never got round to it.'

Harry pushed a hand back through his hair.

'I never asked you why you went to England in the first place.'

'*Why*? They married me off. That's why!'

Harry balked at the news.

'What about your wife? Did she go with you?'

'No. She stayed at Meerut. No money for two tickets.'

'But she knows you went to England, right?'

Again, Bitu's head wobbled.

'Not exactly. She thinking I went to Bombay.'

'And I thought *I* was a screw-up!' Harry bellowed.

Mulling over their troubles, each was lost in his own state of self-imposed misery.

'Now we're cleansed, what to do?' Bitu asked. 'Home to Blackpool?'

'Back to the grey and the cold?' Harry answered, the words pained.

'I love that place.'

'Well I don't. Hate the idea of getting a job… a *real* job… chopping up bones for minimum wage.'

'You could stay in India,' Bitu offered.

'And do what?'

'Magic tricks?'

Harry scoffed at the idea.

'Told you, I'm done with all that. Anyway, you saw for yourself – it went down like a lead balloon.'

Sitting up, Bitu dug the end of a finger into his right ear, coughed hard, and cleared his throat.

'On my travels I've learnt one thing,' he said.

'What?'

'That if you relax, the path opens up.'

Harry looked round at his friend.

'You're sounding like a bleedin' godman.'

'No chance of that!' Bitu said.

After much deliberating, the pair decided to take the train back to Delhi, collect their luggage from the hotel in Connaught Place, and to follow their chosen paths.

Next morning, Harry braved the pit-latrine, and found himself wishing he was a thousand miles away from the Kumbh Mela. It may have been the greatest gathering in human history, but it was short on creature comforts.

Trudging back from the toilet, he found Bitu charging about hysterically.

'It's gone! It's gone!' he cried.

'What has?'

'My money and passport!'

Grabbing the knot of dirty laundry he was using as a pillow, Harry searched for his own valuables.

'*Jesus Christ!*' he yelled. 'They got me as well!'

'I hate this country!' Bitu whimpered. 'Wish I could go home.'

'This *is* your home!' Harry growled scathingly.

Collapsing on their *charpoys*, they sat in silence, wondering what to do. One by one they crossed off all possibilities in their heads.

'We're outcasts,' Bitu said.

'So what do we do – *beg*?'

'This isn't Blackpool! Who's gonna give us money?'

'We could go to a soup kitchen. There's one over where the *sadhus* hang out. Saw loads of pilgrims getting fed for free there yesterday.'

'A bowl of soup is one thing,' Bitu countered, 'but money and passport's another.'

'You mean we're gonna be stuck here at the Kumbh Mela forever?'

'In three weeks everyone will have gone and the waters will roll back with the new moon.'

'So, we're stuffed, right?' Harry muttered.

His friend didn't reply. He just sat on his *charpoy* staring into space.

After what seemed like an age, Bitu looked round.

'The Great Omo-ji can save us,' he said.

Harry mumbled an insult.

41

'Listen to me,' Bitu said, reaching over and tugging his friend's sleeve.

'*Bitu-bhai*! You saw how the tricks went down. No one took any notice.'

'And why not?'

'Because they've got other stuff on their minds.'

'No, no, no,' Bitu shot back. 'Not that.'

'Then, you tell me why no one watched the magic tricks – I did them well enough.'

'Very simple reason,' Bitu said. 'You did them as a stage magician.'

'What's wrong with that?'

'Should have performed them as a godman,' Bitu said.

From: *Godman*

In Old Casablanca

THE ROOF OF Hotel Marrakech was flat, tiled in red bricks, and covered in a spider's web of junk.

There were rusting old bicycle frames and rotting bamboo deckchairs, crates of empty gin bottles, strands of lead piping, threadbare furniture, and a line of refrigerators from the days when home appliances were the size of family cars.

On the south side of the roof there was a small area free from clutter. It was just big enough for a wrought iron table and chair, and an ice bucket arranged on a stand that doubled as an ashtray.

Blaine sat there all afternoon, his gaze locked on the postcard, his mind conjuring fantasies of a lifetime ago.

As his concentration strayed, he found himself wandering the streets of wartime Casablanca. He could picture himself clearly, strolling down the grand boulevard – what was then Avenue de France. The dazzling winter light bathed it all, reflecting off the gleaming Art Deco apartment blocks, the shops below them emporiums of wonder and delight.

And he could picture Bogart passing him, cigarette in hand, grey fedora tipped down low on his brow.

Blaine peered down to the street below and closed his eyes.

He wished he could wind back the clock's hands, slip into the black-and-white postcard world, a realm of unending possibility.

By the end of the afternoon, he knew every detail of the picture – every shadow, every straight line and curve. He admonished himself for falling victim to an old man's story. Then, slipping the card into his shirt pocket, he went down to Cinema Rialto, where the early evening screening of *Casablanca* was about to begin.

His back warmed by the walk, Mortimer Wu arrived at the Marché Central, where he treated himself to a bowl of fish broth and a stale chocolate croissant. He wasn't in the best of spirits, and hadn't been for days, not since the bad business in Marrakech.

As he spooned the thin soup to his lips, holding the bowl in his right hand, he wished he were home in Hong Kong, away from the trouble that had overrun his life.

'Want a shoeshine?' said a voice.

Saed sauntered up to the table with his box.

'I'm wearing sneakers,' Wu replied, 'don't think you'd get much of a shine on them.' He struggled a smile. 'Want half a croissant?'

Leaning forward, as if only half-trusting, Saed took the pastry.

'You are new... new to Casablanca, no?'

'How did you guess?'

'Your shoes... they are dusty. Marrakech dust.'

Mortimer Wu slurped the broth. He motioned to the waiter.

'My little friend here is joining me. Bring another bowl of soup.'

Saed sat down and was soon slurping as well.

'Which hotel you staying?'

'Not sure. I'm travelling to Tangier tomorrow. D'you know anywhere cheap and good?'

The shoeshine boy jerked a thumb behind him.

'Hotel Marrakech,' he said. 'If you don't mind cats.'

At seven forty-five Blaine left the Rialto.

He was still glowing from the final sequence, and was mumbling the dialogue as he went. Drifting through the empty streets on his way to Baba Cool, he noticed a light in Monsieur Raffi's shop, and the shutters drawn up.

Without thinking, he crossed the street and rapped gently on the window.

Raffi unbolted the door.

'Come on in my American friend,' he said. 'I have been sitting here waiting for you.'

'But we hadn't planned to meet.'

The shopkeeper locked the door once Blaine was inside.

'Of course we had, you just didn't know it,' he said, slumping down in his tattered satin chair. 'Now, tell me, how are you getting on with the clue?'

Blaine pulled out the postcard.

'I've spent the afternoon staring at it.'

'And what have you seen?'

'Old Casablanca in a time before the rot set in.'

'That's good,' Raffi said, 'but you are missing the details. And the world depends on details.'

'Believe me, I've seen them all.'

Monsieur Raffi shuddered.

'Seeing is not the same as understanding,' he said.

'Seeing what?'

'The real picture.'

The American frowned. He held the card up to the light and turned it slowly.

'What am I missing?'

'*Everything.*'

Again, Blaine turned it, slower this time. And as he turned, he noticed the edge gleam very slightly, as if it had been glued flat. He assumed it was part of the printing process. But, as he turned it again, he saw that the glue had been added later.

With great care, he pushed his thumbnail into the space where the picture was pasted onto the card. The two sheets separated easily, as if they were supposed to be pulled apart.

Working his way around the entire edge, Blaine found himself staring at the side of the card that had been glued to the image.

The left side was covered in writing, made in a small, neat hand. It looked like a series of directions – directions through Casablanca. The right side was devoted to a very rough hand-sketched map. It featured what appeared to be a main street, with bars, cafés and cinemas, all of them crudely marked.

Blaine's mouth opened but no words came out at first. Then, as if in a daze, he said:

'This is Bogart's handwriting. I'd know it anywhere.'

Monsieur Raffi coughed hard, then blew his nose.

'Now you have the clue, you can begin to unlock the secret,' he said.

A gleaming glass elevator ascended through a sumptuous office building, the floors and walls clad in pallid grey granite, the fittings all polished steel.

Ghita Omary stepped out at the fifteenth floor. Dressed more conservatively than usual, she moved with uncharacteristic urgency.

Striding up to the reception, she tapped a manicured fingernail on the desk. The receptionist, who was talking to her boyfriend on the phone, glanced up.

'I will be with you in a moment,' she said tersely.

'Please tell Mr. Senbel that Ghita Omary is here to see him.'

The receptionist covered the receiver with her hand.

'Would you wait? Mr. Senbel is very busy indeed.'

Turning, Ghita pushed her way fast down the corridor, and began searching for the largest office. She had not visited the lawyer before, but knew full well that jaw-dropping grandeur was expected by the upmarket clientele.

At the end of the corridor stood a thick glass door, a potted bonsai standing proud either side. It was the only one with plants.

Making a beeline for it, Ghita barged in, the receptionist sprinting after her.

Driss Senbel was seated near the window at a teak desk, the wall facing it obscured in diplomas and photographs of the lawyer in the company of the great and the good.

'Forgive me for not making an appointment,' said Ghita, 'I didn't have your number.'

The lawyer looked up from a legal contract. He seemed alarmed at first, but then smiled tautly, waving the receptionist away.

'My dear Ghita, you are a daughter to me, and do not need an appointment. The door is always open to you.'

Ghita sat, or rather she perched, on the edge of a grey leather chair. Coaxing herself to remain composed, she pressed her palms together.

'I am turning to you for help,' she said, 'as my father's close friend.'

Senbel didn't reply at first. He looked at Ghita, his manner taciturn and cold.

'Your father's plan to root out corruption has backfired dramatically,' he replied. 'We all knew it would, and we warned him – but he didn't listen.'

'He is a patriot,' Ghita said, her voice straining. 'He loves his country and is the only one of you willing to stand up against the evil that's eating it from the inside out.'

The lawyer held out his wrists.

'You can take me away if you believe I have done anything wrong,' he said.

'It's not you, but the system… and you're part of it.'

'My dear Ghita, if you chop down the forest, nature begins to fight back. It sends pestilence and plague. This may not be nature, but it's the same thing.' Senbel paused, took a deep breath, and sighed. 'The drugs they found... it wasn't a gram or two of *kif*. It was a massive haul, and of heroin at that.'

Ghita's mouth contorted in a snarl.

'You know as well as I do it was planted there!'

'Of course it was.'

'So what are we going to do about it?'

'*Wait*. We have to wait.'

'Wait for what?'

Driss Senbel groomed a strand of hair over his bald patch.

'Your father's assets have been seized,' he said. 'Everything is frozen. His home, his companies, his private jet... *everything*.'

'So let's get them unfrozen!'

Senbel picked a silver letter-opener from the surface of his desk. It had an ivory handle and a hallmarked blade.

'These people we are dealing with,' he said, 'they are extremely dangerous.'

'What people?'

'The ones your father has so enraged.'

'But who are they?'

'They're gangsters – gangsters with the cloak of respectability.'

'Do they have a leader?'

'All I know are the rumours...'

'And what do the rumours say?'

'That they take their lead from a man known to them as the Falcon.'

'I must meet him. I'll plead with him if I have to.'

'He won't listen. None of them will. And in any case, you'll never find him.'

The lawyer ran the blade across his palm.

'The police, the politicians, businessmen, they all live in terror of him,' he said. 'The Falcon controls the system. He *owns* it... even powerful wealthy men like your father have no hope against him. *Why*? Because his power is not constructed from anything logical. You see, it's power derived from raw fear.'

There was a knock at the door.

The receptionist entered with a memo for Senbel to sign. Striding indifferently through the room, she glared at Ghita as she approached her employer. A moment or two later she was gone.

'There's a huge storm approaching,' the lawyer said. 'It's going to be a tempest, a perfect storm. All I can do is to warn you. Leave Casablanca while you still can. Go very far away.'

'And let my father languish in jail?'

'I suppose so.'

There was rage in Ghita's eyes.

'I'm not frightened of this man, this Falcon,' she said. 'I'm not frightened of anyone.'

Taking the shoeshine boy's advice, Mortimer Wu went across to Hotel Marrakech, and soon found himself installed in the room opposite Blaine's.

Opening the window, he stared out at the flower stalls on the edge of the market. Then he lay on the bed, closed his eyes, and thought back to Hong Kong once again.

An hour or two passed and Wu didn't move.

By remaining completely still he found that the anxiety and the fear subsided. But, as dusk fell over Casablanca, he pushed back his shoulders and pulled himself off the bed.

He glanced down at the market.

The flower sellers were packing up, draining their buckets into the gutters, bundling up the roses for another day.

There were footsteps out in the corridor.

Wu put his ear to the door. He listened and opened it a crack. A man was fumbling for his key at the room opposite.

'Hello,' he said, in a friendly voice – an American voice.

'Good evening,' Wu replied, opening the door wide.

'You new here?'

'Yeah. Just arrived this afternoon.'

'How are you liking the faded grandeur of Hotel Marrakech?'

Mortimer Wu didn't respond to the question. Instead, he asked:

'Is there any hot water?'

'Hot water? Are you crazy?' said Blaine with a grin. 'You're lucky if you get any water at all – hot or cold.'

'Can you direct me to the shower?'

'Sure. It's all the way down the hall.'

'Thank you,' Wu replied, before withdrawing into his room.

Shutting the door, he slid the bolt firmly into place.

Left standing there, his own door open, Blaine plodded down the corridor to relieve himself.

On the way back, he wondered whether to reach out, to invite the newcomer for a glass of *café noir* down at Baba Cool.

He was about to knock when he heard a commotion down in the lobby. The front door slammed hard and was followed by the cacophonous cry of cats.

Leaving his room open, Blaine hurried down.

The ever-present clerk wasn't laid out on the floor in his usual state of delirium. He wasn't there at all. Blaine peered on the floor behind the desk, but there was no sign of the clerk.

The cats seemed uneasy.

A few of them had their ears pricked up, alert, poised low as if ready for flight. One or two had leapt up to higher ground, and were perched on a high shelf. They were quite obviously spooked.

Eventually, Blaine went back upstairs and slipped back into his room. He cursed the damp, the cold, and the stench. Then his mind turned to Ghita. Even though the thought of her made his blood churn; he wished she were there.

Pulling on his Humphrey Bogart raincoat, fedora in hand, he went out into the corridor again.

Across from his room the Chinese backpacker's door was ajar.

Rehearsing a line of invitation in his head, Blaine knocked, pushed the door open and swung his head in.

Mortimer Wu was lying on the bed, face up. There was an odd oily, almost metallic smell, and the curtains were drawn shut. Frowning, Blaine flicked on the light.

He leapt back in terror.

The backpacker's throat had been slashed. His clothing and the moth-eaten blanket were soaked in fresh blood.

Blaine screeched. It was a high-pitched girly scream, the kind from *Tom and Jerry* cartoons, when the woman sees the mouse.

He stood there for what seemed like an eternity, his feet rooted to the bare floorboards, every nerve in his body in shock.

Then he panicked.

Something was telling him to get out, to run.

But do so and he'd be a suspect. This isn't America, he thought. Things don't work like that here!

So, shaking, he ran back to his room, grabbed his satchel and the bin-liner.

Sprinting down the stairs, he rushed out through the front door of Hotel Marrakech.

Patricia Ross had spent the day petitioning Casablanca's governor to release Hicham Omary, but without any luck. Baying for blood, he was in no mood for clemency.

At six she drove back to the Globalcom headquarters, an attaché case under her arm. She was tired, frustrated and fearful. It felt as though the walls were closing in, as though the enemies were everywhere. As the CEO's assistant, Ross knew it was only a matter of time before the authorities tried to implicate her as well.

On the ground floor, five uniformed police officers were standing guard in a line. Ross was no expert on Moroccan law enforcement, but they appeared to be better equipped than usual, armed with semi-automatic weapons.

Before she could get to the elevator, a plain-clothes officer stopped her.

'Where are you going?'

'Up to my office.'

'At this late hour?'

Ross rolled her eyes.

'We're in the news business,' she said. 'The news doesn't stop.'

'What's in your case?'

'Papers, documents, that's all.'

The officer waved her through. She took the elevator up to the fifteenth floor, placed the attaché case on her desk, and looked out at the lights of Casablanca below. In any other job she might have quit right then, but Hicham Omary had been a mentor to her, a boss with a vision.

She sat down, put her head in her hands, and tried to think straight.

How could she help him?

Without meaning to, she thought of the first time they'd met. It was in Paris at the Musée Jacquemart-André.

Omary had been alone, taking a quick tour through the picture gallery between meetings nearby. They had both been drawn to the same painting, a self-portrait of Nélie Jacquemart, her long, graceful form in profile.

From the first moment she saw Omary, Patricia Ross had been struck by his gentleness, and by his love of fine things.

They had taken tea in the museum's salon and, the next thing she knew, she was working for him in Casablanca.

A dozen memories flashed through, all of them featuring Omary, a man of astonishing courtesy and good taste. Ross had never met anyone quite like him, either in an intellectual capacity, or in the way he always seemed to be three steps ahead of the game. The news business suited him more than anyone alive.

Ross glanced at her reflection in the window. She could feel the establishment closing ranks. It was just a matter of time before they took her in. But she knew how Omary had a sixth sense, a sense of how a situation would be played out, a sense learned on the way up from the streets.

Logging into her laptop, Patricia Ross squinted at her emails, and swore out loud. Her account had been hacked. Thousands of filed messages were missing. She was about to slam the laptop shut, when a random email caught her eye.

It was from Jacques Mart.

She clicked on the message. It was blank, except for a single character way down the page – a question mark, highlighted as a hyperlink. She clicked it, and a web site opened. It was password protected.

Without thinking, Ross typed in the name *Jacquemart*.

The screen went blank. Then, a moment later, it came alive with dozens of dossiers, titled with some of the most important names in the land.

'My God, Hicham, you're amazing!' she exclaimed.

Opening one of the files at random, she found scans of secret bank statements, illicit video footage, and proof of bribe-taking on a grand scale.

At the bottom of the page was an instruction. It read:

MAKE PUBLIC AS SOON AS POSSIBLE

For more than three hours Blaine walked the streets, replaying the sight of Mortimer Wu with his throat slashed.

Time and again, he set off back to Hotel Marrakech, each time stopping just short. On the last abortive return, he saw a cluster of uniformed officers standing outside and the stoned-out clerk being interrogated on the pavement, a fluffy white cat pulled tight to his chest.

Blaine's gut told him to bide his time, because whoever killed the backpacker might still be there, waiting for him. He thought of going to the American consulate and explaining it all. But, again, instinct warned against it. He needed somewhere quiet, somewhere he could lie low and think.

He thought of Ghita and her apartment. It may have been wretched, but at least it was silent – the last place he would be disturbed. As for Ghita, she may have been a pain in the backside, but she spoke fluent English.

Making sure no one was following him, and dressed in the fedora and raincoat, Blaine hurried to the apartment building opposite Baba Cool. He slipped into the entranceway and ran up the stairs, groping his way up the curved wall as he went.

There was no light under Ghita's door, but he knocked anyway.

Silence.

Blaine sucked air through his teeth, squatted down on his satchel, his forehead streaming with sweat.

'Jesus Christ,' he said aloud. 'What do I do now?'

At Globalcom headquarters, Patricia Ross copied the dossiers and sent them to WikiLeaks, with an embargo until ten p.m. GMT.

Then she sent them to every newshound she could think of – in Morocco and abroad.

After that, she hurried upstairs to the newsroom and cornered Adam Binbin, the only editor she could completely trust.

'What have you got on the line-up tonight?'

Binbin logged on, skimming the schedule as he stirred his tea.

'A Chinese student's been murdered downtown – it's a suspected robbery gone wrong. Then some political stuff and a whole lot of sport – the opium of the people.'

'I need to ask a favour, a big favour,' said Ross, touching a hand to the back of her head.

Binbin took a sip of the tea, picked another sugar-lump from the saucer and dropped it in.

'I've got a huge story that has to go out… *tonight.*'

'Bigger than a murdered tourist?'

Ross leaned in close.

'This is as big as it gets,' she said.

Ghita had crisscrossed Boulevard Mohammed V all evening, checking the cafés and the dingy drinking dens tucked away in the backstreets. She might have been repulsed by the derelict men who patronized them, but her mind wasn't on judgement. Rather, it was on finding someone who could lead her to the Falcon.

Behind the market she came to an especially run-down bar. There was no name outside. And, in place of a door, a curtain hung – fashioned from what looked like strands of bath chain. Ghita peered inside, into the cumulonimbus haze of cigarette smoke.

In varying stages of inebriation, half a dozen men were reclining on broken chairs, nursing half-empty bottles of Flag Spéciale. A couple of loose ladies were attempting unsuccessfully to drum up business.

On the floor near the bar, a man was having his shoes cleaned. Ghita recognized the shoeshine box, which had a gold cross on the side. She stormed in and tapped Saed on the neck.

'I need to speak to you,' she said urgently.

He looked at her feet.

'I clean those, OK?' he said.

'I don't want my shoes done.'

'*So?*'

'So, I need some information.'

Choking into her hand, her face screwed up, Ghita took a seat at a booth. Saed sat down opposite.

'I'll get you a drink,' she said. 'You want a Coke?'

The boy made a sign to the barman, and a pair of green bottles were slapped down on the table-top.

'You're far too young to drink that!' Ghita said reproachfully.

'No, no, no…' Saed replied. Lighting a cigarette, he blew the smoke out to the side.

'What would your mother think?'

'I have no mother.'

'Your father then… what would he say? I bet he'd spank you!'

'I have no father. No one to do spanking,' said Saed, downing the first beer in one. 'So I am free.'

Ghita's disapproval eased. She lowered her head subversively, her thumb feeling the curved lines of her iPhone.

'What do you know about the Falcon?' she asked.

The shoeshine boy froze.

'Nothing,' he said quickly.

'I don't believe you.'

'Keep away from the Falcon,' said Saed, wiping the froth off his lip.

'I can't.'

'Why?'

'Because he's had my father imprisoned for a crime he's incapable of committing. I need to know where he's being held.'

'Then look for the police commissioner. You need him. Not the Falcon.'

Ghita frowned.

'*Do I?*'

'Yes.'

'Why?'

'Because he knows everything.'

Ghita's eyes widened.

'Should I give him *baksheesh*?'

The shoeshine boy waved a hand dismissively through the air.

'No, no, just drinks. That's what he wants.'

'Drinks?'

'Scotch.'

'How do you know that?'

'I know everything… like the commissioner,' the boy said, reaching out for the second beer.

Ghita tapped a manicured fingernail to the table.

'And where does the commissioner drink his Scotch?' she asked.

Saed winked at the ground.

'Down there.'

'Where?'

'In the tunnels.'

'What tunnels?'

'The ones under the city. There is a world down there.'

'Is there?'

Saed nodded.

'You don't know that?'

'Apparently not,' Ghita replied curtly. 'When can I go there, to buy him the Scotch?'

The boy shook his head.

'You cannot go there. Only... you know... *working* women can go there.'

'Then will you go?'

'Too young for Club Souterrain.'

'So what can I do?'

'Find someone else.' Saed took a gulp of Flag and lit a second cigarette off the end of the first. 'The American?' he said.

'That imbecile? Oh, God no!'

'One of your friends?'

Ghita's expression soured.

'I don't have any friends,' she snapped.

All of a sudden, 'Yankee Doodle Dandy' blasted out from the iPhone. It was Mustapha.

'*Chéri*, I came looking for you!' said Ghita.

'I know you did. My father told me.'

'When can I see you, my dearest? Will you come for me?'

There was hesitation on the other end.

'Ghita, I must inform you that... that...'

'What?'

'That our engagement is off.'

From: *Casablanca Blues*

61

Nasrudin's Misadventures

Oxford, England
Comedic Constipation

Nasrudin was commissioned by a publisher to write funny stories about his life and antics.

Although he had high hopes, having sold the idea in the first place, he wasn't able to come up with anything at all.

Three months after the manuscript was due, the editor called the would-be writer.

'Where's the manuscript?' he demanded. 'We want to print it next month!'

Nasrudin winced.

'I haven't actually started it.'

'Why not?'

The wise fool sighed long and hard.

'*You* try coming up with funny stories about yourself!' he whined.

'I don't need to because I haven't sold a proposal to a publisher.'

Nasrudin slapped his hands together.

'There's only one thing worse than writer's block…'

'And what's that?' the editor asked.

'Comedic constipation!'

Greenland

Bear Talk

On a mission to the north of Greenland, Nasrudin strayed from the track he was supposed to be following and got terribly lost.

Having no communication with his backup team, he was losing hope.

Then, he spied a jagged lump of ice in the distance, upon which was sitting a polar bear.

With no one else to ask for help, he strode over and begged the creature for directions.

The bear looked at the explorer in disbelief.

'Don't you understand my accent?' Nasrudin asked.

'No,' the bear replied politely, 'I understood the question just fine.'

'Then why are you gaping at me like that?'

'Because I've never met a human who speaks perfect polar bear before.'

Paris, France

Miming Full Volume

Flat broke as usual, Nasrudin was strolling through Montmartre when he saw people throwing coins to a mime, who was performing in the bright summer sun.

Taking off his jacket, he laid it on the ground, as the artiste had done, and pretended to be a mime as well.

Although he had no training as an actor, he found the work easy, and he was soon enacting a story of unrequited love.

But, unlike the mime across the street, who'd taken a small fortune in coins, Nasrudin hadn't been thrown a single cent.

Cupping both hands around his mouth, he mimed in full volume:

'Damn you... you cheapskates! I'm giving you my best material!'

Monte Carlo, Monaco
Adulation Wanted
Known as a high roller in the gaming world, Nasrudin had an unprecedented winning streak while gambling at the celebrated Casino de Monte Carlo.

In the establishment's long and distinguished history, no one else had ever accrued winnings on such a scale. And none had come close to the wise fool in disposing of his newly gained wealth.

As soon as he had his hands on the fortune he'd won, Nasrudin went on a spending spree to end all spending sprees.

He bought an enormous villa overlooking the sea, a private jet, a yacht, and a fleet of luxury cars. He'd hand out Rolex watches to anyone he passed, and would allow complete strangers to enjoy the fruits of his winnings.

Worrying that he was burning through his winnings too fast, an old friend cautioned Nasrudin to be careful.

'Before you know it, you'll be how you used to be – broker than broke.'

The wise fool shrugged.

'Whether I am rich or poor is of no concern to me at all,' he replied.

'How could it not be?'

'Because I'm not in it for the money.'

'Then what are you in it for?'

Nasrudin looked at his old friend, smiled vacantly, and answered:

'For the adulation.'

Pavlovka, Russia
The Perfect Time

Following a complicated misunderstanding involving a box of chickens, a felt hat, and a grilled cheese sandwich, Nasrudin had become a fugitive.

Having been chased across Siberia, he'd holed up in the village of Pavlovka, east of Omsk, and was hiding in a log cabin in the woods.

It was only a matter of time before the police dogs caught his scent and tracked him down.

Flicking the switch a megaphone, the commander called out into the darkness:

'We know you're in there!'

There was no answer, so the commander repeated his words.

'But I'm not!' came a soft voice. 'There's no one in here except for my shadow.'

The commander rolled his eyes.

'This is no time to speak such nonsense!'

'On the contrary, it's the perfect time to speak such nonsense,' Nasrudin replied. 'Because, believe me, I've got no sense left to speak!'

Waterloo, Belgium
Over-prepared
Nasrudin decided to cycle around the world, starting in the Belgian town of Waterloo.

The flat landscape there would, he felt, not prove too much of a strain while he got used to a life on the open road.

Having planned the expedition for weeks, he bought himself a first-rate bicycle, panniers, camping gear, and a mass of other equipment.

Despite telling everyone he met about his plans to cycle around the world, he didn't cycle anywhere at all – not even across town.

Eventually, one of his local friends enquired gently why he hadn't gone anywhere at all.

Nasrudin shrugged.

'There was no need.'

'Why not?'

'Because all that preparation got the restlessness out of my system,' he said.

Boston, Massachusetts
Self-duping

Following a series of unlikely coincidences, Nasrudin was recognized as a visionary.

Overnight, almost everyone wanted to hear what he thought would happen to the world over the coming century.

Hoping to capitalize on his newfound fame, a publisher commissioned him to write a book about his prophecies. When the book was released, it sold in its millions, and the wise fool was catapulted to global stardom.

In the days and weeks after its launch, the book led to public hysteria and celebration in equal measure. Part of the reason was that the prophecies included predictions that the Earth would be invaded by blood-sucking aliens, and that geysers raining $100 bills would sprout up all over the place.

While waiting to go on a radio show in Boston, Nasrudin was asked by a technician how he could be so certain all the predictions will come true.

The wise fool shrugged.

'I've got no idea at all,' he replied.

'Then why are you making such claims?' the technician asked. 'After all, they're getting people worked up to fever pitch.'

'Because,' Nasrudin answered, 'by the time anyone finds out I'll be long gone.'

'Don't you feel guilty though, of duping people?'

Nasrudin looked at the technician hard, his eyes cold.

'My friend,' he replied, 'this is an example of people duping themselves.'

TAHIR SHAH

Vienna, Austria
Out-of-Sync-Mania
However hard he tried, Nasrudin never managed to fit in.

His family and friends knew he was an oddity, and they put up with him – at least most of the time. But there came a point at which they grouped together, and suggested the wise fool go in search of treatment for his condition, which was now making their lives intolerable.

The behaviour was characterized by huge mood swings, and by living a life that was strangely out of sync. Nasrudin had taken to sleeping in the bath, bathing in the kitchen sink, and cooking meals in bed.

Packing a few belongings, he bid his friends and family farewell, and zigzagged around the world in search of someone who could cure his condition.

Eventually, he arrived in Vienna, the founding place of psychoanalysis.

A respected psychiatrist named Dr. Plank made an examination, then gave his diagnosis.

'You are suffering from a condition we call Out-of-Sync-Mania,' he said. 'The only way to be yourself again is to have a big shock.'

'You mean like when you get cured from hiccups?'

'Yes, that's right. The most effective treatment is if I frighten you when you are not expecting it.'

Nasrudin agreed, and went about life as usual.

The problem was that he was expecting Dr. Plank to frighten him, so he was always prepared – even when he was asleep.

Days passed, and the condition grew worse, as a result of expecting to be frightened.

Dr. Plank jumped out on a tram and clashed cymbals together, but the wise fool was expecting him. Then, the psychiatrist lurched at Nasrudin in a cinema.

But, again, the assault was anticipated.

Confused why the usual techniques were not working, the expert pondered long and hard.

Then he had an idea.

He phoned the wise fool.

'I would like to visit you this afternoon at 5.36 and 23 seconds.'

'Thank you doctor,' Nasrudin answered. 'You have my address.'

At precisely 5.36 and 23 seconds, the doorbell rang.

'I'm here!' the psychiatrist called out.

The wise fool opened the door.

As soon as he saw the doctor, he screamed, and his Out-of-Sync-Mania was cured.

Nasrudin was greatly impressed.

'How did you know the perfect way the scare me, doctor?'

The physician drew a hand down over his goatee.

'Because in usual circumstances an expected visitor wouldn't be the least bit scary,' he said. 'But, as you were so profoundly out of sync, I had a feeling it was the one thing that would work!'

Ivanovka, Azerbaijan
Gradual Improvement

Nasrudin had been travelling through Central Asia for some time, and had learned a universal fact that linked all the countries in the region.

It was that there was nothing quite so important as having a reputation.

No reputation, and you were likely to be trodden underfoot.

So, before approaching the village of Ivanovka, he gathered together a group of boys and offered them a handful of coins in return for publicizing him there.

'Go to Ivanovka and tell everyone you meet that the world-famous explorer, Nasrudin, is about to arrive. Do you understand?'

Nodding, the boys took the coins, and set off across the fields to the next village.

That evening, they returned.

'You did do as I asked?'

The boys said that they had.

'And were people astonished, delighted, and amazed?' the wise fool asked urgently.

'No, no one was impressed,' said the oldest boy.

'Some jobs have to be done by a professional!' Nasrudin exclaimed.

Next morning, as the dawn broke over Azerbaijan, he dressed in his finest clothing, festooned his donkey in a strand of scarlet silk, and set off over the fields.

Riding tall, he rode into Ivanovka, his chest pushed out like a warrior returning from battle.

No one showed the least bit of interest.

'Here I am!' the wise fool yelled at the top of his lungs.

Still no interest.

'Here I am! Yes, it's me! It's Nasrudin the world-famous explorer!'

'If you're so famous why haven't we heard of you?' a homeless man begging in the main square spat.

'Well, I paid those stupid boys from the other village to tell you about me yesterday!'

The beggar hissed rudely.

'If you were really famous you wouldn't need to pay children to do your publicity.'

'That may be true,' Nasrudin retorted angrily, 'but I'm working my way up the celebrity scale gradually. How d'you expect me to become really famous until I've been moderately famous first?'

Iquitos, Peru
The Pink-toed Tarantula
Having swallowed a bluebottle, Nasrudin had asked everyone he met what to do.

All manner of advice was given.

A dentist suggested he hang upside down in a tree and wait for the insect to fly out.

A chiropodist suggested he learn to speak the language of bluebottles and then make his case.

TAHIR SHAH

Then, Nasrudin's psychiatrist suggested he travel to the Upper Amazon, where a particular species of pink-toed tarantula lived… an arachnid known for its fondness for big, juicy flies.

'Just swallow the tarantula and it'll gobble the bluebottle up,' the physician said.

Never one to do things by halves, the wise fool took the expert's advice.

The next week he arrived in Iquitos, located smack bang in the middle of the jungle.

After days of adventures he reached a longhouse, in the rafters of which dozens of tarantulas were nesting.

Nasrudin lay down on the floor, opened his mouth, stuck out his tongue.

…And waited.

Three days and nights came and went.

Then, just as Nasrudin was dozing off, a plump female tarantula crept over his tongue, into his mouth, and down his throat.

Swallowing hard, the wise fool punched the air.

'That'll teach you, you damned bluebottle!' he gasped.

Rio de Janeiro, Brazil
The Secret of Success
Nasrudin had entered the Olympic Games as an athlete in the two hundred metres.

He may have been well below average, but quotas had to be kept up, and he was given the green light to run.

Just before the start of the race, a journalist called out to the wise fool:

'D'you think you have a chance of winning?'

'Of course I do.'

'But you're the slowest by far.'

'I have an unbeatable strategy!' Nasrudin answered cheerily.

A minute or two later, the starter's gun fired, and the race began.

Right away, two of the athletes tripped over one another and were disqualified.

Then, a hundred metres in, a third was eliminated for straying out of his lane.

And, later, two more of the runners were disqualified for having taken banned substances.

As a result, Nasrudin was given the gold medal.

At the ceremony, the same journalist who'd called out before the race did so again.

'What was your unbeatable strategy?'

The gold medal hanging around his neck, the wise fool grinned ear-to-ear.

'Simple,' he said. 'It's not about me having good fortune, but about everyone else having misfortune.'

Abergavenny, Wales
The Taste of Freedom
Nasrudin was given work as a fruit-picker and, from the first moment of his employment, he did nothing but moan.

The farmer said that if he complained any more he'd be fired.

Undeterred, the wise fool made jokes about the farmer all day long. Within an hour, an informant had reported the subversion.

Nasrudin was summoned to the office.

'You can get out!' the farmer scowled, expecting the employee to beg for a second chance.

Instead, the errant fruit-picker kissed the farmer's hands.

'Thank you so much, O Great One!' he whimpered.

The farmer narrowed his eyes suspiciously.

'Don't think any amount of thanking will get me to change my mind!'

'But, O Great One... I'm not asking you to change your mind!'

'Then what are you thanking me for?'

'For freeing me from my servitude!'

Mato Grosso, Brazil
Ready, Steady
After spending many weeks in deep jungle on the trail of an incredibly rare bird known as Spix's macaw, thought by many to be extinct, Nasrudin spotted one in a clearing.

His heart was pounding so hard that he almost collapsed.

Steadying his nerves, he approached the bird, with his assistant close behind.

When close to the macaw, he didn't pull out his net, as the plan had been to do.

Instead, he cupped both hands around his mouth, and hissed:

'I'll count to ten, then we're coming!'

The wise fool's assistant was both bewildered and shocked.

'So many months in this damned jungle searching for that bird, and you shout that! What are you thinking?!'

Nasrudin smiled vacantly.

'Simply giving him a head start,' he said.

Cheltenham, England
The Cloak of Wisdom

The fact that Nasrudin's brain was wired differently from everyone else's meant that the wise fool was unsurpassed in cracking even the most unbreakable enemy codes.

Having been employed by numerous disreputable countries, he was poached by the British intelligence agency, MI6, and given an office of his own.

After years of service, the wise fool retired, and wrote a book about the systems he had developed for code-breaking.

The work became an instant bestseller... not because anyone could understand it, but because owning it was seen as proof of higher intellect.

The few who managed to get through the volume were feted, and regarded as geniuses in their own right.

With time, the book – which was utterly mystifying – was used by the secret services as a basis for a specialized cryptographic system of its own.

Nasrudin was asked to comment on the success of his masterpiece.

'Every great genius in human history has been a fool,' he said. 'And they recognized themselves as fools, rather than merely pretending to be wearing a cloak of wisdom.'

M'hamid, Morocco
Solar Remote
The wise fool had crisscrossed the deserts of southern Morocco for weeks, travelling with nothing but a pair of she-camels, a couple of water skins, a bed roll and a little food.

Priding himself as a traveller in the mould of the great adventurers of the past, the wise fool regarded himself as the kind of man who could endure flies, thirst, and being roasted by the sun from morning until dusk.

As he tramped through the vast wasteland, certain ideas flashed onto the stage of his mind. Most of them were nonsensical but, once in a while, he had an idea that had promise.

One day, while heading to an oasis three days east of M'hamid, he had an idea that had the possibility of making his fame and fortune.

He would devise a remote control with which to modulate the sun's heat.

Ecstatic beyond words at the idea – which had the potential to change the future of humanity – he hurried to M'hamid, and then took the bus to Casablanca.

Once there, he rented a workshop in Ain Diab, and started turning his idea into reality.

Every day, he would toil from morning until night, working with all manner of technical equipment.

Weeks passed.

After returning to the drawing board a hundred times, he solved a series of mathematical problems which, in turn, allowed him to build a prototype of the device.

Although he hoped to scale it down in size, the prototype was the size of a city bus.

A local man who had befriended the wise fool, and invested in his idea, suggested that the apparatus be tested first of all outside the workshop, where it had been built.

Nasrudin shook his head.

'There's only one place to test it... the desert where I first had the idea!' he cried. 'I shall have a trailer built, and will take the machine down there, and test it *in situ!*'

And so the huge machine was transported first to M'hamid, then across the salt flats, and far beyond them to the next horizon... with the investor and a team of engineers following close behind.

Once he was standing in the exact spot at which he'd had the idea in the first place, Nasrudin gave the order for the giant remote control to be lowered onto the sand.

This was done.

The wise fool peered up at the sun, then at his watch.

Five minutes before noon.

Taking a deep breath, he turned a dial to the left, then jerked the big red lever on the side, and waited.

Nothing happened.

Then he pulled the lever up and down.

Still nothing.

'Doesn't it work?' the investor asked.

Nasrudin insisted that the machine worked, but that it would need to cool down for a few hours before they could try again.

'We will have another go at dusk,' he snapped.

At six-thirty that evening, he had a second go, just as the sun was disappearing below the horizon.

'It works!' the wise fool declared. 'My creation works!'

'The air's cooling,' said the investor, 'not because of your remote control, but because night is approaching.'

Nasrudin, who hated being caught out, glowered at his companion.

'No invention works perfectly right from the start,' he said. 'At the moment, it's working well at the beginning and the end of the day. With a little more time I'll have it working a hundred per cent.'

From: *The Misadventures of the Mystifying Nasrudin*

The Ladder of Mithras

THE PRESIDENT'S PRIVATE secretary corralled Emma and Will down into the palace basement. Agitated, his face was dripping with perspiration.

'We are relying on you to instruct us which treasures are most valuable,' he said. 'You will find a lot of second-rate items, most of them gifts to the late emperor from other African leaders.'

The private secretary broke off at what sounded like an infantry charge outside. Tugging off his horn-rimmed glasses, he wiped them fitfully with a damp handkerchief.

'The protestors are gaining ground!' he exclaimed, his voice trembling. 'We will hold them off. But I must implore you to work with speed. Do you understand?'

Will signalled that they did.

The private secretary unlocked the reinforced steel door to the vault and stepped back.

'I will leave you to your work,' he said. 'The president's guard shall be down in a few minutes to pack up the most valuable pieces. The helicopters are due very soon. One already left this morning with a dozen crates.' The private secretary paused again, as his ears caught the clamour of protestors nearby. 'The people of Ethiopia thank you,' he said solemnly.

Inside the treasure vault, Will and Emma found rows of shelving, packed with artefacts amassed through eight centuries of imperial rule.

A central display housed the crowns of the emperors. Crafted from fine gold, they were laden with precious gems. There were solid silver tureens as well, and dinner sets bearing the imperial seal of the Lion of Judah; and racks of ornate weaponry, orbs and sceptres, ornamental clocks, caskets brimming with ancient coins, rock crystal vases, and coronation robes.

'This is outrageous!' Will yelled.

'I've never seen anything like it.'

'Start looking for the Ladder.'

'Got any idea – size, shape, anything?'

Will shook his head.

'Just look for something that could have come from ancient Greece.'

They spread out, combing the stacks for the Ladder of Mithras.

Emma pointed to a robe in a glass case – black wool embroidered intricately with gold.

'I've seen that in old photos,' she said, impressed. 'It was worn by Haile Selassie, last emperor of Ethiopia, at his coronation.'

'How come they have emperors rather than kings like everyone else?' Will asked.

'Because they claim descent from King Solomon.'

'Solomon and who?'

'Solomon and the Queen of Sheba. To the Rastafarians he's God incarnate.'

'*Rastas*, you mean like Bob Marley?'

'Yup. They're named after him – *Ras Tafari*.'

'So what happened to the last emperor?' asked Will.

'Bustled away during a coup d'état in a Volkswagen bug, smothered with a pillow and buried under President Mengistu's toilet.'

There was a clatter of automatic fire outside. Short bursts, louder and more frequent.

'We don't have much time,' shouted Will. 'I've got a feeling this is the wrong place to be right now!'

Emma was only half listening. She had spotted something in a carved teak box – a silver and gold helmet, adorned with what looked like a ladder motif.

'Could this be it?'

Will rushed over.

'I'd love to say it was, but…'

Will's sentence was cut short by an explosion. He and Emma were flung to the ground, as the palace shook on its foundations.

At the far end of the vault, the shelving collapsed, choking them in clouds of dust.

Will grabbed Emma's hand.

'You OK?'

'Yeah, you?'

'Just about.'

Another blast ripped through. It was followed by cries of anger and pain, more gunfire, and by the dull thud of helicopter rotor blades in the distance.

'Sounds like they're gonna try and land out there.'

'It'll be suicide.'

Emma turned to the door.

'Ladder or no Ladder, we have to get out of here!'

Will thrust out a hand.

'*Wait!*'

'There's no time!'

Will didn't react. He was standing in front of a display case, its glass front smashed by the blast. Inside, covered in dust, was a mannequin decked out in imperial robes. Skewed on the head was a solid gold crown ornamented with polished gems.

Snatching the crown, Will tossed it onto the floor. Then, with care, he reached in and pulled a silver pendant from the mannequin.

With Emma watching, he put it around his neck.

Just then a third explosion hit.

A Russian-made RPG fired at close range.

Deafened, enveloped in smoke and dust, Will and Emma spotted blue sky through the ceiling of the vault.

Choking, Emma led the way.

'Follow me!' she cried, clawing her way up over the sea of rubble. As she scrambled up, Will made out a line of rioters in blurred silhouette heading straight for her.

'Look out!'

Will tripped, his ankle trapped between two blocks of masonry. Emma reached back and yanked him free.

Inexplicably, the rioters were gone.

'Where are they?'

'Must have been shot,' yelled Emma, her blouse drenched in blood.

'They get you?'

'No, it's not mine.'

Will took Emma's hand. Together, they clambered through clouds of dust, up over the bodies and out into the daylight.

Protestors were streaming towards the palace from all directions, as the clamour of a Super Puma deafened them.

Against the odds, the pilot managed to perch it on the roof, the massive rotors sweeping invisibly round.

Will choked out a lungful of dust.

'Looks like the president's making his grand escape.'

'What do we do now?'

'How about getting out of here fast.'

'Where to?'

'The US Embassy. It's our only bet,' said Will.

Way in the distance Emma spotted a taxi approaching. A battered red Lada, its windscreen a spider's web of cracks. As it neared them, she flagged it down, surprised when the driver stopped.

They leapt into the back.

'To the American Embassy!'

The taxi driver spun round. He was about to say something, when a towering figure wearing military fatigues shattered the passenger window with the butt of a .44 revolver.

Without the faintest hint of emotion, he emptied three chambers into the driver's head.

Her face spattered in blood, Emma was screaming.

'What the…?!' cried Will.

The man in fatigues motioned to the passengers.

'Get out! Get out now!' his voice boomed over the clatter of gunfire in the palace behind.

Hands above their heads, they got out of the car.

'Put your hands down,' ordered the man, stuffing away his weapon. 'I've just saved your lives.'

Reaching through the shattered passenger window, he seized a 9 mm pistol from the driver's right hand.

'He was about to finish you off.'

Will felt faint. The man grabbed his shoulder, steadying him.

'Come with me! We'll go to where it's safe.'

'Who are you?'

'Solomon.'

Will touched Emma's hand.

'Can we trust him?' he whispered.

Jerking back as though he had overheard, Solomon's face lit up in a grin.

'Yes, you can trust me!'

'Why?'

'Because I have been sent for you.'

'Who by?'

Solomon sponged a hand over his face, wiping away the sweat.

'By Mr. Hannibal Fogg,' he said.

Slaloming through the lines of rioters, Solomon steered the Lada away from the centre of town at breakneck speed. Without giving the killing a second thought, he had thrown the driver's body out onto the ground unceremoniously.

Behind them came the intermittent clatter of Kalashnikov gunfire, followed by an almighty explosion. It was accompanied by a plume of black smoke, mushrooming up into the heavens above the Ethiopian capital.

'Must be the palace arms dump going up,' said Solomon, spinning the wheel fast through his hands.

Will didn't hear him.

'Don't understand,' he stammered, his mind reeling. 'How could Hannibal have sent you?'

'It's a long story,' Solomon replied. 'And I'm not the man to tell it.'

'Then who is?'

'My grandfather.'

Craning her neck to the right, Emma caught her reflection in the driver's mirror. She broke down in tears.

'Look at me! I'm covered in blood!'

'Relax,' said Solomon calmly, aiming the vehicle at a double line of protestors. 'We'll be at the safe house in a minute.'

Will clapped his hands.

'No! We want the American Embassy!'

Solomon launched into a crazed laugh, blinding white teeth stretched between his ears.

'The embassy got hit this morning,' he said.

The safe house was guarded by a pair of figures with the same sinewy build as Solomon. They were both clutching cut-down AK-47s, their double magazines bound together with silver duct tape.

'My brothers Jonah and Yohannes,' Solomon said by way of introduction.

Will and Emma were taken inside, where they found themselves in a fortified room. The windows were blacked out, and the walls and floor made of concrete. A cluster of rickety old school chairs and an upturned packing crate did for furniture.

Solomon flicked a switch, and the room was bathed in neon light.

'I'm surprised there's still electricity,' he said. 'It won't last for long.'

Will was shaking.

'Never been under fire before?'

'Take a wild guess.'

'The adrenalin's used up all your blood sugar. Eat some of these.'

Solomon ripped open a packet of wholemeal biscuits and passed them to Will. Chewing one, he strained to swallow. His throat was too dry to eat.

In reflex, he thumped a hand to his chest, his fist striking something hard. In all the excitement he had forgotten about the pendant. Digging it out from under his shirt, he took it off and nudged Emma.

'Look at this.'

'It's the monogram.'

'Yeah, but that's not all… it's a key as well.'

Just then, one of the guards outside wolf-whistled twice. The sound was followed by the silhouette of a man at the door. Unlike Solomon and his brothers, he was weak. Hunched low over a cane, he was presented as Tewodros.

'How do you do?' he enquired politely. 'I am very pleased to make your acquaintance, Mr. William Fogg.'

Will scanned the man's wrinkled face, taking in his cataract-clouded eyes.

'How do you know who I am?'

Tewodros laughed.

'I knew your grandfather, Mr. Hannibal Fogg.'

'He was my great-great-grandfather.'

The ancient took in the floor vacantly. 'I suppose that is right,' he said. 'After all, it was a very long while ago.'

Emma balked.

'You knew Hannibal?'

'Yes, indeed. When I was a young man, I was his assistant on one of his Abyssinian expeditions. He used to come here often and loved our country, although it almost stole his manhood on one occasion.'

The comment was lost on Will. He was still thinking about the bloodbath back at the palace, and about the pendant clutched in his hand.

'I don't understand,' he said again. 'How do you know who I am?'

Tewodros drew a long fingernail down his nose. He didn't reply. Will was about to repeat the question for a third time, when the old man spoke.

'Because Mr. Fogg left instructions,' he said. 'He made me promise to commit this day to memory. He said that nothing was so important as today... 18th May 2017. Back then I did a calculation on my fingers, remember it clearly. "If I live that long, I shall be one hundred and five years old!" I said.

'Mr. Hannibal Fogg slapped me on the back, and promised that I would live. He said it with such certainty that over the years I almost wondered if he had seen the future.'

'What instructions did he give you?' asked Will.

As if summoning a stream of memory, Tewodros pressed a hand to his wrinkled brow.

'He told me to make my way to the Presidential Palace in the afternoon, and to look for a young man – a white man.' Tewodros sighed. 'I'm getting old,' he said sorrowfully, 'and as you have seen it's chaos. So I sent my grandson, Solomon, to find you.'

Emma turned to Will.

'How could he have known?'

'I know... it's incredible, even for Hannibal.'

Tewodros touched a hand to his throat and began coughing. He coughed so long that the others thought his time might have at last come. But the coughing eventually eased.

'And now,' he said, 'I will take you to the room.'

'Which room?'

'The one you have come to see.'

Will looked at Tewodros.

'I don't know what you mean,' he said. 'What room?'

'Mr. Hannibal's Abyssinian Chamber, of course.'

Solomon prised open a storm grate in the Mercato quarter of town. Two hundred yards to the south of where he was crouched with a crowbar there was carnage.

Kitted out in third-rate riot gear, a dozen soldiers were attempting to stave off droves of looters and hold their ground against the legions of protestors. Molotov cocktails and debris were flying through the smoke-tinged air, cries of rage drowning out the military sirens.

Once the storm grate was open, Solomon motioned to Emma and Will.

'Get in there quick!' he barked, just as a vigilante Jeep reeled full tilt towards them.

Dropping to his knees, Will shuffled up to the hole, swivelling the lower half of his body inside. Rusted iron rungs were set into the concrete casing. His hands grasped them, and were at once covered in roaches.

'God damn it!' he shouted, lowering himself down into the darkness.

'Miss Emma, you next!'

'What about Tewodros?'

Solomon let out a grunt, an expression of brute strength.

'I'll carry him down.'

Once Emma had disappeared behind Will, the old man curled both arms around his grandson's back, and together they descended – Solomon's giant hand heaving the storm grate back into place just in time.

'How far down is it?' called Will, his voice echoing up the tunnel.

'Just keep going!'

Solomon's words were lost in the roar of the vigilante Jeep rattling over the storm grate above.

One hand after the next, they descended. Will was thankful for the darkness. It prevented him from actually seeing the cockroaches, or the rats – which were everywhere.

In a frail voice Tewodros cried out, instructing Will to wait at the bottom.

A moment after that, all four of them were in the sewer pipe, their feet slipping in sludge.

Solomon clicked on his torch and, gagging, Will wished they were in darkness again.

'Just a little further,' Tewodros intoned.

'How can you be sure it's still there?'

The old man shrugged.

'I can't.'

'When were you last down here?'

'With Mr. Fogg.'

'But when?'

Taking the torch from his grandson, Tewodros staggered ahead.

'In the summer of 1936,' he said.

Reaching back, Will felt for Emma's hand. He squeezed it reassuringly.

'Here's the passage,' said Tewodros, aiming the light's arc high. 'This one, off to the left.'

One at a time, they followed, the stench of raw sewage unbearable.

'Here it is.'

Tewodros rapped a knuckle to an iron door. Fumbling, he pulled out the key hanging around his neck.

'I've worn this almost my entire life,' he said with a sigh. 'It's three keys in one.'

'Quickly, open it,' Will pleaded. 'I'm covered in roaches.'

The lock's mechanism clicked and a steel bolt slid back.

Gently, Tewodros pulled the handle.

The steel door swung open on greased hinges.

In single file they entered.

When the door was firmly shut and locked behind them, Tewodros pushed open a second portal. The rats and the cockroaches were gone now, replaced by a clinical room. Small and bare, it smelled of ammonia and was lit by electric lights.

'Is this the Abyssinian Chamber?' asked Will, a tone of disappointment in his voice.

Tewodros pointed at a third portal. Unlike the first two doorways, it was made from stone.

'In there,' he said. 'Mr. Fogg sealed it to prevent decay or corrosion.'

Stooping down, he slid the key into the lock and turned it twice.

A gushing sound came and went.

'What was that?' asked Emma.

'The hermetic seal being broken,' Tewodros replied. 'The air's rushing back in.'

He signalled for Solomon to open the door.

Stepping forwards, his grandson wrenched the handle downwards and pulled with all his might.

The door was immensely heavy – crafted from a single slab of granite – balanced perfectly on a complex hinge mechanism. As it swung open, Hannibal's Abyssinian Chamber was revealed.

Fifty-five feet square, it was bright, illuminated by shafts of natural sunlight searing in through blocks of glass set into the roof. Tewodros entered first, blinded by the sudden light.

The others followed close behind. As their eyes adjusted to the light, they caught a first glimpse of the equipment.

There must have been fifty crates filled with expedition gear, weaponry and specialist supplies. All of it in mint condition and monogrammed; it was a time capsule of ingenuity.

'Hannibal!' cried Will in disbelief. 'You've done it again!'

Tewodros fluttered a hand at the crates dismissively.

'Tip of the iceberg,' he said with a toothless grin.

'Huh?'

'Follow me.'

The old man cocked his head at a stack of crates piled up against the far wall. 'Get those away,' he said.

Will and Solomon did as they were told, revealing a low door.

Tewodros punched a number into a mechanical display. A system of gears unlocked, and the door opened.

A moment later, he and the others were standing in a far larger room. Much of it was taken up with equipment. But it wasn't the gear that caught Will's attention.

In the middle of the chamber, its tyres raised an inch off the ground, was a vehicle.

Emma burst out laughing.

'This has been the wildest day,' she said.

'How the hell did he get this old thing down here?' asked Will.

'Old?' said Tewodros. 'What are you talking about? It's brand spanking new!'

Circling it as in a dream, Will took in the cloth top, the bucket seats and the running boards.

'What make is it?'

Tewodros reached out and, brushing his fingers against the driver's door, he breathed in.

'It's a Rolls-Royce,' he said.

1936

A semi-circle of thatched huts stood in the middle of the plain, their baked mud walls affording little shade from the blistering African sun.

A stone's throw from the hamlet, some boys were tending the clan's sheep, the parched mud beneath their bare feet a shattered mass of cracks.

It hadn't rained in the Afar Desert for years.

Hannibal Fogg was seated in a chair under a sprawling thorn tree – the only natural shade for a hundred miles. He was dressed in khaki, a safari outfit of his own design. On his lap was a notebook, the pages ruled in neat columns, each one filled with phonetic symbols.

Standing an arm's length away was a tall Ethiopian man of about twenty. Unlike Hannibal, he appeared distressed by the sweltering heat.

'Tell me, Tewodros, what's the Amharic word for buffalo?'

'It is *gosh*, Mr. Fogg.'

'Ahh, that's right. And tell me, how does one say, "How long does it take?"?'

'*Sent gizea yiwesdal.*'

Tewodros had turned his back to Hannibal's chair.

He was standing stock still, as if listening to the wind.

'What do you hear?'

'It's not what I hear, sir.'

'Then what?'

'I smell the Danakil, Mr. Fogg.'

'Oh hush, there's no Danakil for fifty miles.'

'Where Danakil are concerned it is unwise to take a chance, sir.'

Hannibal circled a phonetic notation with his pen.

'And what does *kulfu* mean?'

Slanting his face into the breeze, Tewodros breathed in through his nostrils.

'I must plead with you, sir,' he said. 'I can smell them very clearly. They are near.'

'Nonsense!' said Hannibal. 'Come on... *kulfu*...?'

Tewodros had nothing but respect for his employer and would not normally have made a fuss. But the Danakil were not a normal tribe.

'I believe you know what they prize more than anything else, sir.'

'*Testicles?*' said Hannibal, the word rolling off his tongue with delight.

'Yes, sir. But there's one kind of testicle they prize above all others, for their trophy necklaces.'

'And what kind of testicle is that, Tewodros?' asked the Englishman studiously.

'A white man's, sir.'

Groaning, Hannibal went back to his notes.

'You know I don't believe that mumbo jumbo,' he said.

Tewodros was at the point of pleading.

'Danakil can follow the scent of a lion crouching on the savannah three horizons away,' he said.

Glancing up from his notebook, Hannibal seemed distracted. He was about to reply, when something caught his attention – the frozen mask of terror wrapped over Tewodros's face.

He looked at the horizon.

In the distance, sweeping over the plain at impressive speed, were a thousand Danakil warriors. They looked like a plague of insects at first, one blurred into the next.

But, as they got rapidly closer, Hannibal could make out their rhino-hide shields, and the elongated spears wielded ferociously above their heads.

As they drew even closer, he discerned the individual faces and the strands of human testicles worn around their necks.

In a single deft movement, Hannibal lurched up from the chair, tossed down the notebook…

…and ran for his life.

*

'MR. FOGG HAD the Rolls-Royce modified for Abyssinia,' Tewodros explained. 'It started out as a Silver Ghost Tourer, but was stripped down to the chassis and completely rebuilt. The engine is a straight-six, the suspension reinforced and the panelling is fully armoured.'

'Armoured?'

Hannibal's former assistant tapped a fingernail to the bodywork, the details crystal clear to him despite his advanced age.

'Bullet-proofing all round,' he said. 'But that's just the start. There are stun grenades in the doors and a water-cooled Vickers .303 machine gun mounted under the bonnet. You pull that lever when you're ready to deploy it.'

'How did he ever get it down here?' asked Emma, for a second time.

'More to the point, how do we get it out?' said Will.

Tewodros gesticulated at another stack of crates.

'There's a door behind those,' he said. 'Takes you on a purpose-built track... comes out near the Church of Saint George.'

Next morning, after a night stretched out on the floor of the safe house, Will, Emma and Solomon set off in the Rolls-Royce, driving north out of Addis Ababa. The vehicle had started on the first go, filling Fogg's secret Abyssinian Chamber with fumes.

In the hours of darkness, the presidential palace had been burned to the ground, the ancient wealth of the Ethiopians looted.

Steering through the suburbs, Solomon zigzagged between the bodies of dead protestors, and others caught in the crossfire.

As the vehicle progressed into the wealthier suburbs, Will spotted the plumes of smoke rising from the mansions where the president's henchmen had lived in luxury until a few hours before. Some of them had escaped to neighbouring Djibouti or even to Europe, as their leader himself had done. Those less fortunate were hanging from the trees, trussed up by their ankles by the mobs of vigilantes baying for blood.

Leaning back, Will tested the ropes holding the luggage. He had followed Solomon's advice and taken along only what they could be certain to use.

As Solomon explained, in a war situation nothing was so precious as provisions or fuel. The Rolls-Royce was laden with plenty of both, its mighty engine growling under the weight of it all.

The suburbs gave way to the open road, and Will's thoughts turned to the Ladder of Mithras.

As if the task of locating it wasn't challenging enough already, Ethiopia's political situation was disintegrating hour by hour.

Wishing them well on their journey, Tewodros had revealed one last nugget of information entrusted to him in person by Hannibal Fogg:

'Seek out the Cross of Lalibela,' he had said, 'and the Ladder will be near.'

A day and a half of jolting and juddering, and the Rolls-Royce swerved west off the main road. The last fifty miles had been strewn with bandit positions, and many more bodies strung from the trees.

While Solomon deployed the stun grenades and opened up the Vickers to clear the path, Will took the wheel.

'Lalibela's only a few miles now,' said Solomon.

'Thank God for that.'

'Oh, no…'

'What is it?'

Solomon cocked his head to the distance.

Will had been so busy swerving around the potholes, some of them as deep as a man's height, that he had forgotten to keep his eyes on the road ahead.

Two hundred yards beyond them was a roadblock. Beside it, a beer truck was burning on its side.

Solomon pulled the Vickers into position.

'Hold tight!'

Emma thrust out a hand from the back seat.

'They're just kids!'

'This is war,' Solomon countered.

'I'll ram it.'

Will's voice was lost against the sound of the Rolls's engine gaining speed.

As they approached the barricades, the child soldiers raised their weapons in disbelief.

'They've got AKs!' Solomon yelled. 'They'll shred us!'

Will forced the accelerator to the floor.

'Heads down!'

Aided by the gradient, the Rolls-Royce picked up speed.

It was pushing sixty by the time it struck the burning barricades. Against the clatter of Kalashnikov fire, the Rolls barrelled ahead, its bodywork raked by razor wire.

'We're through!' Emma shrieked.

Will breathed out, whooped, and got a flash of the predictable life in San Francisco he had left behind.

An hour later, the Rolls-Royce reached Lalibela.

'So where's the Cross?' Emma asked.

'This way, in the Church of Saint George,' Solomon said.

It was then they caught a first obstructed view of the rock-hewn church. Like all the others in Lalibela, it was carved into the pancake-flat plateau – every inch of it hollowed in a true wonder of pious dedication.

If the church had been anywhere else on earth there might have been security cordons and tourists.

It being Ethiopia, there was gunfire instead.

'Maybe this isn't such a good idea,' Will said, clambering out of the vehicle.

Solomon unclipped a stun grenade from its mooring in the driver's door.

'Be prepared for anything,' he said, leading the way to the viewpoint.

Once at the edge, he held up a hand to halt Will and Emma. Together they peered down at the Church of Saint George. A singular feat of architecture and endurance, it was carved from the rock plateau in the shape of a perfect cross.

'This is it,' said Solomon. 'The Cross.'

'Not quite what I had in mind,' said Will.

One by one they climbed down to the door of the church. Inside, a group of priests were performing a ritual in the darkness, the rock-hewn interior pungent with the smoke from burning myrrh.

'We should speak to the priest,' said Solomon.

'Which one is he?'

'That one over there, reading the Bible.'

Emma was about to add something, when a white man in military camouflage leapt through the door, a long-shafted mace grasped between outstretched hands.

Lunging at Will, he missed his shoulder by an inch.

Solomon pulled the pin on a stun grenade, but held back from hurling it. They would all have gone down if he had.

Will ran out of the door into the blinding light. The assailant was after him, the mace twirling above his head like a lasso.

Stumbling, Will fled behind the church.

The hit-man was closing in.

Zigzagging left, then right, Will ran fast, like a gazelle hunted on the savannah. Turning, he looked back in utter consternation.

The attacker was lying dead on the ground.

His throat had been torn open below the Adam's apple; the blade had gone all the way through the neck.

Will felt adrenalin surge through his bloodstream.

He fell to his knees.

'What the…?!'

Sprinting up fast, Solomon kicked the assailant over with his boot.

'Thank you,' screeched Will.

'I didn't kill him.'

'Then who the hell did?'

Emma reeled forward, her eyes wide open in shock.

'I threw the knife,' she said, her voice trembling. 'Don't know how I ever hit him.'

'You saved my life,' said Will, straining to breathe.

'I killed a man,' Emma replied in horror. 'I can't believe I killed a man.'

'He wasn't local,' said Solomon.

'He was coming for me,' Will added. 'Oh my God, he must be the enemy Hannibal warned me about.'

'Who?'

'The Magi.'

The priest seemed unsurprised at there being an attacker in the church compound. Wizened, with a balding head, his body was gnarled, wrapped in linen robes.

In Amharic, Solomon asked him about the Ladder of Mithras.

The lids lowered over the priest's eyes, and he thought for a long while.

'The Ladder will only be found by the man who does not search for it,' he said.

Will rolled his eyes.

'That's just great,' he said sarcastically.

The priest uttered a line of Amharic with slow deliberation, pronouncing each syllable as though vitally important.

'What's he saying?'

'That the Ladder of Mithras connects Man with his destiny.'

'But *where* is it?'

'Above the mines.'

'What mines?'

'The gold mines of Ophir.'

Another full day of driving through choking dust, and the Rolls-Royce Tourer reached the starvation camps.

On presidential orders, thousands of tribesmen and their families had been herded together in pens. The government's fear was for the world to once again catch sight of the stark truth – starvation in the Highlands of Ethiopia.

Word of the president's inglorious departure had spread rapidly from mouth to ear. As it did so, the army deserted en masse. The starving clansmen of the Highlands might have fled too. But, with no food, there was little chance of escape.

'Was Live Aid for nothing?' Emma asked reflectively.

Solomon huffed.

'D'you really think that money ever reached these people?'

'What happened to it, then?'

'The Derg – Mengistu's dictatorship – that's what happened. Most of the cash was siphoned off to Switzerland long before it ever reached Ethiopia.'

'What's the hope?' said Will.

'There isn't any.'

'So?'

'So they'll die here,' Solomon remarked, his voice even and cold.

'We can share out our supplies,' said Will, realizing at once the stupidity of the remark.

'Feed fifty thousand people with a few tin cans?' Solomon said.

'What's gone wrong here?' Emma asked.

'These people you see are from the wrong tribe.'

'What do you mean?'

'They're not Tigrayans – not from the dominant tribe.'

'So what?'

'So they've been abandoned on the scrap heap of life and left to rot.'

Three hours beyond the starvation camps, the track came to an abrupt end.

Far in the distance stood a freestanding outcrop of rock, a slender plateau running its length. Solomon thrust an arm in its direction.

'We'll walk from here.'

'Do you know the way?'

'That way.'

Hours of stumbling followed, over boulders and through parched scrub. They had hidden the vehicle in a thicket of thorn trees. As they left it, traipsing off in the direction of the horizon, Will wondered if they would ever see it again. In a landscape so devoid of luxury, a Rolls-Royce made for an incongruous travelling companion.

Eventually, as they neared the plateau, they caught the muffled hum of voices.

'Don't see anyone,' said Emma.

Solomon patted the air in front of him.

'Wait.'

Approaching the plateau's base cautiously, they curved around it from the far side. The boulders gave way to a steep slope. Scrambling up it, they found themselves staring down into a man-made canyon.

It was filled with people.

Thousands of them.

Men, women and children – all digging with their hands.

'My God,' said Will. 'It's like something out of the Old Testament.'

'The mines of Ophir,' Solomon said, 'where the ancient Egyptians got their gold, and King Solomon, too.'

Dressed in little more than rags, the miners paid no attention to the outsiders. They were far too engrossed in their work – gleaning a few grains of gold dust from the alluvial lode.

'The system hasn't changed in four thousand years,' Solomon explained. 'Not since the time of the pharaohs. Look at the sluices – those were invented in ancient Egypt.'

Will nudged a hand over to the far side of the pit.

'What's going on over there?'

'They're digging shafts. They send the children down because the tunnels are so narrow. It's dangerous work, and there are frequent cave-ins.'

The timing of the remark was uncanny.

For, at that moment, one of the miners began yelling. The sound preceded a frenzy of commotion. Everyone stopped digging and hurried over to a bore-hole.

From a distance Will, Emma and Solomon watched as the miners scrabbled to save a young life. One group frantically dug a second tunnel down through the clay. Another opened out the original hole.

But it was too late.

A woman's voice ripped through the canyon. The shrill sound of anguish – a mother's instinct. Somehow she already knew her child was dead.

A few minutes passed.

Then, the limp body of a boy was heaved from the ground. The miners dropped their shovels and froze. Careering through the mud, the mother collapsed on reaching her son.

Despondently, Solomon shook his head.

'All this for a few pennies' worth of gold,' he said.

The body was carried from the pit at shoulder height, dozens of miners following behind, heads bowed in respect.

An hour or so passed and the digging began again, the atmosphere more sombre than before.

'We must get up there,' Solomon said, pointing at the sheering rock face.

'How the hell do we do that?' asked Will. 'It's a vertical climb. We'll need ropes and harnesses, and that gear's back in the car.'

Nearing the cliff face at its widest point, they shielded their eyes from the dazzling afternoon sunlight.

Will spat on his hands.

'We could try climbing without ropes.'

Solomon laughed.

'Who are you, Spiderman?'

Just then, a man's voice called down from the top of the plateau. They looked up into the sun.

'What's he saying?'

Solomon cupped a hand to his ear.

The voice came again, a little louder.

'He says to wait down here.'

Little by little, a thick leather rope slithered down the precipice like a great fawn-coloured serpent.

One at a time, they tied the rope around their waists, and were heaved up the sheering cliff face.

Will went first.

As the rope jerked him higher and higher, he looked down at the sprawling canyon, the miners no more than specks in a no-man's land of sludge.

Up on the plateau, he spotted a clutch of crude stone buildings, and half a dozen priests heading to their shade.

Solomon began the prolonged greetings that tended to accompany the arrival of a visitor.

'Ask about the Ladder of Mithras,' Will whispered urgently.

'First we must take coffee with them.'

They were led to a spacious reception room, decorated with cartoon-like murals of King Solomon receiving the

Queen of Sheba. At length, coffee was served, the colour of straw. Drinking it, they praised the taste and gave thanks.

Another hour of greetings slipped by.

Then Solomon cleared his throat. Sitting up, fumbling awkwardly, he posed a question while motioning something long and thin with his hands. The priest appeared concerned. Standing up, he bowed, and walked backwards to the door.

'Something's going on,' Solomon said.

'What?'

'Not sure.'

Outside, there was indistinct conversation, and *pat-pat-pat* of bare feet running fast.

More voices. More running.

Will glanced at Emma.

'I can't stop thinking about that man down in Lalibela,' she said. 'The thought of taking a life is so dreadful.'

'But he would have killed me.'

'I know, but even so.'

Will stared at the mural of Solomon and Sheba, his vision blurring as he remembered the attack.

'The Magi,' he said in a chilled voice. 'I didn't believe they existed.'

Dusk approached, ebbing into darkness.

'Looks like we'll have to sleep up here,' said Solomon.

Will got up and strode to the doorway.

He peered out.

'A priest's coming,' he said.

Father Anthony had the physique of a weightlifter, his squat, muscular frame furled up in a white cotton vestment. As soon as he spotted the visitors, he welcomed them cordially in English.

'I have been told you have come for the Ladder,' he said once introductions were over.

Will nodded.

'We were told that you keep it here.'

Father Anthony scratched a hand to the back of his neck.

'Our community has existed up on this plateau for a thousand years,' he said. 'The monastery was founded to protect the Ladder. We have always known that one day an outsider would come and ask for it. Such is the legend. But you must forgive our surprise that this day has at last arrived.'

'Can you give it to us?'

The priest dipped his head.

'Are you ready to receive it?'

'Yes we are,' said Will firmly.

'Then come with me.'

Emma and Solomon got to their feet.

'Your friends must wait for you at the bottom of the cliff.'

'They can't come?'

'No. Only you may stay here. Your friends must leave.'

Will followed Father Anthony across the plateau, Simien wolves howling in the darkness far below.

'How big is it?' Will asked as they walked.

'I do not know.'

Will frowned.

'You've never seen it?'

'None of us have.'

'Why not?'

'Because it's a sacred relic.'

Edging around to the plateau's rear, they crossed a field of alfalfa, and reached the mouth of a cave.

'This is the place,' said Father Anthony, leading Will to a sacred alcove set into the side of the cave. Lit by burning torches fuelled by ghee, it was thick with smoke and packed with handwritten volumes in Ge'ez.

The priest tugged a burning torch from its bracket and handed it to Will.

'You will find the Ladder at the end of the passageway,' he said. 'I wish you luck.'

'Aren't you coming?'

In silence, Father Anthony turned and left.

Cautiously, and with small steps, Will paced down the rock-hewn passageway, his hand stretched out, the torch vanquishing the dark. Cold air streamed over his face, the flames rippling in the draught.

Filled with the stench of bat excrement, the passageway narrowed.

Will staggered ahead.

Another fifty feet and it was too low to stand. Straining to keep the flames from his face, he shuffled ahead, to a stone doorway.

Scrambling through it, he emerged into what seemed to be a natural cavern, the ceiling thick with bats. Alarmed at the intruder and the light, they swooped to and fro.

Offset in the chamber there was an altar.

A hand protecting his head, Will approached it. As he did so, the torch's fire was snuffed out. He swore, the exclamation lost against the screech of the bats.

A voice was calling out in his head, reminding him to use the night-vision goggles. Hannibal had patented the invention under the name 'Darkness Dispelling Viewing Device'.

Fumbling in the daypack, he grabbed the goggles and pulled them on.

A flick of the switch and darkness was replaced by turquoise light.

Will drew closer to the altar, squinting to get a view of its upper surface. Laid out on the stone slab was a pair of human skulls, a silver orb and a bronze box upside down – each object smothered liberally in centuries of bat droppings and grime.

Lifting the box in his hands, Will turned it over. Fixed to the top was a sheet of card, adorned prominently with Hannibal's monogram. Under the card was a keyhole.

Fishing the key from under his shirt, he inserted it into the lock and turned twice.

The box opened.

Inside, wrapped in a disintegrating scrap of velvet, was an object – a double helix crafted from solid silver.

'The Ladder!' he bellowed. 'Hannibal! I've got it!'

At that moment the bats fell silent.

Stuffing the helix under his arm, Will looked up.

The altar fell away, plunging into an abyss, followed by much of the floor.

Will screamed out for help, but there was no reply.

Summoning courage, leg muscles clenched tight, he prepared to jump to the other side.

Something stopped him – Hannibal's voice.

Do the unexpected.

Huh?

Jump!

What?!

Panicked, Will gaped down through the turquoise mist. There was no way of telling how far the drop could be. It looked like certain suicide.

Sorry, Hannibal, but I'm going with gut instinct.

Once again, he clenched his leg muscles, readying himself to leap across the void.

But, wait.

Flame and shadow were racing down the passageway from where he had come, the light flaring through the goggles. Enraged at the prospect of losing their relic, the priests were pouring into the cavern in a blur of turquoise rage.

Will looked down into the abyss.

What to do?

No time to deliberate.

Hugging the helix to his chest, he took a deep breath, and jumped.

Down.

Down.

Down.

The rock streaked turquoise as he fell, his voice a single prolonged shriek of terror.

Suddenly, he plunged into ice-cold water.

A pool.

Instinct told him to flail his arms. But the helix – he had to keep hold of it.

Struggling with all his strength, Will swam upwards into the dark, the relic clutched tight in his hand.

Ripping off the night-vision goggles, he swam to the edge of the pool and struggled out. A voice echoed somewhere in the darkness. Will opened his mouth a fraction to hone his hearing, as his father had taught him to do.

He listened. Must be the priests coming for him.

His chest tightened with fear.

But it was a woman's voice. What's more, it was speaking English.

Thank God. It was Emma.

From: *Hannibal Fogg and the Supreme Secret of Man*

Scheherazade's Quest

As the travellers quenched their thirst and feasted on a meal of roasted goat, the queen explained why they'd been summoned.

'Despite your varied lives and adventures, the three of you are heroes in a collection of tales... the greatest treasury of stories ever set down by humankind.'

Aladdin peered at Scheherazade through the campfire's flames.

'What's its name?' he asked.

'It's called *The Thousand and One Nights*,' the queen replied. 'Or, rather, it will become known as that. You see, the story has not yet been told – so its very existence hangs in the balance, as does mine.'

'How so?'

'Because, unless the telling continues,' Scheherazade explained, 'my life, and those of countless other queens, will be snuffed out as sure as night follows day.'

Aladdin pushed a hand back through his hair.

'Don't know about the others, but I'm not a character from a storyland,' he said. 'I'm a man who has a past and a future.'

The queen rolled her eyes.

'That's what you think,' she said. 'Of course you had no idea of who or what you really are, just as you had no notion of each other's existence – or that my voice, guided by certain forces, has conjured you, and shaped each one of your tales.'

Tossing down a mutton bone, Ali Baba spoke for the others:

'If you're not a jinn, then what are you?'

'I am a queen – a queen married to a ruthless king. If the tale I tell falters, as it has apparently done, he'll execute me, and a thousand more women.'

Sindbad reached for another morsel of meat.

'And why should it have faltered?' he said. 'After all, a story's a story.'

Scheherazade peered out into the darkness, her mind reliving the predicament in which she found herself.

'The story's been diverted by a sorcerer in the employ of the king. He's thrown it out of kilter. As a result, the only certainty is my appointment with the executioner and his axe at dawn. Once I'm gone, King Shahriyar will marry a fresh bride each sunset and bury her each dawn.'

Aladdin frowned.

'In what way has the story been disturbed?'

Scheherazade sighed.

'In our love for tales, we overlook how they work,' she said.

'They work because a storyteller speaks, and someone listens. It's as simple as that.'

'No,' the queen replied. 'If that were true, then we wouldn't be in the quandary we're in. You see, when a tale is begun, a seed is planted, a seed from which the story grows and grows. Sometimes the seed ripens into a little story – a handful of words. But, at other times, it matures into a fantastical reflection of wonder.'

'What's the seed got to do with any of us?' Ali Baba asked.

'All three of you are heroes in a vast and intricate tale, a story that's a labyrinth of astonishment – the most complex tale ever told. Although I have only just begun recounting it, the twists, turns, and each individual adventure is contained within the story seed. Hide the seed, and the tale goes awry.'

'How would anyone hide a story's seed?' Sindbad snapped. 'It sounds preposterous, as though it were out of a story itself!'

'Of course it sounds as though it's from a story,' Scheherazade cried, 'because it *is*! As for how the seed of a story can be hidden, it's done through supernatural means. In this case, by the King of the Jinns.'

The sailor winced.

'I wish you luck,' he said. 'But I have a voyage to attend to.'

'And I have a shop to run,' Ali Baba mumbled.

'If you don't help me,' said the queen, 'I could have you both thrown into the deepest, darkest dungeon in any of a dozen kingdoms.'

Silence prevailed, eventually broken by Aladdin:

'Nothing would please me more than to be part of your quest,' he said with a smile.

Begrudgingly, the other two agreed, too.

'Excellent,' Scheherazade said. 'We leave at dawn.'

'Where to?' the sailor asked.

'To the City of Brass!'

Long before the first blush of desert light warmed the travellers' faces, Scheherazade woke the others one by one.

During the few hours of rest, dreams transported them far from the freezing, flea-infested caravanserai.

Sindbad dreamt he was in a palace in distant China.

Aladdin imagined he was in a fantastical treasure cave.

Ali Baba fantasized he would one day own the most colossal marketplace for goods from all corners of the world.

Before they set out, Scheherazade explained that the City of Brass was the destination because the kindly Blue Witch had revealed it was from there the story's seed had been taken. On hearing the information, Sindbad clenched his hands into fists.

'You speak of witches, and claim to have power over us,' he said, straightening his back imperiously, 'but how do we know your power until we've seen it?!'

Scheherazade rolled her eyes.

'I am the teller of the story, of *your* story,' she replied. 'So I can control each one of you as I wish.'

With that, she pointed to the sailor.

'And the queen pointed to Sindbad the Sailor,' she said, 'her right hand clenched as a fist. Twisting it, she caused him to rise from the ground and turn in mid-air, hanging there like a bird in flight.'

As she spoke, Sindbad rose from the ground, and turned upside down.

'Put me down!' he cried.

'With pleasure,' said Scheherazade.

She clicked her fingers, and the sailor fell head first onto the sand.

Ali Baba stepped forward.

'Your Magnificence,' he said, fawning, 'I would be most obliged if you wouldn't use such necromancy ever in our presence.'

Aladdin and Sindbad seconded the request.

'Are you certain that's your wish?' Scheherazade said.

The three travellers nodded in unison.

'Please swear it in an oath,' they said all at once.

'Very well. I, Scheherazade, reluctant wife of King Shahriyar, pledge on all I hold sacred that while in your presence I shan't use the powers at my disposal as a storyteller.'

With that, the procession pushed out of the caravanserai.

As the first rays of dawn light broke across the horizon, three dozen camels moved over the vast emptiness, a giant shadow thrown by each one.

Scheherazade led the way, the travellers behind her, and a retinue of pack animals and their attendants following at the rear. The frail light of dawn was quickly replaced by the piercing blaze of late morning, and heat so intense that it scorched any skin left unprotected.

Their heads furled in turbans, the ends tied over their faces, the humans were hopelessly unprepared for life in the parched wasteland.

Time and again Sindbad lost his balance and fell from his mount, to the amusement of the others.

'I'm a man of the sea!' he bawled. 'Put me on the ocean and you will know my skill.'

The sailor may have been unsure in his footing, but his aptitude for navigation was second to none. Charting the way by the night sky, he pointed out the constellations to the others, regaling them at the nightly campfire with tales of his voyages.

'I have crossed seas with waves as great as mountains,' he said, 'and with whales that would swallow an entire ship if they had the will. I've sailed to the ends of the earth, swum with mermaids, and listened to the cries of the great *bahamut*, the immense sea creature which holds up the earth.'

'And what did you learn in all your adventures?' asked Scheherazade.

The sailor didn't reply at first. He stared into the embers, his mind zigzagging through all the narrow escapes.

'I learned to treat every day as the greatest wonder imaginable,' he answered.

Aladdin wiped a hand down over his youthful face.

'And what have *you* learned in your adventures?' he asked the queen.

She smiled.

'To understand the power of stories,' she said.

For seven days the caravan crossed the desert, scorched by day and frozen to the bone at night.

Each one wished they could be transported to their destination by magical means, or that they would wake to find they'd been dreaming all along.

As one day slipped into the next, the travellers' skin grew increasingly blistered, their bodies ravaged by lice. Not wishing to be considered soft by the others, each one of them put on a brave face, and pretended the going was good.

On the seventh evening, Sindbad stared up at the firmament, his eyes fixed on its tapestry of constellations. While the desert was immense, the night sky hanging above it was incomparable. Billions and billions of pinpricks, as though the sun was being shone through a baker's sieve.

At length, the sailor surveyed the darkness beyond the makeshift camp.

'A sandstorm's approaching from the east,' he said. 'Wind as strong as any I have encountered on the ocean.'

Ali Baba asked the question in everyone's mind:

'How do you know?' he said.

Throwing his head back, Sindbad the Sailor gazed at the heavens.

'The wind powers my sails,' he said. 'It sings to me, and scorns me. But, most importantly, it never lies.'

'When will it reach us?' Scheherazade asked.

Slowly, the sailor filled his lungs, then exhaled.

'At first light,' he said. 'It will come at first light.'

All night long, the travellers prepared for the wind.

Supplies were unpacked and repacked, secured beneath great sheets of canvas, and dug down into the sand. The camels had their hobbles untied, and their heads wrapped in long strands of cloth.

Scheherazade climbed up onto a high dune overlooking their makeshift encampment, sparks from the fire below spitting up into the night. The moon was full, casting an eerie aspect over the rippled surface of the sands. She thanked Providence for saving her neck, if only for a few hours longer than was planned.

She thought of her mother and father, her beloved sister, Dunyazad, and of the ruthless man she'd married out of selflessness rather than love.

Perched up on the dune, she removed her turban so as to tie her hair back. As she did so, a stray strand of hair blew over her face. A moment later, she felt coolness on the back of her hand. Then, far in the distance she heard the faintest rumble of noise. A hissing sound, like a child blowing hard through a clenched fist.

The sailor called everyone to gather around.

'It's coming,' he said sombrely. 'Dig yourselves down as I showed you, and don't dare emerge until the uproar has come and gone.'

Aladdin asked how long it would last.

'No way of knowing,' Sindbad answered. 'All I can say is that once it's passed by, we shall all be ripened by the experience.'

So each one of the travellers dug themselves in, as the first gusts reached the encampment, fanning the fire as though they were flames from the inner reaches of hell.

An hour of utter tranquillity came and went.

Then the full force of the sandstorm tore through in an ultimate performance of nature's rage.

All night it howled and bayed, screaming like a pack of wolves ten thousand strong. From time to time it would ease, then revive six times as forcefully as before.

At the height of the impact, a pair of the camels careered away and were soon engulfed. Breaking orders to dig in, one of the attendants went after them. Every inch of clothing, then skin, was stripped from his body, like a shaft of wood whittled beside a winter fire.

Through the next night the sandstorm raged on, and all through the following day. Her ears ringing, and her bones shaken until they were numb, Scheherazade prayed for tranquillity. But, the more she did so, the more the winds whipped up, howling with incandescent rage.

Three days and nights after the strand of hair had first blown across Scheherazade's face, the wind ceased. Not a gradual cessation, but rather an immediate end, leaving those who had experienced it wondering whether it had ever taken place at all.

Sindbad the Sailor was the first to emerge.

His muffled voice was heard by the others, calling them to come out.

'It's over! It's over!' he cried triumphantly.

One by one, the other travellers unfurled themselves, the blinding light dazzling them. Bewildered like victims from some forgotten war, they were reunited.

'I hate the desert,' Sindbad said. 'Take me to the sea!'

The remaining camels were calmed and attended to, and the supplies dug out from the pools of sand. Then, the sun blazing from an indigo sky, came the shrill sound of a voice in exclamation.

'Come! See! Quickly, all of you!'

Fearing another onslaught of nature's wrath, the other travellers followed the voice and were soon scrambling up a steep dune. Aladdin was standing at its apex, a hand shading his face.

'What is it?' Ali Baba yelled. 'Do you see the City of Brass?'

The boy pointed to the distance.

One by one, the others climbed up and set eyes on what he had discovered.

'Never in all my voyages!' yelled Sindbad.

'By what supernatural incantation…?' added Ali Baba.

Scheherazade said nothing.

Flabbergasted, she stood there, gazing out at the plateau stretching from the hillock to the horizon.

Through days and nights the wind had stripped the desert away, revealing a colossal city, entombed, like a wonder from the pages of a child's fantasy. Every single grain of sand had been sucked out – millions and billions of tons of powdered rock.

The result was a city deserted of all life, but preserved in entirety, as though everyone had crept away and never returned. Like dreamwalkers lured by curiosity, the four travellers hurried down into the metropolis.

Too awed to say a word, each one seemed to glide forward as though silenced by a spell. Descending into the maze of streets, they found shops filled with their wares, the workshops of scribes ready for clients, guard posts neat and orderly, and carpenters' yards ready and waiting.

'Where are all the people?' Aladdin asked.

'*Dead*?' suggested Scheherazade.

'How could they be?' Ali Baba answered.

'They're not dead, but gone,' Sindbad said.

Aladdin balked.

'Gone *where*?'

'Who knows?' murmured Sindbad.

'A jinn,' said Scheherazade. 'This is the work of a jinn. A city as great as any in all the world, transported to nowhere – for the senseless amusement of a jinn.'

Aladdin was pointing again.

'Look, the shops are filled with merchandise.'

A mask of the most terrible fear swept down over Scheherazade's face.

'Do not take a thing! Not a single thing! D'you hear me?!'

'Why not?' Ali Baba asked.

'Because this scene smacks of diabolical sorcery. We can't risk unleashing the rage of whoever, or whatever, cast such a despicable spell.'

Exploring the streets, they marvelled at the bolts of cloth in the tailors' shops, the coloured goblets neatly arranged in the glass-blower's studio, and the cabinets of gold jewellery on display in a bridal emporium.

'To think we would have simply marched across it, not knowing it was here,' Aladdin voiced in wonder.

'It must have lain here for centuries,' Sindbad replied.

Scheherazade gazed up at the sun.

'We must get the camels ready and keep going,' she said.

Making their way back through the streets, the travellers began ascending the steep dune back to where their camp was pitched.

As they climbed, there was a clap of thunder.

'The wind! The wind!' Ali Baba yelled. 'It's coming back again!'

His face cloaked in fear, the sailor pointed upwards.

'It's not the storm,' he said.

One at a time they looked upwards, their heads cocking back hard as they followed the mountainous trunk of a creature's form.

As wide as a building, it seemed to rise up into the heavens, swathed in a filthy, blood-splattered robe. In places the garment was so badly torn that the travellers caught a glimpse of the flesh beneath. Scaled and wart-ridden, it was like the hull of a ship that had been at sea for many months.

Far above the creature's trunk were four arms, each one grasping a blood-soaked scimitar, and finally a head so monstrous it defied description – except to say it was crowned by a pair of razor-sharp horns.

Before any one of the group had mustered a sentence, the creature spoke, his voice booming with fury:

'Who dares steal from the Black Jinn?'

Standing tall, Scheherazade replied:

'Oh great and mighty creature from the heavens, please rest assured that none of us would take a single grain of rice from the city that lies below. We merely explored it, and marvelled at the power that transported it to this distant realm.'

'Nooooooo!' cried the Black Jinn, all four arms raised above his head, scimitars flashing like demons. 'One of you has stolen, and all of you shall pay!'

Quickly, Scheherazade conferred with the others.

'I took nothing,' Sindbad affirmed.

'Nor I,' Ali Baba added.

Aladdin swallowed anxiously.

'The tiniest little button,' he whispered, opening his fist. 'The smallest memento. I'm sorry… it just caught my eye.'

'You wretched boy!' the sailor growled. 'For your stupidity we'll lose our heads!'

High above them, the Black Jinn rankled with rage, his anger boiling over to fever pitch.

Again, Aladdin spoke to the others:

'If our storyteller used the powers she possessed, then we might have a chance at living!'

'But what could she do?' Ali Baba moaned.

'She could tell the tale in another way!'

All eyes turned to Scheherazade.

Arms crossed, the queen shook her head left, right, left.

'On your orders I made an oath on all I hold sacred!'

'Then we shall die,' said Ali Baba. 'Slaughtered like the wretches we surely are.'

His prey the size of vermin on the desert's face, the Black Jinn heard their voices as humans hear mice.

'What's with all this bickering?!' he cried.

The travellers froze.

Then, finding humour in their predicament, Aladdin broke into fits of laughter.

'We're just blaming the storyteller among us for not changing the story.'

The jinn frowned, lowering his head until it was in line with the travellers' faces, a single grotesque eye straining to focus on them.

Each one of them grimaced at seeing the eye, and smelling such truly abominable breath.

'Storyteller?!' he called. 'Which one of your vile excuses for life is a storyteller?'

Without fear, Scheherazade raised her hand.

'I am.'

'Then you shall die first!'

The queen shrugged.

'Might I ask what you have against storytellers?'

The Black Jinn's scimitars slashed left and right, narrowly missing the travellers.

'I shall hack you into morsels, grind your bones into dust, then blow it to all four points of the compass!'

Scheherazade held her ground.

'You didn't answer my question,' she yelled. 'What do you have against the noble art of storytelling?'

His face no more than a few yards from the group, he said:

'For a thousand years I have been the butt of every joke spoken by storytellers' mouths. I have been ridiculed, maligned, and called a stinking, wretched excuse of life!'

'I'm sorry that's what others have called you,' Scheherazade said. 'But I myself have sung your praises, and named you as the handsomest, proudest, kindest jinn that ever walked the roaming sands of Arabia.'

'Nonsense!' cried the Black Jinn. 'You're as bad as all the rest of them, and you shall perish first!'

Irked that he was to die in the desert and not the sea, Sindbad the Sailor spoke:

'O Great Jinn, O towering pillar of life and extinguisher of evil! By freeing us, you will prove your good, and will be regarded as a saint evermore by spinners of yarns, and tellers of tales!'

An expression of meekness slipped over the creature's face.

'Is that true?' he asked.

In the blink of the Black Jinn's eye, the four travellers were pinned out on the desert sands with leather bindings, spreadeagled like skins at a tannery left out to dry.

'Damn you, Aladdin!' the sailor bellowed. 'There's no honour in dying here, like this!'

'He couldn't help it,' Ali Baba broke in. 'Any one of us might have allowed their hand to stray.'

'It was such a lovely little button,' Aladdin moaned.

Again, all three men begged Scheherazade to retell the tale, without the Black Jinn.

'I can't and I won't!' she shouted. 'So don't ask me again!'

Aladdin began cackling once more.

'We're not going to get a chance to!'

Curious that anyone but a madman would find humour in their fate, the jinn lowered his head inquisitively.

'Why does the young one laugh?' he asked.

'Because the storyteller over there could paint you in words as a picture of wonder and delight,' said Sindbad, 'but she refuses to do so.'

'And why is that?' the Black Jinn enquired.

Ali Baba explained:

'Because she had made an oath on all she holds sacred,' he said, 'and unlike the rest of us she won't break it, even though her neck's on the line.'

The jinn gazed at Scheherazade pinned out on the sand.

'I loathe storytellers more than any form of life... even more than the Turquoise Jinn from the Kingdom of Astamagar.'

Doing her best to be diplomatic, the queen said:

'Beloved Black Jinn, who holds our lives in his hand, what if we could change the way others regard you?'

'Are you offering to describe me differently?' he asked, his brow furrowed deep.

'No,' Scheherazade answered. 'Your story has already been told.'

'Then what's there to be done?'

'Well,' said the queen softly, 'my friends and I would like to clean you up, and dress you in clothing fit for a jinn as distinguished and handsome as yourself.'

The Black Jinn growled.

'What good would that do?'

'It would make others wish to be near you for a start, and would give you back your sense of self-respect.'

'How can you be sure it'd work?'

'Well, if it doesn't, you could simply stake us out on the desert again.'

The creature brooded long and hard.

Then, he clicked his tongue. Instantly, the leather bindings vanished, and the prisoners were free.

With the Black Jinn's permission, the travellers led half a dozen camels down into the deserted city, and loaded them up with merchandise.

Late in the day they returned, the beasts burdened under the weight of cloth, leather, soap, and perfume. All night they scrubbed the jinn, chipping away at centuries of filth. They trimmed his talons and cleaned his horns, shaved his face, brushed his teeth, and cut his hair.

All the while, the Black Jinn watched with annoyance, his single eye widening with disapproval.

'If I don't like it, I'll peg you out again and leave you to die!' he'd call from time to time, until Scheherazade barked back at him.

'Will you *shush*?!' she spat. 'In case you haven't noticed, we are doing this to help you, and to make others like you.'

'But what if I don't want anyone to like me?' the Black Jinn snapped.

'Well, then you'll turn into a sad, good-for-nothing old jinn! And you won't have lovely clothes to wear, like the ones my friends are making.'

The creature raised its head inquisitively.

'Show me the clothes,' he said.

'No! Not until they're finished. You'll like the surprise.'

Again, the Black Jinn growled.

'I hate surprises,' he whimpered testily, 'almost as much as I hate storytellers!'

Scheherazade, who had been sitting on the top of the creature's head, brushing back his hair, climbed down onto his shoulder. From this vantage point, she made her way onto his nose and peered into his eye.

'Why all the hatred for storytellers?'

'They're horrible!' the Black Jinn growled. 'He said horrifying things about me.'

'*They* or *he*?'

The jinn rolled his eye.

'*He!*'

'He *who*?'

'*He* the unkind storyteller in the market in Damascus.'

Scheherazade leant in close, her voice directed into the creature's ear.

'What did he say?' she asked tenderly.

'That I was ugly and stupid, and that I was the runt of my mother's litter.'

'Is it true? Were you the runt?'

The Black Jinn shook his head.

'No. I was the strongest from the day we were born.'

There was a whistling from the ground.

'Ah,' Scheherazade said, 'it's ready.'

'What is?'

'Come and see.'

Expert at making sails, Sindbad the Sailor had used his skill to craft a robe colossal in its proportions, sewing dozens of bolts of cloth side by side. Aladdin had trimmed the garment in gold beading, and had even embroidered *Black Jinn* on the front, surrounded by flowers. As for Ali Baba, he'd fashioned a pair of moccasins from forty goat skins.

Turning their backs to give the Black Jinn a little privacy, the travellers waited while he dressed himself. When he was ready, he materialized a pool of crystal-clear water in the desert, and peered into it.

'Don't you like it?' Scheherazade asked hesitantly.

The jinn snarled, growled, and snarled again, his face reflected over the surface of the water.

A single tear welled up in his eye, and rolled down the right side of his face.

'You've made an old jinn happy,' he said.

Sindbad the Sailor spoke up:

'You could have done all that yourself with magic.'

'Of course I could,' the Black Jinn retorted.

'Then why didn't you?'

'Because the pleasure is knowing that others cared,' he said.

'Does that mean we're free?' Aladdin asked.

'I suppose it does.'

The travellers let out a wail of joy, then Ali Baba asked the Black Jinn what his plans were for the future.

'Thought I'd go down to Africa and roast a few kingdoms,' he muttered dreamily.

Scheherazade shook a fist.

'If you want to be liked,' she scolded sharply, 'you have to be likeable. And roasting innocent people for no reason at all is no way to be likeable!'

Once again, Aladdin conferred with the others, and they all agreed.

'Why don't you come with us?' he asked.

'Where to?'

'The City of Brass.'

'That's a long way.'

'Not for you!'

The Black Jinn nodded.

'If I click my tongue, we'd get there right away.'

'No!' Scheherazade cried. 'No magic! You must promise it on all you hold sacred.'

'But why?'

'For the same reason I didn't escape your clutches by retelling the tale.'

'What's the reason?'

'Because there's more honour in it.'

Sindbad was staring out at the horizon. Turning he cried out:

'Think of it as a new beginning!'

TAHIR SHAH

The Black Jinn smiled – the first time he'd done so without causing harm to others.

'Very well,' he said. 'I shall come with you.'

Ali Baba raised an arm.

'As our travelling companion, is it too much to ask your name?'

Self-consciously, the Black Jinn touched a paw to his head, grooming back his hair.

'My mother named me Baibar,' he said modestly.

Scheherazade stepped forward and extended her hand.

'Pleased to meet you, Baibar,' she said.

From: *The Arabian Nights Adventures*

The Prism

THE PRISM WAS a vast inverted pyramid, fashioned from triangular sheets of impregnable glass.

A mile wide, and twice as high, it lay at the heart of the Abyss, divided and subdivided into an infinity of octagonal cells.

Rotating on its vertical axis, it clattered, lurched, and screeched, as it swept round and around, powered by the fugian wind.

Three pairs of immense iron sails kept the Prism turning, by powering an elaborate machinery.

Cantilevers and clockwork bearings.

Oscillators and mainsprings.

Drive wheels, cams, and coaxial gears.

And, most important of all, the pendulum of the great escapement.

The mechanism was as dependable as time itself. Because of it, never once had the Prism stopped turning. So the rogue jinn remained as prisoners – trapped in their cells by the penitentiary's cloak of metamagnetism.

As a result, there was peace.

Before the Prism's conception, through centuries of fear, jinn had terrorized every dimension. A dominant life form since the dawn of time, jinn had ruled the Realm – with rogue jinn the preeminent masters.

But, gradually, they were pursued.

Outwitted, then trapped, they were imprisoned by the bravest and canniest legion of warriors.

The Jinn Hunters.

The balance of good and evil was maintained by the fact that so many rogue jinn were interned within the Prism's transparent walls.

But the prison was only strong if it turned.

Cease for a fraction of a moment, and it would lose its impregnability. If that were to happen, the jinn convicts would gain their freedom.

Escape was unthinkable though, because the Prism was managed by an army of guardians devoted to an ancestral cause.

Known as 'malbinos', their fraternity had been bred in antiquitas – in a time before records began. Duty was hard-wired into them – the duty of ensuring no imprisoned jinn ever escaped.

Living as long as three centuries, malbinos were short in stature, and blessed with extraordinary physical strength. On either hand they possessed five fingers and a pair of thumbs. Their hunched forms were obscured head to toe in coarse white bristle, over which was secreted an unctuous lilac slime, which they knew as 'fusilia'.

Set all the way round each malbino head was an arrangement of oversized eyes.

Nine of them, each one a different size.

Multiple eyes made the malbino custodians especially suited to the guardianship of the Prism. Nothing escaped their untrammelled gaze. Yet, despite such perfect sight, no malbino had ever possessed an ear, let alone a pair of them. Through a complex telepathic faculty they could discern most sounds.

Only the musings of jinn were out of range. The lack of ears meant malbinos were immune to the constant whispering of their prisoners.

It was the perfect arrangement.

For, listen through ears to a rogue jinn whisper, and even the most attentive malbino would be instantly driven insane.

*

As the students filed towards the door at the end of class, Dr. Moss motioned a hand towards Oliver Quinn.

'Got a minute?'

As usual, Oliver was lost in his own world.

'Um, sure,' he grunted hesitantly, once the question had been repeated.

'What d'you make of the images?' Moss asked.

'*Huh?*'

'The images – the ones up there on the wall.'

Oliver combed a set of long fingers back through the mop of rowdy blond hair. He got a flash of the dhow, and of the blood-red sea.

'Wild,' he said doubtfully.

'*Wild?*'

His gangling form leaning back against the wall beside the desk, Oliver managed an anxious grin.

'They were like gateways,' he said.

'*Gateways?*'

'Yup.'

'Gateways to what?'

'Dunno. Just that they were amazing.'

'Any idea what they were designed for?'

Oliver shrugged.

'Have a guess,' prompted Moss.

'Something to do with spying, maybe.'

'Spying?'

Oliver yanked his daypack from the floor, up onto his shoulder.

'They were obviously somewhere remote,' he said. 'Even though they were related to high-tech, it was kind of low-tech high-tech, if you see what I mean. Something outdated. But kind of cool.'

Moss looked at Oliver hard.

The Institute had never had a student like him. Oliver Quinn may have been lost in a dream world much of the time, but he could recognize patterns hidden to everyone else.

'Have a go,' Dr. Moss coaxed. 'Guess what they were designed for.'

Oliver pinched the end of his nose.

Glancing down at the floor, his eyes took in the worn felt furrows in the low-grade carpeting. As he thought of the random patterns he'd seen projected on the classroom wall, his mind was mapping the beige carpet square.

However hard he tried to prevent it, the pattern returned him to the dream world, and to the Kingdom of Avenged Hope.

Professor Moss's voice broke through, jerking Oliver back to the present.

'Oh, er. Um. I'd say they were a way of calibrating satellites,' he said. 'Chinese spy satellites. It's out-dated technology. These days you'd be able to make the calibration with a pattern on a postage stamp.'

Moss took a step back.

'How did you know that?' he enquired incredulously.

Oliver looked up from the beige carpet square.

He smiled.

'A lucky guess,' he said.

*

OF ALL THE malbinos, none was more trusted or expert in the dark and devious ways of rogue jinn than Morrock.

The most experienced malbino of all, he had toiled at the Prism for a century and a half, and hailed from a preeminent line of ancestral guards. He knew every inch of the Prism's labyrinthine passages, just as he did its deepest secrets. But, most importantly of all, he understood how rogue jinn thought.

Revered by his fraternity, and even by some of the prisoners, it fell to him to train the new generation.

Morrock didn't care for youth.

He regarded it as a dangerous condition – one more likely to lead to calamity than it was to success. A long career of guarding the Prism had proved that youthful zeal was pointless without a solid foundation – one of understanding.

At dawn the newest trainee reported for duty at the stone cleft – the point at which all careers in guardianship began.

Bright-eyed, eager, and enthusiastic beyond belief, he had dreamed of pursuing the ancestral calling from childhood. From the moment Morrock caught sight of the boy, he knew he would have to begin at the beginning.

'What's your name?' he spat gruffly, his spoken words seeping telepathically into the lad's head.

'Jaspec, son of Sofulec.'

Morrock let out a grunt.

'What do you know of rogue jinn?'

'That they're a threat to the Realm and mustn't be trusted.'

'D'you fear them?'

Arching his back perfectly straight, young Jaspec swallowed hard.

'*No!*' he called out, his face snarling. 'I have no fear of them at all!'

Morrock frowned, each of his nine eyes colder than the last.

'You must always fear the prisoners!' he bawled. 'If you do not, they will get the better of you. Do you understand?!'

Jaspec blinked awkwardly.

'Yes, Brother Morrock. I understand.'

'You must learn to think like the prisoners, because only then can you know what they are planning.'

'But, Brother Morrock, how do rogue jinn think?'

The veteran malbino raised a hand.

'I'll tell you everything,' he said. 'I will speak and you will listen. Do you understand?'

The student blinked a second time.

When all nine of Jaspec's eyes had closed, then opened, Morrock grunted.

'First things first,' he said. 'Follow me.'

'Where are we going?'

'To see the reason you must fear,' said Morrock.

'Are we going to the Prism?' Jaspec asked eagerly. 'Are we going to where rogue jinn are trapped in the cells? Am I to see them for myself?'

Turning, the veteran malbino limped off through the stone cleft, the young trainee guard close on his heels. Jaspec's questions came thick and fast, but all were left unanswered.

Limping through the twists and turns, as though the route were second nature, Morrock caught a flash of himself making the journey for the first time so many decades before: bright-eyed, a slender waistline, nimble feet, and an insatiable zest for life.

It was hard to believe, but even he had been young and sprightly once – a time when he hadn't set eyes on the creature destined to become his nemesis.

All of a sudden, Morrock stopped, the sheer stone walls rising up on either side, their shadows as cold as death.

Half a pace behind, Jaspec froze.

'What is it?' he asked urgently.

'Listen to everything I tell you,' Morrock countered. 'Remember every detail, so that the knowledge becomes you as much as you are yourself. Most of all, sense my fear, and learn from it.'

'But why must I fear, Brother Morrock?'

'Because if you do not fear the prisoners,' the veteran malbino said, 'they will swallow you whole, spit out your bones, and dance on your soul.'

*

In the Courant Institute's afternoon session, Dr. Moss dropped the lights again and projected the morning's lead story from the *New York Times* website on the back wall.

Scrolling beyond a headline blaring news of the Bank of England heist, he paused on a photograph – a detail of pattern.

The pattern etched into the walls, ceilings, and the floors in each one of the Bank's now-empty bullion vaults.

'Have a good look,' he urged the class.

'What the heck?' blurted the student who had suggested aliens during the morning session.

'As you can see, they're calling it the "Heist of the Century",' said Moss. 'Billions in gold bullion evaporated, and nothing but this pattern left in its place. No intruders, and the alarms didn't even go off. What do you guys make of it?'

The prudish Russian at the front put up her hand.

'Reaction-diffusion pattern sequence,' she said.

The professor nodded.

A Chinese student near the back called out:

'A diagonal matrix of diffusion coefficients.'

Moss paused.

'I'd say you're both right.'

He nudged the side of his hand towards his star pupil.

'What do you think?'

Until then, Oliver had been silent, his mind zoning in and out of fantasy.

'Hmm?'

'The pattern found at the London bank heist,' Moss recapped. 'What's your take on it?'

Pushing a hand back through his hair, Oliver scanned the newspaper article and then the pattern. With the entire class waiting for his answer, he took a moment to reflect.

Conclusions tended to come to him effortlessly, even to the most complex problems. But, for the first time in a long while, Oliver had no answer. He just sat there, while the class waited for him to deliver another dose of characteristic genius.

On the surface, he appeared calm, if baffled like everyone else.

Yet, deep down, something was stirring inside him.

Something as unexplainable as the bullion heist.

*

143

LIMPING DOWN GULLIES little wider than himself, Morrock led the way to the low vaulted tunnel that formed the gateway to the Prism complex.

The colour and texture of rock-hewn lapis lazuli, the walls were dark blue, covered in quastular bats. Hanging in clusters, they squealed in alarm at intruders, their wings glowing gold from fear.

Pacing after the old malbino guard, Jaspec shot out a fresh volley of questions.

Like all the others, they went unanswered.

At the end of the tunnel, Morrock halted and turned sharply.

The eyes on the front of his brow regarded Jaspec with disdain.

'We have reached it,' he snapped. 'From here you must do exactly as I say. Do you understand?'

Less confident than before, Jaspec nodded.

'Very well,' Morrock replied. 'We shall begin.'

Lowering himself onto the tunnel's flooring, he squeezed through a tight aperture, groaning and grunting.

Inches behind him, Jaspec took the last stretch of the shaft with ease.

All of a sudden, the passageway came to an end, opening out into a space.

The Abyss.

Desolate, vast, and utterly mesmerizing, it seemed to defy the laws of scale and possibility.

At its heart lay the Prism.

Rotating on its vertical axis, as it had done for centuries, the great glass penitentiary clattered round – powered by iron sails, the sails driven by the fugian wind.

Jaspec's lower jaw dropped at the sight.

For as long as he could remember he had heard tales of the Prism. Like all other malbinos, he had been weaned on them.

Until that moment, having not seen it for himself, he'd never understood the scale.

Peering round at the young trainee, Morrock felt a twinge of nostalgia, as he remembered the first time his own nine eyes had feasted on the sight.

The veteran malbino limped up to the glass bridge spanning the chasm – from the tunnel to the Prism itself.

'There are seven levels to the penitentiary,' he mumbled, as though the information was almost inconsequential. 'Each one is reserved for an order of jinn. Do you understand?'

Jaspec nodded.

'Yes, Brother Morrock.'

'The uppermost cells contain Species One,' the elder explained. 'They are dull-witted, and can't think more than fifteen seconds ahead. As a result, they're hopeless, hapless, and are easily trapped.'

Reaching the end of the bridge, Morrock leaped down onto the Prism itself.

'When we go past,' he whispered, 'do not look at them directly.'

'Why not, Brother Morrock?'

'Because they scare easily and, when afraid, they swallow themselves.'

The Prism's impregnable glass surface stretched out until it touched the darkness. Brilliantly illuminated from within, it was rock solid, like the surface of a planet, gyrating through space.

Raising the tip of his nose with a thumb, Morrock sniffed the air long and hard. Then, having let out a grunt of satisfaction, he disappeared down a foxhole between the sheets of triangular glass.

Unnerved, Jaspec followed, doing his best to appear brave.

The hole emerged into a long galleried passage.

Identical octagonal cells spanned out on either side, above, and below. The lighting was bright, the air tinged with the faintest touch of haze. A pungent smell lingered there – a mixture of burned honeysuckle and sworp-sworp soap.

Morrock gesticulated at the cells.

'Species One,' he said with loathing. 'All of them imbecilic.'

Jaspec held up a hand.

'What are they here for, Brother Morrock?'

The old malbino cocked the side of his face at the first cell.

'That's a wart jinn from the Kingdom of Smod,' he replied. 'Been here for as long as I can remember. A danger to society, and to himself.'

'What was his crime?'

'Devoured the royal family, after mistaking them for a bowl of mos-mot.'

'*Mos-mot?*'

'The porridge wart jinn like to feast on in the season of Candlemas.'

A creature was curled up behind the glass, its iridescent skin pocked with suppurating warts. Either side of a long bristled snout, a dainty eye was welling with tears.

'How long will he be in here?' Jaspec asked.

Morrock scowled at the question, his back teeth exposed in rage.

'That is no concern of ours!' he roared. 'We are merely guardians in the service of Zonus. You would do well to remember it, do you understand?'

Dipping his head in terror, Jaspec bared his jugular – the malbino way of signalling subservience.

Growling and grunting, Morrock limped on down the passageway.

Either side of it, the glass cells were uniform and empty of anything but the inmates. The cubicles may have been identical, but the rogue jinn prisoners they housed were anything but similar.

Some were as small as marbles, while others were far beyond gigantic. In the same way that an immense black hole is compressed in on itself, even the most unwieldy jinn were contained in a standard-sized cell.

Jaspec followed in Morrock's footsteps, his apprehension doubling with every pace. For the first time in his life he experienced real fear. Suffocating, perplexing, and utterly grim, it was bitter as the sourest grapes from the Kingdom of Kríx.

Peering into the cells, one by one, he was struck by the rogue jinn's astonishing range in form and size.

Some seemed vaguely like malbinos – two arms, legs and a single head. A great many more bore features for which jinn were often known – serpentine scales, barbed fur, serrated talons, hooves, horns, tentacles, and row upon row of shark-like teeth.

They ranged wildly in colour.

A few were pinkish-grey, while others were the shade of pickled walnuts, or blazing red, or any other of ten thousand hues – constantly changing, depending on their mood.

Having passed dozens of cells, Morrock paused, and motioned to the glass floor between his feet.

'That one in there was caught by Epsilius,' he whispered.

Jaspec frowned.

'*Epsilius?*'

'The greatest living Jinn Hunter,' Morrock replied. 'Remember the name and honour it as you honour your own ancestors!'

The young malbino peered down into the cell.

Inside, nudged up against one wall, was a trembling mass of turquoise fur. Somewhere near the middle was a single eye, resembling an ostrich egg cracked into a soup tureen. Off-centre below it was an oversized mouth, filled with drool and uneven-shaped teeth.

Moving down along the glass wall, Jaspec's gaze reached the fur and the yellow eye.

Without meaning to go against Morrock's orders, the

young malbino found himself drawn in. Before he knew it, he was staring into the pupil, sucked in, as though hypnotized.

Having limped ahead, Morrock froze.

He swivelled round.

As he did so, the turquoise jinn opened its mouth as wide as it could. With teeth gnashing and amid a tidal wave of drool, it began ingesting itself.

Nothing in his wildest dreams could have prepared Jaspec for the sight of a rogue jinn swallowing its own body.

Crying out, the young malbino pounded at the glass with his fists.

Face flushed with rage, Morrock dived forward and punched an octagonal emergency button set into the floor.

Within an instant, the jinn was paralyzed.

A moment later and a dozen malbino guards were on the scene, armed with giant callipers, tridents, and nets.

'I didn't mean to,' moaned Jaspec despondently. 'Didn't mean to look at him, but I couldn't help it.'

Morrock spat a salvo of orders at the guards.

Then, stepping close to Jaspec, he sighed.

'Young malbinos like to think of me as cruel,' he intoned tenderly. 'I'm not. But the way I view life in the Prism has been shaped by experience. These nine eyes of mine have witnessed the most terrible sights – the kind which no malbino should ever see. Memories so fearful they haunt my waking life and all my dreams. I have witnessed terrible events take place because of simple mistakes. Mistakes that spiralled out of control.'

Morrock reached out a hand and touched a pair of

thumbs to Jaspec's shoulder. 'Never disobey me again,' he said. 'If you do, unthinkable terror will befall you.'

*

HALFWAY THROUGH THE afternoon session, Oliver excused himself and made a beeline for the restroom.

Hunched down over the washbasin, he soothed his face in a stream of cool water. He was feeling both hot and cold, focused and awry, elated and downcast, as though something had tampered with his internal settings.

All of a sudden, he caught sight of himself sitting on a brick wall with Bill Lewis, his best friend since fifth grade. They must have been about twelve. Bill was showing off a prized baseball mitt bought with his savings.

'It's awesome!' Oliver gasped. 'I'm green with jealousy.'

The words had hardly left Oliver's mouth when Bill jerked the mitt off his hand and passed it to his friend.

'For you,' he mumbled.

'What? No! I can't take it! You delivered papers for weeks to earn that!'

Bill's face soured.

'You have to accept it,' he said. 'And you must remember something and never forget it.'

'*What?*'

'That I'm always here for you, just as you are always here for me.'

*

Jaspec close behind him, Morrock slipped down a second foxhole.

After twists and turns, they emerged in another sector of the Prism.

'This is where Species Two are kept,' the veteran guard explained. 'A little more intelligent than the ones above, they're easily trapped. They're panicked by small objects – like grains of sand, buttons, and even by little jinn. There's very little remarkable about them, except their expertise in shape-shifting.'

Jaspec peered into the first cell, in which a lugubrious rodent-like creature was sprawled out. As soon as it spotted the malbinos, it transformed itself into a steel strongbox.

Morrock motioned towards a lumpy odd-shaped protrusion on the side.

'Take notice,' he said.

Jaspec leaned in towards the glass.

'What is it?' he asked, squinting.

'A kind of nostril,' said Morrock. 'Every Species Two jinn are born with an olfactory gland on the bottom of their left foot. No amount of shape-shifting can ever conceal it.'

'Why's it there?' asked Jaspec.

The seasoned malbino guard shrugged.

'Why is any of it as it is?' he replied. 'No one knows – not even the fopula slugs… and they know everything… or, at least, everything worth knowing.'

'Fopula *who*?'

Morrock turned to the young trainee, his multiple eyes wide.

'You don't know anything, do you?' he snapped.

Jaspec didn't reply.

'Have no fear,' said Morrock, leading the way towards another foxhole, 'you will learn everything soon enough.'

As they descended through the layers of octagonal cells, the Prism's glass grew thicker, and the guards on duty more seasoned.

On every passageway, malbino sentries were stationed at regular intervals, each one alert for the tell-tale signs of dereliction. Checking and rechecking the cells in an endless routine, they regarded everyone and everything with suspicion.

Such was the ingenuity of convict jinn, especially those housed on the lower levels, that nothing was taken for granted. Fifty times a day, the inmates and their cells were inspected. The malbinos on duty were checked as well. After all, the most likely way to escape would be for a shape-shifting jinn to assume the identity of a guard.

Morrock and Jaspec descended deeper into the depths of the Prism.

Every duty guard and official they encountered saluted the malbino elder, before bowing down low in respect.

'How do they know you're not a jinn in disguise?' asked Jaspec, as he strode slowly down the short passageway.

Morrock felt his back warm with anger at what he regarded as youthful insolence. But, rather than lash out, he replied:

'They know it is me because of the secret.'

'*Secret*?'

'The secret known only to them and me.'

'Will you tell it to me?' Jaspec squirmed. 'Will you tell me the secret?'

Again, the veteran's back warmed and, again, he calmed himself.

'With time you may learn that secret and many others,' he said.

'How long will it take before the secrets are revealed?'

Morrock was tiring of the trainee and the perilous condition of youth.

'A wise malbino would never wish to know any secrets,' he answered, frowning hard.

'But why not, Brother Morrock?'

'Because secrets are accompanied by grave danger.'

Pushing his shoulders back, Jaspec remembered how brave he had claimed to be.

'I'm not frightened,' he said.

'*Really?*'

The young malbino did his best to appear defiant.

'Yes.'

'Not frightened of anything?'

Jaspec shook his head.

'Nothing.'

'Then I'll show you something,' said the old malbino calmly.

'What?'

'Come with me.'

A warren of interlinking furrows, passages and gangways

came and went, as Morrock and Jaspec clambered further and further into the Prism.

As they descended, the atmosphere grew heavier, as though it was somehow weighed down with terror.

With each level, the passages were shorter, until they were hardly passages at all.

Eventually, they reached the lowest point, where the Species Seven jinn were housed.

The nadir of the inverted pyramid.

Drinking in Jaspec's youthful vigour, Morrock turned to the cell and blinked.

'Go on, have a look.'

'What's in there?'

'The jinn I guard.'

The young malbino craned his neck to look inside.

All he could see was the faintest outline of a form.

His eyes scanning the creature slowly, Jaspec felt a force pressing down on his chest.

'Can't breathe,' he choked, doubling over.

'Is that all you feel?' asked Morrock.

Panting, Jaspec looked towards the cell.

As he did so, he was overcome by a second sensation.

Slipping into his muscles and flesh, it coursed through capillaries and veins, across synapses, and into every fibre of his fur-covered frame.

The sensation was fear.

Pure, perfect fear.

Shaking, Jaspec collapsed onto the glass floor, all nine eyes bloodshot, his palms streaming with sweat.

'*Whhhhhat… what… what's that?*' he wheezed, fighting to make the words audible.

Morrock retreated from the cell's wall, as though even he were not safe.

'It is Nequissimus,' he said.

From: *Jinn Hunter: Book One – The Prism*

An Acquired Taste

THE OFFERS OF work kept coming for weeks.

And the more that arrived, the more Dr. Kaine began to wish he could crawl under a rock and hide. He thought of taking a sabbatical, or of writing another book. But, as Mrs. Phelps often reminded him, now that he was a celebrity in his own right, the public owned a little piece of his soul.

The only comfort was the dining club.

In its company the surgeon indulged himself, revelling in his passion for obscure gastronomy. He would long for the first Tuesday of the month, counting down the days, and then the hours. Secretly, he wished he could tell its members the truth about the curious pastries he had sampled on his visit to Bhochnivia. But the taboo was so great he felt sure that even the seasoned gastronomes of his beloved fraternity would disapprove.

In the weeks since journeying to Vladimir Drusnev's pleasure dome, Kaine had become increasingly fixated with the notion of ocular cannibalism. He knew it was depraved yet, at the same time, he was fascinated by the apparent effect the human eye had had on his body and his mind.

For a full month after eating the pastries, he had felt like a new man. His hair had grown through thick and black. His skin was rosy pink, and his back pain was entirely gone. But best of all was the transformation in mental capability.

The surgeon found that he could do almost any mathematical calculation in his head. He could write poetry too, and consider the most complex intellectual arguments from numerous angles. He managed to pick up basic Mandarin by studying an hour a day, and he mastered the violin as well.

Then, one morning, he awoke to find his skin a tired and sullen shade of grey. His bald patch had returned in the night, and his back was aching terribly. Over breakfast, he struggled to complete a single clue in the *New York Times* crossword. The day before he had finished the entire exercise in ten minutes flat.

It was as though an invisible switch had been turned off on the back of his head. Rather than being his old self again, he was half the man he had been before eating the supreme leader's pies.

All that morning the usual stream of VIP clients came and went, with Kaine doing his best to accommodate them. He scheduled surgeries for some, examined others, and whispered reassurance to yet more.

But his mind was far away in the Central Asian capital of Moslok.

Worst of all was the craving – the desperate, unhinged craving for the pastries. All he could think of was how to get more.

He considered calling Drusnev's chief of staff to ask for a batch to be sent through the diplomatic bag, or even for a follow-up trip to Bhochnivia. After all, the invitation to go prisoner-hunting had been an open one.

That evening, Amadeus Kaine stayed at work a little later than he had planned, finishing a medical paper for a learned journal. The essay assessed a question of ethics in ophthalmology, a subject that the initial effect of the pastries would have made far easier to debate.

After struggling for a good long while, the surgeon stood up, leaned back on the desk and picked up the gold-plated orb. Weighing it in his hand, he decided then and there that a little prisoner-hunting was the only solution.

He would call Drusnev's office first thing in the morning.

That night Kaine dreamed of his ex-wife, Francine, the one woman in the world who had the ability to make his blood boil. He dreamed that she was on a chain gang deep in the opal mines. And he dreamed that her hazel eyes were plucked out and stuffed into pastries for Drusnev's table.

The nightmare woke Kaine.

In a cold sweat, he reached for his glass of water in the darkness and wondered whether he should see a therapist.

Clambering out of bed, he went online and checked the news. Reading world events did wonders for taking his mind off the ins and outs of his life.

The lead story carried a grotesque picture of a headless body. Drenched in blood, it was missing its hands and feet as well. The corpse was labelled with an attention-grabbing headline:

MAD-DOG DRUSNEV SLAIN IN
MIDNIGHT ATTACK

The story explained how the supreme leader's impoverished people had risen up against him. Hundreds had been slaughtered, most of them members of Drusnev's own family. Realizing that the odds were overwhelming against them, the army had joined the mob and turned their weapons on the misguided aristocracy.

Within hours, Drusnev was captured and killed. His body was dragged through the streets and then decapitated, its eyes apparently swallowed by an onlooker in the crowd.

Kaine clicked on the link, to find a gallery of images of Moslok in both turmoil and jubilation. There were pictures of the presidential palace being looted, of a Rolls-Royce ablaze, of droves of blind prisoners being led up from the opal mines, and of people dancing in the streets.

Damn it, the surgeon thought to himself, I'll never get any of the pastries now.

A few days passed, and Kaine excised the right eye of a Canadian billionaire.

The procedure was carried out using a piece of equipment that he himself had designed and patented, known as the Kaine Excisor. It consisted of a pair of elliptical blades and a kind of ventouse suction device. The apparatus had been regarded as a revolution in its own right, so much so that every eye surgeon worth their salt now used one.

When the operation was over, the patient was wheeled through to post-op, and the surgical team waited to be dismissed. Dr. Kaine thanked them. He was about to leave, when he noticed the excised eye looking up at him from a kidney dish.

There was something irresistible about it.

'Is that bound for the incinerator?' he asked one of the nurses casually, his mouth watering.

'Yes, doctor.'

'I'd like to make an analysis of this one. I'll send a rundown of what I need. Keep it on ice.'

'Very good, Dr. Kaine.'

Three days went by and the analysis arrived. The surgeon had it sent to his office, where Mrs. Phelps brought it in with his morning coffee and a copy of the *Wall Street Journal*.

'There's a piece about you on page twelve,' she said.

Kaine waved the newspaper away. Opening the envelope, he squinted at the figures.

'Oh,' he said softly. 'Now that *is* interesting. Who would have thought?'

The receptionist was hovering.

'Something unusual, doctor?'

'It must be due to the amino acid content of the melanin, an associated effect of the tyrosine. I'm certain of it.'

'Certain of what, doctor?'

'The taste.'

Mrs. Phelps frowned hard.

'Excuse me?'

Kaine looked up. He had been lost in his own world and was half imagining he was talking to himself.

'Um, er, nothing,' he said, faltering. 'Nothing of importance anyhow.'

The receptionist sauntered back to her position, and when she was gone Kaine looked up the effect of tyrosine on the human sense of taste. That was it, surely. The human eye contains complex arrangements of amino acids, and tyrosine has a profound effect on the metabolism and on neurotransmission in the brain.

Staring out of the window, Amadeus Kaine watched the commuters hurrying into work. He pitied them for living wasted lives stripped bare of uproar, the kind that visited him on a regular basis.

Stirring his coffee six times to the right, and then to the left, he began to think about the taste again. That taste – succulent, well-rounded, and so utterly taboo. It was like nothing he had ever experienced before, as perfect as its consistency, and made all the more appealing by the thought it was the ultimate forbidden fruit.

Stepping over to the mantel, the surgeon checked the time on the Jaeger Atmos clock, his most prized object. He had bought it in an antique shop in Vilnius fifteen years previously.

It was eleven minutes past nine.

Kaine checked the time against his wristwatch, then walked through to where Mrs. Phelps was sitting at the reception desk.

'What time is my next appointment?'

'Not until eleven-fifteen.'

'Who is it?'

'The Ambassador of Hungary. He's come up from DC especially.'

'OK. I'm just running out, but I'll be back in time for him.'

The doctor hurried downstairs and hailed a cab.

'72nd and Broadway.'

The driver didn't answer. He sped off fast and was soon cruising through Central Park.

Kaine looked out at the face of winter in the trees – the bleak austerity and the cold. It reminded him of Moslok, and that reminded him of Drusnev and the banquet, a memory that reminded him of the eyes.

Everything reminded him of the eyes.

The more he thought of them, the more he craved them. He couldn't work out what he yearned for more – the texture or the taste. They were yin and yang, two inseparable halves of the whole.

The perfect food.

The despised – and now deposed – supreme leader had, without realizing it, happened upon the food of the gods.

The cab rumbled over Central Park West and down 72nd Street. Kaine's gaze jarred from building to building, but he wasn't seeing anything at all. He was thinking – thinking about the genius of Drusnev.

The one man who had understood the passion.

The taste. The craving.

The taxi crossed Broadway and began to slow.

'Which number?' yelled the driver.

'245… that one there… with the green awning.'

Kaine fumbled for change, then jumped out onto the kerb. He closed his eyes, breathed in gently, savouring the patch of street where his youth had been played out. He knew every inch of pavement. Well, he knew every inch of how it had been. It was all gentrified now, awash with glass-fronted emporiums and name-brand stores.

The only one left from the old days was at 245 – Bill's Butchery.

Amadeus Kaine blinked and cleared his throat. A moment later he was inside.

Bill's was an institution, a fourth-generation family business. It had been founded in the twenties by William McMarsh, an immigrant from the Scottish Highlands. His son, grandson, and now great-grandson had all borne the same name in a firm that prided itself on tradition.

Those who patronized Bill's Butchery could rest assured that the customer was always put first. But most important to the discerning clientele was the fact that successive generations of the McMarsh family made every effort to source exotic meat.

And exotic meat had always been the name of the game at Bill's.

Every scrap of wall space hung with trophies, a kind of gruesome 3D catalogue of what was available.

There were camels' heads and those of crocodiles and kangaroos, gemsbok and zebra, wildebeest and kudu. And, for regular clients, or those in the know, there was the Black Book.

The book was kept behind the counter and its pages contained a cornucopia of wildlife that had at times been sourced for special clients. The inventory included everything from the big cats of the African savannah, to the exotic birds and reptiles of the Mato Grosso plateau.

As soon as he saw Kaine step over the threshold, William McMarsh IV lurched up from his stool. He swept round from behind the counter and gave the eye surgeon a rib-crushing hug.

A giant, round-shouldered hulk of a man, he had a tangled grey ZZ Top beard, and a voice so gravelly that it was near impossible to make sense of anything he said. He and Kaine had been childhood buddies. They had grown up together, running errands up and down the West Side.

The surgeon massaged his hands together once the pleasantries were over.

'I'm doing some tests,' he said, 'and need some animal products. One or two things from the Black Book.'

Bill took it from the drawer under the counter and handed it over. It was an inch thick, more of a folder than a book.

The doctor flicked through with concentration.

'They're ophthalmological tests,' he said absently. 'So what I'm after are some eyes.'

'That shouldn't be a problem. It'll take a few days though, depending on what you're after.'

Kaine looked up from the book.

'I need as wide a range as possible.'

'What are we talking about?'

'Some big game, and some more standard stuff.' He sniffed, pinched the end of his nose. 'I'll make you a wish list,' he said, 'and you see what you can get.'

Bill McMarsh teaselled a hand down through his beard.

'Since they're for experimentation I'm assuming they can be, you know... a few days old.'

Kaine's face seemed to tense. He wagged a finger in the direction of his old friend.

'No, no, it's absolutely imperative that they're completely fresh,' he said.

Two days passed and there was still no word from Bill's Butchery, and so Kaine asked Mrs. Phelps to check up on the order.

'He says he needs another week, and that your list is the challenge of his life.'

The surgeon didn't reply. He simply leaned back in his chair and re-enacted the Central Asian banquet in his mind. Amadeus Kaine had never taken drugs in his life, and had never even been tempted. But, for the first time, he understood the anguish of the serious user. The worst thing was the social condemnation of it all, the sense of being an outcast for craving something so proscribed. Then again, as he reasoned it, drug addicts had it easy. They could find a dealer on any street corner ready and willing to supply them the hit.

All of a sudden, the telephone rang.

It wasn't the black one that Mrs. Phelps called on, but the red one – reserved for VIP clients. Kaine let it ring six times. Always best to make them think you're busy.

He picked up.

'Hello?'

'Is that Dr. Amadeus Kaine?' asked a thickly accented voice.

'Yes, it is.'

'I am Obunda Malinku of the People's Republic of Tenin.'

Kaine racked his memory but couldn't place the country. He typed it quickly into Wikipedia, and found it nestling to the west of the Congo.

The People's Republic of Tenin.
Capital city: Bayotville.
National population: 1,247,000.
Currency: Tenin Dollar.
Language: English and tribal dialects.

'Good afternoon to you, sir. How may I be of assistance?'

There was a muffled screaming sound, as though someone of high authority was extremely displeased. The line went dead. Kaine hung up. He rolled his eyes. Then, after a long pause, the phone rang again.

'Hello?'

'I am sorry,' said the voice. 'There are some communication difficulties.'

'Don't worry about it.'

'I am calling you on behalf of the prime minister's office,' the accented voice explained.

'I see.'

The voice chuckled.

'Well, Mr. Julius Marimba does not!'

'*Julius*...?'

'Marimba... our prime minister.'

'And what exactly is the matter with Mr. Marimba?'

'Hello?'

'I said what is his condition?'

'He has been shot.'

'Where?'

'In the right eye.'

Kaine winced.

'Has an eye surgeon examined him?'

'Yes, sir. I mean no, sir.'

'Well, you need to get a doctor to send me a report. Is that possible?'

The line went dead and Kaine got on with his work. Then, an hour later, the red telephone rang again.

'This is General Oscar Omamba, Chief of Armed Forces in the Republic of Tenin!'

'Good afternoon.'

'I hear you are the best eye surgeon in the world.'

'I don't know about that,' Dr. Kaine replied modestly.

'A bullet has pierced the right eye of our prime minister. We need you to come at once.'

Kaine may have had pity for the Madison Avenue commuters, but there were times he wished he was one of them.

'I need to speak to a surgeon,' he said, repeating himself.

General Omamba's voice seemed to rise in pitch.

167

'We are in a challenging position,' he said. 'We are fighting insurgents.'

'Listen, General, I don't want to seem uncharitable, but neither I nor any other surgeon I know is likely to come to a hostile situation. Can you not have the prime minister moved? Could you bring him to New York?'

There was the sound of a desk being thumped with a fist, followed by more shouting.

Another voice came on.

'Dr. Kaine? This is Obunda Malinku. I called you before.'

'Yes, Mr. Malinku.'

'Dr. Kaine, the prime minister is not going to leave. His feet must remain on Tenin's soil. Sir, we are willing to pay you for your services. You can name your price!'

'I can't promise that I shall be able to do anything at all,' Kaine replied. 'The eye has most likely been totally destroyed, and possibly large portions of the brain as well. Is the prime minister conscious?'

'Yes, sir.'

'Well, that's a miracle in itself. What surgical set up do you have there?'

'*Surgical*?'

'Do you have a hospital?'

'Yes, there is a hospital, sir.'

'Are there flights between New York and Tenin?'

Obunda Malinku cleared his throat.

'An aeroplane just left, sir. It will reach New York by nightfall.'

Kaine stood up. He looked hard at the portrait of George III, his eyes counting the buttons on the monarch's coat.

'I shall come for forty-eight hours, and not a moment longer. Do you understand?'

'Yes, sir.'

'And even then, I am coming to make an examination and nothing more.' He paused, clicked his neck. 'As for my fee... I am sure we can work something out.'

Service on the Challenger 601 was low on frills.

There wasn't champagne, caviar, or even peanuts.

The jet, which was almost twenty years old, had seen much better days. The seat stuffing was coming out, and there were what looked like large bloodstains on the floor of the galley.

'We are borrowing it,' said the pilot awkwardly, as Kaine boarded that night. 'From another African government.'

'Hasn't Tenin got its own aircraft?'

'It had one, but it was destroyed last week in the uprising.'

Kaine had sat down in his seat and thought twice about fastening the buckle.

'*Uprising?*' he whispered.

The pilot shrugged.

'Insurgents. You know. They're all over Africa these days.'

'Is there fighting?'

'Nothing to worry about. It's all over now.'

'Are you sure?'

The pilot didn't answer. He slipped into the cockpit and locked the door firmly behind him.

Nine hours later, bright African sunlight was streaming in through the windows. Despite the lack of refreshments, Kaine had slept well. He finished reading a novel on his Kindle, and then half wondered why he was bothering with Tenin at all.

The answer was that there was something about Africa, something deviously magical, something alluring. The Dark Continent was in his blood, and it touched him like nowhere else on earth.

The Challenger jet banked steeply to the right and started to descend fast through the pale blue sky. The pilot announced that landing would be in five minutes. They were still tremendously high. But suddenly, in nothing short of a nosedive, the jet hurtled to the ground.

It tailed off in the nick of time.

Once on the ground, they taxied past the terminal building towards a ramshackle old Nissen hut. All around the airport there was dense, luxuriant vegetation. And there was smoke, too. At first Kaine had assumed it was mist. But as soon as the door was opened, he could smell it. There was a tang of sulphur about it, as though a large stockpile of ordnance had gone up.

As soon as the steps were folded down, three men ran out from the Nissen hut. Two of them were in military fatigues and were armed with Chinese machine guns. The third was dressed in a business suit. He seemed alarmed, his face and clothing drenched with perspiration.

'Welcome to Tenin, Dr. Kaine,' he said. 'I am Obunda Malinku. We spoke on the telephone.'

The surgeon was about to ask something, when Malinku held up a hand.

'There's no time to talk now,' he said urgently. 'The insurgents are closing in on the airport. We must get away.'

They clambered into an old Land Rover with Kaine's voluminous luggage piled in the back, where there was an M60 machine gun mounted. The vehicle was badly damaged and appeared to have caught fire in the recent past.

'Shall we go straight to the hospital?' asked the American.

Malinku shook his head.

'It was hit last night. So we will go to the palace. The prime minister is resting there.'

'What treatment has he received?'

'Valium.'

'Is that all?'

Malinku's reply was drowned out by a huge explosion in the near distance. It rocked the ground like an earthquake, and was followed by a second blast, and then a third. The driver accelerated down the rutted dirt road in the direction of the explosions.

'Is it wise to go this way?' Kaine shouted.

'It's the only road,' Malinku replied, climbing into the back to man the M60.

The jungle foliage gave way to shanties and then to low-rise buildings as they approached the outskirts of Bayotville. The air stank of more sulphurous smoke and burning oil. There were too many burnt-out cars and buildings to count.

As for people, there were plenty of dead, peppered all over the ground – men, women, children. The only live people were the soldiers manning the endless checkpoints. At each one they waved the Land Rover quickly through.

From time to time small arms fire rang out. Malinku released the M60's safety catch and returned fire in short, steady bursts.

Clutching the handrail, Kaine was white-knuckled and terrified. There was nothing he disliked more than weaponry or warfare. His blood was so charged with adrenalin that he could have taken a bullet in the ribs and hardly known it.

He got a flash of Drusnev's headless body being pulled through the streets. What if the prime minister was overthrown while he was there? That's all it would take for him to be hacked into mincemeat along with an entire rotten regime. The only difference between him and everyone else was that he couldn't even pronounce the prime minister's name.

A series of extra-large defence barriers came and went, each of them armed more heavily than the last. At the final one the sandbags were stacked four deep, and were finished off with electrified razor-wire and double machine-gun posts.

The Land Rover was waved through fast.

After crossing an open stretch of ground, the vehicle screeched to a halt outside the palace. The American was hurried inside, where General Omamba was awaiting him.

'Thank you for coming to Tenin, Dr. Kaine,' he said in a grave voice. 'I am sorry that the circumstances are not more favourable. If it is any consolation, we have this morning captured the rebel commander.'

'Would you take me to the prime minister?' said the surgeon.

'At once.'

Even on the scale of unscrupulous African dictatorships, the palace was colossal. It boasted three hundred and nine bedrooms, six ballrooms, fifteen kitchens, and its own cathedral. The water in the Olympic-sized swimming pool was imported from the source at Evian, and the walls of every room were overlaid with sheets of twenty-four carat gold.

Amadeus Kaine might more normally have made an effort to show interest in the furnishings, but the fact that the insurgents were closing in disturbed his attention.

Outside, the sound of mortar fire was growing louder and more thunderous, the intervals between the explosions shorter and shorter still. From time to time there was the agonized wail of a man who had had his legs blown off, or his stomach riddled with lead.

The eye surgeon quickened his pace from a fast walk to a jog, and then to a sprint. As if in a nightmare, the more ground he covered, the further there was to go. Just as he was giving up hope, the general thrust an arm towards a grand doorway.

They entered, zigzagged through a cluster of anterooms, and emerged in a vast bedroom. Octagonal in shape, it had a domed ceiling which could slide away with the flick of a switch. The floor was made from a single sheet of optical-quality glass, allowing a view straight through into a giant aquarium below.

In the middle of the room, the prime minister was lying in a great golden bedstead, fashioned in the shape of a huge, brooding eagle. He was propped up, his head copiously bandaged. A drip had been fitted into the leader's arm. Remarkably he was conscious, although in a dreamlike state – a result of the Valium.

Stepping forward calmly, Dr. Kaine introduced himself. He asked for his equipment, and for everyone but the general to leave. Experience had taught him that there was nothing quite so wretched as having hangers-on loitering during an examination, especially one in testing conditions.

On his instructions, the lighting was turned up and the air conditioning was set to super-cool. Having taken a moment to change into sterile clothing and to scrub up, he removed the bandages from the prime minister's head.

The bullet had penetrated at an angle, grazing the nose and entering the middle of the right ocular cavity. Fortunately, it had hit the target when almost spent of energy. Were it to have collided with bone, it would probably have left nothing but a bruise. It seemed as though the bullet, a 9 mm round, had entered the prefrontal cortex, where it was now lodged.

There was no question of the patient ever seeing again through the injured eye, or of the bullet being removed without a full team of specialists.

Kaine stepped away from the bed and beckoned the general to join him.

'The good news is that, with the right treatment, the prime minister will live,' he said. 'But left here, he will die.'

'He cannot leave Tenin!' the general stammered. 'If he does so, our country is lost.'

The surgeon leaned forwards conspiratorially.

'You said, did you not, that you have taken the insurgents' commander alive?'

'Yes, we have. He's in the jail below this palace.'

'I am not a military man,' said Kaine. 'But I have a suggestion.'

'I am listening,' replied General Omamba.

'You could put a sack over the prime minister's head, pretend he's the rebel commander, and send him back to New York with me. He'll get the best treatment there – I'll make sure of it. The insurgents' morale will falter because they'll believe their leader has been taken away. And, when he has recovered a little, the prime minister can make a triumphant return.'

The general held a hand to his chin.

'It sounds as though you have experience of similar situations,' he said.

'I've been around,' replied Kaine. 'You know how it is.'

The prime minister was made ready for the journey, and a sackcloth hood was brought from the jail below. Kaine gave him 300 mg of Valium.

There was the sound of heavy gunfire in the immediate vicinity. Then an explosion. It was so strong that the windows were blown in.

The general brushed the glass off his uniform.

'We must move into a more secure area,' he said, as the prime minister was transferred into a wheelchair.

Again, Kaine found himself jogging down a great corridor, the chandeliers swinging from the continuing barrage of explosions. His face taut, the general led him down to the vault at breakneck speed. The armoured subterranean chamber doubled as a wine cellar.

Inside lay many thousands of bottles of 1er Cru Beaune, Saint-Émilion and Margaux. An entire anteroom was devoted to champagne, most of it Louis Roederer Cristal. The only exception were thirty bottles of the 1907 vintage Heidsieck, destined for Tsar Nicholas II and recovered from the depths of the Baltic Sea after a German U-boat attack.

Taking refuge in the vault, Kaine wondered why Tenin had no air force to mount an aerial attack on rebel positions. As he pondered it, there was the deafening sound of rotor blades. A Puma helicopter roared above the palace, raining fire on the insurgents.

Within half a minute there were dozens of dead. Their bodies were scattered around the palace complex, mangled by the high-intensity assault.

The general gave a thumbs up.

'That's what we needed,' he said.

'Shall we go now?' the eye surgeon asked.

'It's better to wait until darkness. You'll be taken to the airport by helicopter.'

The soldier popped the cork on a bottle of Cristal and passed it around.

'I suppose this is a good time to ask about your fee,' he said.

Kaine took a swig, wiping the bubbles from his mouth.

'There's something I'd rather have in place of money,' he replied. 'Something hard to get back home in New York.'

'Diamonds?' said the general with a smile. 'We have sacks of them down here.'

'No, not diamonds. Something a little more unusual.'

JFK had never seemed so sweet as it did on the night that the old Challenger 601 landed in dense fog on runway 4L.

Prime Minister Marimba had slept most of the flight. He lay outstretched on the floor, his breathing shallow, and his clothing drenched with sweat. Midway over the Atlantic, Kaine had administered another shot of Valium. Then, as the aircraft began the descent, he checked the leader's vital signs and whispered words of encouragement.

'We're nearly there now. Just a little longer and you'll be living it up at Mount Sinai.'

As for himself, Kaine had never felt better. He was floating on cloud nine, his senses buzzing through a kind of primitive alchemy. Throughout college his friends had taunted him to try drugs – but who needed drugs when you could knock back a dozen or two human eyes?

The effect was immediate and far more profound.

General Omamba had thought nothing odd about the surgeon's request. Fulfilling it had been far easier and cheaper than making a wire transfer from a Swiss bank, or even packing up a bag of precious gems.

At dusk he had sent a couple of his men out into the darkness beyond the palace. They were given instructions on what to do, and ordered to use their bayonets with care.

Only one of the conscripts had returned.

The other had been shot through the head by a sniper lying low in what was until recently the Café Royale. The soldier who survived had filled his helmet with fresh eyes. There must have been forty of them, a harvest from twenty dead insurgents. Surprisingly, there was very little blood. Rather like a child's illustration of a strange creature from the deep, they were disturbing but utterly fascinating. Kaine couldn't take his own eyes off them.

'That was fast,' he had said. 'How many did you get?'

'Plenty,' mumbled the conscript.

'Good work,' replied the general, taking a long swig of Cristal. 'Go and find a box and we'll wrap them up.'

On the return flight, the doctor had waited for the Challenger to climb to cruising altitude and for the crackle of gunfire to subside. Then he had switched on his seat's lamp and, a little cautiously, had picked up the box. It was sitting on the coffee table.

Untying the string, he'd pulled away the lid. What touched him first was the smell. It was difficult to describe – metallic, oleaginous, and succulent. Even before his mind had made sense of the eyes, his mouth was salivating.

Amadeus Kaine had unbuckled his seatbelt and walked back to the galley. He'd pulled open one or two drawers and found a silver-plated soup spoon and a crystal salt-shaker.

Back in his seat, he had put the box on his lap. Without any apprehension he had begun shovelling the eyes into his mouth.

Whereas President Drusnev's pastries had contained cooked eyes, the ones from the urban battlefield of Bayotville had been raw and extremely fresh.

As soon as the first one had touched his tongue, Kaine had realized that although remarkable at the time, the supreme leader's delicacies paled in comparison with the real thing.

And the real thing was raw, stripped bare of pastry and seasoning. Its texture was similar in softness to a well-cooked poached egg. But, unlike the egg, there was a variety in consistency. The cornea was a little tougher than the back of the eye, and the muscles on the sides more meaty than the rest.

As for the taste, it was not dissimilar to *marron glacé*, with a hint of *maguro* sushi thrown in. The more Kaine devoured, the more he had begun to appreciate the subtleties between one eye and the next. Some were a little more astringent on the back of the throat, as if somehow unripe; while others melted in the mouth, their juices disgorging themselves like the finest Beluga caviar.

By the time the aircraft landed at JFK, the surgeon was digesting the meal. He had felt full but not bloated, and had found himself wondering how he could ever stomach what was considered to be normal cuisine again.

But the most remarkable thing was the effect the illicit food was having on him. As before, in Moslok, he could feel the blood pumping in his muscles, and the colour returning to his cheeks. His mind was racing, as though he could compute any mental calculation, or discuss an idea of the most intense complexity.

The fresh eyes had not only tasted far more delicious than their Central Asian counterparts, but their effect was more immediate and far more rejuvenating, too.

As he sat back buckled up in the seat, the doctor could actually feel his bald patch growing over and his back pain easing once again. The sensation would have astounded any medical man, but it was all the more amazing to Kaine, who had devoted his professional life to the study of the very organ that effected this change.

At JFK, an ambulance met the private jet.

An hour and a half after landing, Amadeus Kaine began the complex operation to remove the bullet from behind the prime minister's eye. A surgical staff of fifteen assisted in a procedure that took six hours.

When it was over, Kaine took a cab home to his apartment and locked himself away. He left a message for Mrs. Phelps, asking her to cancel all his appointments and to inform anyone enquiring that he was unwell.

The truth was quite the opposite.

It was as though the world outside was too lethargic, too languid, that it couldn't keep up. With each hour that passed, Kaine felt stronger and more mentally agile, until every fibre was vibrating with electrical energy. Never in his life had he felt so vital, so astonishingly spirited and alive.

On the first day he wrote an entire symphony. After that he dedicated himself to considering world hunger. He created a blueprint for a new kind of society – one that was truly fair but without the glaring pitfalls of communism. The next day he devoted himself to writing a five-hundred-page masterwork. Entitled *Eye Spy: A Surgeon's Vision*, it was a cultural consideration of sight from prehistory to the present. The day after that, he designed a machine to create free plentiful energy from seawater.

On the fourth day, Kaine returned to work.

Mrs. Phelps offered consolation at his illness. The eye surgeon shooed her away. He looked through his mail and asked if there was anything that couldn't wait.

Touching a finger to a name on her memorandum pad, the elderly assistant said:

'This gentleman keeps calling.'

'Who does?'

'This journalist from the *LA Times*.'

'What does he want?'

'A comment on the outbreak of oculosis.'

Amadeus Kaine tossed the pile of mail he was holding onto the desk.

'Where is it – the outbreak?' he asked quickly.

'Up in Maine. It's been headline news for a week.'

Striding over to his laptop, Kaine punched up the story.

'Just what I predicted!' he exclaimed.

The next morning, Bill's Butchery delivered.

The eyes were packed in polystyrene, cooled with crushed ice and were labelled – URGENT.

Mrs. Phelps took the delivery and assumed the doctor was having a dinner party. She brought the sealed package through to the office.

'Where would you like this, doctor?' she asked.

Kaine looked up. His mind was on oculosis, the mystery eye disease that had appeared from nowhere. As soon as he saw the label, he jolted out from his chair.

'Put it in the lab, would you?'

'Yes, doctor.'

Having finished reading the first comprehensive report on the outbreak, he called a fellow surgeon up in Augusta. Then, washing his hands, he slipped back into the lab. Once alone, he bolted the door and cut away the packing tape with a scalpel blade.

Inside the box, the various eyes had been individually wrapped in protective transparent containers. They made for quite a beautiful sight. Bill McMarsh had outdone himself, sourcing the freshest examples, and carefully labelling each one.

Before dining, Kaine went to the sink and washed his hands a second time. And then a third. After that, he counted backwards from one hundred in multiples of three. It was at moments of heightened anticipation that his OCD was at its worst.

Calming himself, he applied a moisturizer, and thought back to the days when he would wrestle Bill McMarsh out on the street. He sat down, his movements unhurried and considered.

And then with care he opened the first package.

A miniature label read – *Kangaroo*. Kaine popped its contents into his mouth. It went down smoothly, rather like an oyster. On a notepad he jotted:

Kangaroo: Muscular, congealed. A hint of tobacco and cinnamon.

Next, he opened the package containing a lion's eye – no doubt, he imagined, sourced from the overstocked hunting grounds of San Diego Zoo. It tasted a little saltier than the first, rather more bitter than he liked, with an infusion of nutmeg. The third eye was from a male kudu, the fourth from a crocodile, and the one after that was from a wild boar. Each one was quite different in both consistency and taste – a point that interested the doctor greatly.

By the end of the degustation, he had filled three sheets with notes and had swallowed fifteen eyes. The most delicious had been without doubt the llama's eye, and the oryx had been the worst.

But none of them had been nearly as enjoyable as a human eye.

When he had consumed all the samples that Bill McMarsh had sent over, Amadeus Kaine went back through to the office and sat in his chair. His mind was racing again, and he considered the strange predicament in which he now found himself.

This new and unknown superfood was, as he reasoned it, one that was unlikely to be discovered by anyone else.

But the human variety alone had provided the seemingly miraculous effect.

There were plenty of diets rich in melanin, but synthesizing the amino acid content didn't appear to be enough. Kaine tried desperately to think of a trustworthy confidant in the world of medicine with whom to discuss the subject. The last thing he wanted, though, was a lecture on ethics. He knew that consuming human tissue of any kind was regarded as abhorrent, wrong, and would be considered as utterly distasteful by his peers.

Yet, if it had had such an intense and transformative effect on one man, imagine what effect it could have on an entire society. Surely there was a way of creating an analogue, of replicating the effect with human tissue.

Leaning back, Dr. Kaine swivelled around and gazed through the window. Madison Avenue was awash with ant-like figures, as it was on most afternoons.

All those people, Kaine thought to himself. They end up dying, and their eyes go to waste. It's as simple as that. A few may be used in surgery, but not the eyes of the masses, the people who die every day. He rocked back and forth thoughtfully. Surely there was no great harm in sacrificing a few eyes if it meant a brighter future for all?

From: *Eye Spy*

Nasrudin's Peregrinations

Ulaanbaatar, Mongolia

Weapons of Choice

During solo travels in Mongolia, the wise fool had experienced more than his fair share of misfortune.

While crossing the steppe on horseback, two of his animals had gone lame.

Then, he'd been poisoned at a well of brackish water.

After that, while camping in the middle of nowhere, he was robbed in the night.

The last straw was when, on the southern bank of the Zavkhan River, he was challenged to a duel by a local landowner.

The man who had thrown down the gauntlet was feared by everyone for miles around.

'He's killed a hundred men!' one villager informed Nasrudin.

'He can stop an enemy's heart merely by staring into his eyes,' said another.

The night before the duel, the wise fool repaired to his yurt, and calmed himself by reading an old book of Mongolian culture he'd brought along.

At midnight, a muffled exclamation of rapturous joy was heard to ring out from the yurt.

The next morning, Nasrudin was up bright and early, and appeared to be in the very best of spirits.

'Aren't you fearful that you're about to be slain?' asked one of the villagers.

'Not in the least,' responded the wise fool.

'But he's never lost a duel,' another quipped.

'Well, there's always a first time for everything!' Nasrudin cackled.

An hour after that, the farmer who'd challenged the traveller to the duel strode out of his yurt, glared at his opponent, and then at the assembled crowd of villagers.

'Are you ready?!' he bellowed.

'Absolutely,' Nasrudin replied, a book in his hand.

'You'd better put your book away,' the farmer snarled, 'because you're about to die!'

Turning to page 235, Nasrudin read:

'It says here that, under standard Mongolian culture, the person who has been challenged to a duel is permitted to choose the weapons that'll be used.'

'That's right,' snapped the farmer, 'so choose your weapons!'

Nasrudin held up two pairs of running shoes.

'These are my weapons of choice!'

Mexico City, Mexico
Other Side of the Gate
One afternoon, while strolling through the leafy Chapultepec Park in the Mexican capital, a conman approached Nasrudin.

'Señor,' he lisped, 'I have here in my hand the ancient title document of the Palacio Nacional, the Presidential Palace... a document that dates back to the time of the Aztecs. If you buy it from me, you will be the rightful owner of the palace.'

His eyes wide with excitement, Nasrudin enquired how much the salesman was asking for the title deed.

'Someone just offered me a thousand dollars,' he answered. 'But I turned him down.'

'Why?'

'Because he did not have noble blood.'

'Well, neither do I,' said Nasrudin.

'Of course you do, señor... look at your long aristocratic nose and your deep-set eyes. They are the mark of royalty!'

'What's the lowest price you'll go to?' the wise fool asked.

'Twenty dollars.'

Fumbling in his pocket, Nasrudin pulled out a used twenty-dollar bill and handed it over.

Unable to believe his luck, he went straight to the Palacio Nacional, and called through the bars for the guards to unlock the gates.

Almost instantly, a sentry in an official uniform marched up and ordered the foreigner to stop threatening, or else he would be arrested.

'I'll have you know that I just purchased this building from a gentleman in the Chapultepec!'

'I won't tell you to leave again!' the soldier bellowed.

Nasrudin waved the title deed and his fist.

'Be careful how you address me!' he warned. 'Or I'll have you posted to the desert when I'm on the other side of this gate!'

Buenos Aires, Argentina
Personality Swap

Nasrudin had been lured to the Argentine capital by the news that there were more psychologists registered in the city than anywhere else on earth.

Known for his many neuroses, the wise fool was thrilled.

The day after arriving, he was lying on the couch of a leading psychologist off Avenida Santa Fe.

'What is the nature of your disorder?' the doctor enquired studiously.

'Well,' Nasrudin explained awkwardly, 'I get fantasies.'

'What kind of fantasies?'

'Fantasies that I'm a psychologist, like you.'

'Really?'

'Yes, doctor.'

'Tell me more.'

'Well, just this morning I fantasized I was an Argentine psychologist who was observing a patient as you are observing me right now, in an office just like this.'

'I've got an idea that I think will help you,' the doctor said. 'I'd like you to sit here in the chair, and I shall lie down on the couch.'

'You mean, we'll do role reversal?'

'Yes, that's right.'

A minute later, Nasrudin was in the chair, pad in hand, and the psychologist was lying outstretched on the couch.

'You have a most interesting disorder,' the doctor said, even though he was now lying on the couch.

'But... but...'

'But what?'

'But it's *not* a disorder!' Nasrudin stammered. 'It's reality!'

Lying back, the doctor cleared his throat.

'You must remember that it is *me* who is the psychologist,' he said sternly, 'and *you* are the patient.'

The wise fool cackled with laughter.

'That's a good joke!'

'Oh, but it's not a joke.'

'Of course it is,' Nasrudin replied. 'After all, I'm sitting in the chair and you're on the couch.'

The psychologist got up. 'Get back on the couch.'

Nasrudin did as he asked, and the psychologist sat back down on the chair.

'Again, *I* am most definitely the doctor and *you* are the patient,' the psychologist said firmly, 'and you must always remember that.'

'Yes of course you are,' Nasrudin answered. 'At least for the purposes of our session. You're in the chair and I'm on the couch. That's how I always arrange it when doing role play with my patients.'

Yakutsk, Russia
Russian Roulette

Amid a journey of extraordinary hardship, the wise fool arrived at Yakutsk in eastern Siberia.

With no money for food, let alone a bed for the night, he found himself begging on the streets. As he huddled in a doorway, a passer-by approached.

Hoping for a coin, the wise fool put out his hand, his fingers frozen with cold.

'I shall give you all the money you need,' the man said. 'But you'll have to earn it.'

'As you can see, I'm in no position to negotiate, and so I will do anything if it means a warm meal, and somewhere to sleep for the night.'

The benefactor led Nasrudin around the corner.

Soon they were sitting together in a restaurant, the aroma of delicious roasted meat wafting through from the kitchen.

'What is it you want me to do?' the wise fool asked, so that he could get it over with and then feast.

'Play a game with me,' the man replied.

'A game? What game?'

'A game of Russian roulette.'

In any other circumstance, Nasrudin would have turned and fled, but such was his hunger that he agreed. Accordingly, he watched as the man took out a revolver, loaded a single bullet, and spun the barrel.

'D'you want to go first, or second?' he asked.

'First,' Nasrudin replied. 'I always go first.'

'*Always?*'

'Yes, always.'

'How many times have you played Russian roulette before?'

The wise fool thought for a moment.

'Oh, hundreds,' he answered absently. 'Maybe even thousands.'

The other man seemed impressed.

'And, pray tell, what's your secret to surviving... good luck?'

Nasrudin rubbed a thumbnail to his cheek.

'Quite the opposite,' he countered. 'You see, my survival has relied on terribly bad luck.'

'How can such bad luck have kept you alive?'

'The kind of bad luck that's always seem to put a bullet in my opponent's head rather than mine!'

Havana, Cuba
Perfectly Crab

Nasrudin was seen walking sideways up and down the beach.

A fisherman asked what was going on.

'I'm learning to think like them,' the wise fool responded.

'Like who?'

'Like crabs.'

'Why?'

'So I understand them, and catch them like no man has ever caught them before!'

'But why don't you just go and buy a crab net and some bait?' the fisherman asked.

Nasrudin laughed at the thought of doing the obvious.

'Unlike other fishermen,' he said conceitedly, '*I* am a perfectionist.'

Paris, France
The Real McCoy

Although conscious of the fact he was not a born artist, Nasrudin relocated to the French capital, and set himself up in a studio on the Left Bank.

Having dressed the part, in a striped shirt and a black beret worn at a slant, he heaved his heavy easel to the Beaux Arts quarter early one morning.

Whereas all the other street artists exhibited the most fabulous work, Nasrudin was conspicuous for the astonishingly poor nature of his oeuvre.

All day long, groups of tourists sauntered by. And, without exception, they lavished praise on the wise fool's competitors. Never once did they stop to admire his work.

By late afternoon, Nasrudin's ready smile was waning.

On hearing an American tourist complimenting another artist's sketches, the wise fool marched over and made his feelings known.

'How come you didn't check out *my* work?!' he demanded.

'Because,' the American answered sharply, 'we're only interested in the real McCoy.'

Nasrudin recoiled.

'If anyone here is the real McCoy, it's me!'

'No offence,' the tourist quipped, 'but when you see the real McCoy, you recognize it.'

'And how's that?' Nasrudin spat.

'Because the real McCoy doesn't have to tell you he's the real McCoy – that's why!'

The Sunderbans, India
The Tiger

A little time passed after Nasrudin swallowed the laughing hyena – time in which his digestive tract gurgled and groaned as it had never gurgled and groaned before.

The wise fool was considering an operation to root out the hyena, the octopus, the mongoose, the rat, the spider, and the bluebottle.

But the thought of being sliced open with a scalpel was too terrible for Nasrudin's delicate nerves.

So he went to the Sunderbans instead.

A vast marshland in India's north-east, the region was said by one and all to be populated by the wildest tigers in existence.

Having paid an especially brave boatman to paddle him out into the marshes, Nasrudin lay on his stomach, opened his mouth, and waited.

He waited, and he waited.

And he waited.

Then, just as he was wondering if there were any predators there at all, a huge male tiger sprang from the reeds, and jumped down Nasrudin's throat.

Leaping up, the wise fool thrust a hand in the air and cheered.

'Paddle us back to the shore at once!' he bawled. 'And put your back into it!'

The boatman paddled as hard as he could, but his craft hardly moved.

'I don't understand how we are not moving,' he said.

'It's because you're not strong,' Nasrudin replied. 'And because I have a little added weight. You may not realize it, but you are rowing you and me, and a tiger, a hyena, an octopus, a mongoose, a rat, a spider, and a damned bluebottle... which has so much to answer for!'

Buenos Aires, Argentina
Faster Than Fast
Nasrudin had enjoyed a long day exploring the backstreets of Buenos Aires, and was just crawling into bed when there was a knock at the door of his hotel room.

Opening it, he found a ragged man with a revolver in one hand and a sack of money in the other.

'Señor, please help me!' he exclaimed. 'I've just robbed a bank and the police are chasing me.'

Having been a fugitive himself at one time on his travels, he let the man in and slammed the door.

'I'll protect you, my friend!' he cried.

Five minutes of silence passed.

Then the police pounded at the door.

'Open up in the name of the law!'

The fugitive was shaking. Despite feeling fear as well, Nasrudin kept his calm.

'I promised to protect you,' he affirmed, 'and that is what I shall do.'

The police thumped at the door, louder than before.

'If you don't open up at once,' one of them called, 'we'll knock the door in!'

'He's not here!' Nasrudin yelled.

'Who isn't?'

'The man you're searching for.'

'How d'you know we're searching for someone?'

'How do you know that I know?' asked Nasrudin.

Paris, France
Roller Rink Art

Nasrudin made his way through security at the Louvre as soon as the museum had opened.

While other visitors were gazing at the paintings, the wise fool clipped roller-skate wheels to his shoes. Then, to the utter consternation of the guards, he began zigzagging at top speed through the galleries, whooping at the top of his voice.

More and more members of staff laid chase.

Within a few minutes they had arrested him.

'What on earth were you thinking?' the security chief demanded to know. 'Skating like that in the most sacred museum in the world breaks a thousand rules!'

'Museum?' answered Nasrudin in confusion. 'I assumed it was a roller-skating rink with an art show combined!'

Oakland, California
Big Picture Thinking
Nasrudin had heard stories of how all the most successful tech firms in Silicon Valley had started in a garage.

So, hoping to follow tradition, he rented a fabulous quadruple garage with a tiny apartment attached.

Once the lease was signed and secured, the wise fool kitted out the garage with workbenches, computers, water fountains, ambient lighting, and even a punch-bag.

A few days passed in which the wise fool added the final details.

Then, when everything was perfect, he called his best friend to come and check the garage out.

'It's amazing!' his pal exclaimed. 'Not even Jobs and Wozniak had a space like this. Tell me, what's your plan for it?'

'What d'you mean?' Nasrudin said.

'Well, now that you have a top-end garage, what's the start-up you're planning?'

Nasrudin had spent so much time getting the garage right that he hadn't given any thought at all into what he'd do there.

'Unlike the trailblazers who came before me,' he said, 'I'm getting the little details sorted, so the big picture takes care of itself.'

Berlin, Germany
The Procrastination King
Nasrudin was supposed to be writing a report on German statistics, but he found the subject so tedious that he started writing a poem about porcupines instead.

But, after working on the poem for an hour or so, he was so bored with it that he went over to the sink and began doing the washing up.

Then, tiring of doing that, he picked up three oranges and began teaching himself how to juggle.

And, finding it far harder than he imagined it would be, he tried to hold his breath and count to a hundred.

Through the afternoon he started on at least fifty things, but found each one was more tedious to master than the thing before.

Finally, he went back to the report on German statistics.

'Don't pretend to me that you're interesting!' he growled at the page of numbers. 'Because I know you're boring as sin. I'm only doing you because everything else I can think of is even more dreary than you!'

Naples, Italy
All in the Details

After hunting Nasrudin for weeks across southern Italy, the Neapolitan Mafia caught him, took him to a building site, and began making him walk the plank over wet concrete.

'How can you end my life?' he shrieked.

'Because you insulted Don Lambrusco! And anyone who insults Don Lambrusco is as good as dead!'

'But...'

'But *what*?!'

'But, if you kill me, you'll never find out the location of the treasure!'

'What treasure?'

'The one that only I know about!'

The hitman gave a signal for the condemned man to pause.

'Where's this treasure, then?' he asked.

'Not far from here... in the mountains.'

'And how are you expecting us to believe you?'

Nasrudin put his hand on his heart.

'I have no need for a vast treasure,' he said. 'Imagine what problems it would give a man like me.'

'So, how are you expecting us to find it?'

'I'll draw you a map.'

Ten minutes later, the wise fool was off the plank with a pencil in hand and was sketching out a map on a sheet of paper.

'There you are,' he said jubilantly. 'Take that to Don Lambrusco, and he's likely to kiss your cheeks.'

The hitman snatched the map away and held it to the light.

'But there are no names on the map.'

'Names are mere details,' Nasrudin answered, 'as you can see, I've left out a lot of details. If you want names, it's quite easy to fill them in yourself.'

Copenhagen, Denmark
Worry You, Worry Me
Nothing could stop Nasrudin from worrying during the time he spent in Denmark.

The condition was sparked off by the high cost of living in the Danish capital. And although it had started in a modest way, the worrying snowballed.

Within a week, the wise fool was worrying at fever pitch.

The more he worried about how he'd stop worrying, the more he worried.

As time passed, he worried about everything – from waking up in the morning to brushing his teeth, and from chewing with his mouth shut, to the sound his feet made as he walked along the street.

Eventually, he was taken to a doctor.

Looking the patient in the eye, he asked:

'Tell me, what are you worrying about right now?'

Nasrudin gasped.

'I'm worrying about you worrying about me!' he said.

Manhattan, New York
Plan of the Plan

Having left his village and travelled by land across Central Asia, the Near East, Europe, and the Atlantic, Nasrudin eventually reached his ultimate destination – New York City.

From the first moment he was admitted into the United States, he told everyone how he planned to make his fame and fortune.

'By this time next year I'll be a billionaire!' he bragged over and over.

Most of the people he accosted had no time for fools and were keen to be on their way.

The only person who was interested was a bum lying outstretched on a bench in Central Park.

'Fame and fortune?' he said approvingly. 'That sounds big.'

'Oh, yes,' the wise fool answered. 'I'm going to be richer than in my wildest dreams!'

The bum sat up.

'So, what's your plan, then?'

'Just like I told you, it's to become a billionaire.'

'No, no… I mean what's your plan to get rich?'

Nasrudin's expression froze.

'Don't rush me,' he said brusquely. 'That's the plan of the plan. As things stand, I'm still working on the plan.'

Panguitch, Utah
Retrained Hands

While driving cross-country along Highway 66, Nasrudin was stopped for zigzagging all over the road.

The officer who'd pulled him over was wild with anger.

'In forty years patrolling this stretch of highway, I've never seen driving as bad as that!'

Gasping apologies, the wise fool explained that in the land where he was from, everyone drove in that way.

'Well, you're not in your godforsaken country now! D'you understand?'

Nasrudin nodded nervously.

'Sincerest apologies, officer,' he muttered. 'But even though I tried to retrain my brain, my hands are finding it a challenge to learn new ways.'

Tucson, Arizona
Discount Skunk Hound

Nasrudin had always been a cat-lover, and so it was surprising that, while living in Arizona, he became obsessed with dogs.

He spent all his time learning about rare breeds and ways to teach man's best friend new tricks.

During his dog infatuation, the wise fool was approached by a crook who was in need of some quick cash. Having heard of his preoccupation with rare breeds, he convinced Nasrudin that the skunk he had on a leash was in actual fact an obscure breed of lapdog.

'He's certainly got fine markings,' the wise fool crooned, taking in the white stripe running nose to tail.

'I can see you know your dogs,' the conman answered. 'And that's why I knew you'd be interested in this competition gold-medal-winning skunk hound.'

Thrilled at the flattery, the wise fool enquired about the price.

'I was going to ask $500,' the crook replied, 'but, since you have such a discerning eye, I'm willing to part with her for $250.'

'My very own pedigree skunk hound for half price!' exclaimed Nasrudin, handing over the money.

Ten minutes later, the skunk hound and its owner were ordered to leave a local shopping mall.

'What kind of lunatic would have a skunk on a leash?!' an elderly lady screamed in the parking lot.

'I can't imagine,' Nasrudin responded absently. 'In fact, I'm amazed anyone would ever keep anything but a skunk hound as a pet.'

From: *The Peregrinations of the Perplexing Nasrudin*

Parisian Paradise

THE NEXT MORNING, an antique cloisonné mantel clock struck eight times, waking Miki from her slumber.

Breathing in sharply, she focused on the nightstand, her gaze moving up slowly over the curtains, the dresser, and onto the chandelier. Her back warmed with pleasure and with fear, as she remembered where she was.

And, as she lay there, the dream slipped back into her mind. She replayed the moment in the café once and then again, the moment of the handover. Frowning, she wondered what her grandfather's secret had been.

There was a knock at the door.

A steward entered, easing a trolley before him through the vestibule and into the spacious salon. It was laden with warm croissants and little pots of jam, a plate of scrambled eggs, fresh cut fruit, orange juice, coffee and toast.

'I am in Paradise,' Miki said in French.

'*Oui, mademoiselle*,' the steward replied, 'the paradise of the George V.'

When the steward had left, Miki sat on the corner of the bed. Clenching her fists, she pulled them up under her chin and began hyperventilating. The delicious food, the luxurious room, the sunshine, and the fact that she was in

Paris, were leading to an alchemical reaction, the likes of which she had not experienced before.

Faster and faster she breathed.

And, as she did so, her body began shaking like a crack addict going cold turkey.

Suddenly, it reached a critical threshold.

Sliding off the bed, Miki fainted and fell to the floor.

*

IT WAS PUN-PUN who discovered her lying at the foot of the imperial-size bed.

Furious that she had been invited into the hallowed corridors of the George V, he had arrived to give the order that she swap her suite with the chairman's standard room.

The steward had left the door ajar, and Pun-Pun barged in.

'What are you doing lying there!' he growled.

Confused and dazed, Miki struggled to open her eyes and make sense of what had happened. The blurred elegance of the room was replaced by Pun-Pun's distorted face leering close, the wart like a big red mountain on a wide plateau.

'Get up at once!' he ordered. 'And how dare you behave so badly! You have disgraced the good name of Angel Flower!'

Miki started to cry. She struggled up, fell down again, and strained to stand a second time.

'I am so sorry,' she said. 'I think I fainted.'

Her superior clapped his hands, more out of rage than out of anything else.

'If I could have my way, I would make sure you were sent home to Tokyo this morning!'

'I promise to behave,' Miki said in a soft voice. 'Please let me stay. This is my dream, a dream I have longed to come true my entire life.'

'You are to swap this suite with the chairman's modest room!' Pun-Pun hissed. 'As soon as you have done that, you are to go downstairs. I will give you five minutes. And...' he spat, as he stormed out, 'be sure that I shall tell the chairman of your embarrassing behaviour!'

*

RUSHING DOWN TO the lobby, Miki found that the rest of the tour group was not yet there.

In her hand she clutched the wad of pages inscribed with the list, the places she was so desperate to see. Out of the three hundred and forty-five names, only nine had been crossed off.

As Miki riffled through the pages, Mr. Nakamura arrived.

'Good morning,' he said.

Miki looked up.

'Good morning, Nakamura-san.'

'We have a busy day planned. There is still much to see.'

Miki held up her list. 'I am frightened that I will not be able to get to it all in time!'

Mr. Nakamura leaned back on his heels.

'Sometimes it is best to keep something for the next trip,' he said.

'Oh, but I do not know if I will ever be able to come back to Paris,' Miki explained. 'You see, I do not have a job that pays well. I am not rich like other people, and I do not work in the travel business.'

The tour leader smiled very gently, the kind smile of someone who genuinely cared.

'Perhaps you should think of getting a job as a tour guide like me,' he said. 'Then you could come to Paris often.'

Until that moment, Miki had been downhearted – the result of Pun-Pun reprimanding her yet again. But it was as though a light switch had been suddenly flicked on, and the world was illuminated for the first time.

Miki raised her head slowly. Her face was vacant at first but, gradually, it came to life, as if an artist had pencilled in an expression of utter delight.

'Yes! Yes! Yes!' Miki exclaimed. 'That is it! That is the best idea I have ever heard! Yes! I will become a tour guide and I will marry Comte Hugo-san!'

The duty manager looked up from his desk. Miki froze. She apologized for speaking so loudly.

And then the chairman arrived. After him came the others. 'I heard you fell,' he said tenderly. 'Are you alright?'

Miki began trembling. She bobbed her head low, indicating subservience.

'I am so sorry, sir,' she moaned. 'I was just tired, tired from all the excitement. I promise to behave.'

'Do you want to see a doctor?'

'No, sir. I am well. Again, I am sorry to have caused an embarrassment to Angel Flower.'

Mr. Nakamura stepped forward and gave everyone yet another plastic pouch bearing the name and logo of Paradise Tours.

'Today is the most important day of all,' he explained. 'Because we are going to travel back in time and visit the Cathedral of Notre Dame. And we will meet some more real French people.'

'Will we go shopping, too?' enquired Miki in a whisper.

'Yes! We will go shopping on the Champs-Elysées!'

The trio of housewives tittered with merriment and, when they had finished cooing, Noemi clapped her hands.

'Champs-Elysées! Champs-Elysées! I want to go to Champs-Elysées!' Miki got a flash of her dream, of her *ojiichan* kissing the woman with bright red lips. She blushed, and then thought of the coin pouch, and of Louis Vuitton, the headquarters of which were located on the Champs-Elysées.

At last she would be able to fulfil her promise. She was touched by a sense of destiny. Unable to stop herself, Miki jumped up and down like a schoolchild in a sweet shop.

The thought of going to Louis Vuitton at last, and the newly conceived idea of getting a job as a tour guide, had filled her with the kind of joy that she had never known. What could be more perfect a job than devoting one's life to showing Paris to other Japanese?

Mr. Nakamura bowed to the group.

'If you are ready, we can go now,' he said. 'The minibus is waiting for us.'

One by one, the visitors stepped through the wrought iron and glass doors into the sunshine.

As they walked over to the Mercedes minibus, a posse of paparazzi jumped out from nowhere. With cameras clicking and flashguns flaring, they clustered around the group from Paradise Tours.

'They must have the wrong people,' said Pun-Pun anxiously.

'We are not celebrities,' the chairman tried to explain.

But then one of the photographers held up a sign. It bore a short slogan in *hiragana*, which read:

PARIS LOVES ANGEL FLOWER!

Mr. Nakamura herded his group into the bus.

Once they were in their seats, everyone fussed and clucked at the thought that they were regarded as celebrities and were being hounded by actual paparazzi.

'Maybe they will put the pictures in a magazine,' said Noemi, hopefully.

'Maybe we will be very famous!' Miki said in a loud voice.

'Oh, but you *are* all famous,' Nakamura-san replied, as he gave an inconspicuous thumbs-up to the photographers. 'Didn't you see – the people of Paris love Angel Flower!'

*

TAKING A DETOUR on the way to Notre Dame, the minibus trundled down rue de Longchamp. As it did so, Mr. Nakamura said something to the driver in French. The vehicle slowed, then pulled over outside a plain stone-fronted building.

'Welcome to the most famous pastry shop in France!' the tour leader declared, 'the Pâtisserie des Rêves! It is where all your dreams will come true!'

The group trooped down off the minibus and filed into the shop, while Mr. Nakamura placed an order for seven pastries.

'We will taste the choux cream,' he said, 'the very best choux cream in the world!'

'Choux cream!' the housewives cooed in a single voice. 'We love choux cream! It is very, very good!'

'It's my favourite!' said Noemi ecstatically.

'Mine too,' added Miki.

The pastries were passed across the counter to Mr. Nakamura. Bowing, he served them to the members of his group, and then went out to the minibus to make a telephone call.

One at a time, the tourists sank their teeth into the cakes.

And, one by one their expressions soured.

'It is a little too sweet,' said one of the housewives, bashfully.

'And a little moist,' mumbled another.

'Mine is very rich,' the chairman said.

'I cannot finish this,' whispered Pun-Pun. 'It is making me feel sick.'

'The choux cream in Tokyo is much better than this!' Noemi grumbled.

Then all at once, the group condemned the pastries as miserable imitations of the real thing. After all, choux cream is well regarded as a Japanese delicacy, one unmatched by anyone else – even by the French, who invented it.

More normally, Miki would have fallen into line and condemned the pastries as well. But she felt a sudden pang of Gallic patriotism in her stomach, patriotism tinged with an overdose of fresh cream. Stuffing the pastry into her mouth, she chewed for a moment, swallowed, then shook her fists frantically and yelled:

'That was perfect, so perfect! I love Paris! *Vive la France!*'

*

A LITTLE LATER, having taken in the solemn wonders of Notre Dame, the Angel Flower tour group was led by Mr. Nakamura out of the cathedral and into the sunlight.

Squinting, shading eyes with hands, they felt the warmth on their faces.

'It is a very old building,' said one of the housewives.

'It is beautiful,' said another.

'Very big,' said the third.

Noemi was about to make a comment, when Pun-Pun pointed to a homeless man lying on a park bench. He was dressed in endless layers of soiled clothing, with many bags of worthless possessions in a heap beside him.

As they watched, the man got up, pulled down his trousers, and pooed on the grass.

'He should be arrested,' said Pun-Pun angrily.

'It's a disgrace,' said Noemi.

Miki took a step forward and put her hands over her mouth. She didn't approve of the man, but disliked the fact that others were criticizing him. So she waved her hands, as if calling everyone else to listen.

'He is ill, a poor ill man,' she said stridently, 'and that is why we must all feel sorry for him.'

Pun-Pun shook his head in disbelief.

'That man is shameful and there is only one thing for such a shameful man – *prison*.'

'He will get nice food in prison,' Noemi said.

'And a proper bed,' one of the housewives chirped.

'Good clothing as well, clothing which is clean,' said another.

'No!' shouted Miki, her hands now gripped into fists. 'This is Paris, where everyone has rights! *Liberté, Égalité, Fraternité!* Everyone has the right to behave as they like!'

The chairman pointed at the homeless man.

'Does *he* have the right to behave like *that?*' he asked.

Miki's fists waved all the harder.

'Yes! Yes!' she yelled. 'It's his human right... his *French* right!'

*

AFTER THE OUTBURST at Notre Dame and at the patisserie, Mr. Nakamura was becoming worried. He had been watching Miki's obsession for the French capital grow in momentum, and he feared that it was about to disrupt the harmony of the group.

Taking the Angel Flower's leader aside, he said:

'Perhaps it would be best for Miki to rest at the hotel for a little while, until she is feeling better.'

The chairman agreed, and the minibus made a beeline back to the George V, where Miki was off-loaded.

'We are all going to take a siesta,' Nakamura-san lied. 'It is a tradition in France. After all, we will be staying up late tonight, for the floor show at the Lido.'

Clutching her camera to her chest, Miki let out a pained squeal.

'But I want to go to Louis Vuitton,' she said. 'You told us that we would go shopping!'

'There will be plenty of time for that,' the tour leader replied in a reassuring voice. 'I promise that you will leave Paris laden with bags!' He smiled, dipped his head a little, and said: 'Sometimes the city can be overwhelming, because there is so much to do and there is never enough time.'

'But I want to see *everything*,' Miki announced, holding up her crumpled list. 'And we are moving very slowly. I wish we could move faster – much, much faster. And I don't want to be laden with shopping. All I want to buy is a coin pouch from Louis Vuitton.'

The tour leader gave a secret signal to the others, and they all went inside. As soon as Miki had been chaperoned up to her new room, the group hurried back down to the minibus.

'She should be sent back to Tokyo immediately,' said Pun-Pun. 'She is a shame on the good reputation of Angel Flower!'

'She is just a little tired,' the chairman replied. 'Young women are like that. All silly and excitable.'

The minibus sped away. A moment or two later it was pulling up outside Louis Vuitton.

Meanwhile, up in her room, Miki lay on the queen-sized bed and tried to sleep. She wanted to be obedient and, although she had little affection for Angel Flower, she appreciated that the firm had brought her to Paris.

All of a sudden she remembered something.

The Musée Nissim de Camondo.

She had promised the kind clerk in the Kinokuniya bookshop that she would visit it. Snatching the list of sights from her nightstand, Miki thumbed through it until she came to the museum.

She gasped, then choked.

And, without knowing quite why, she ran to the door and put on her shoes.

Gripped with panic, a raw, terrible panic, she felt as if iron doors were closing all around her.

In a fluster, Miki fled from the room and down to the lobby, then out onto the street. She was dazed and fearful, uncertain whether to laugh or cry, or whether to follow orders and go back upstairs and rest.

The doorman asked if he could help her with directions. Miki tapped a finger to the Nissim de Camondo on her list. 'This one. I would like to go to this one.'

'Walk up to the Champs-Elysées,' the doorman said courteously, 'and then straight over, and on for a kilometre or so until you reach rue de Monceau.'

Bowing, thanking, apologizing, Miki set off at a fast pace.

By the time she crossed the main thoroughfare, she was jogging. Within a block or two more, she was sprinting. Unsure why she felt it so important to reach the museum right then, it was as though something deep down inside was willing her on.

Had Miki looked to her left as she reached the Champs-Elysées, she would have seen Louis Vuitton's flagship store, the one place she had curiously forgotten. And, had she gone inside, she would have met the members of her own tour group, who were shuffling around the displays in a state of timorous awe.

As she ran down rue Washington, Miki saw a huge heap of litter piled up on the side of the street. A cluster of homeless men were rooting through it with their dogs, spreading it around in their hunt for food.

Miki frowned in surprise.

Saito-san had never mentioned garbage or the homeless, and neither was ever shown in the coffee-table books featuring the highlights of the French capital.

Forcing the thought out of her head, Miki kept on running. Within a few minutes she reached number 63 rue de Monceau, and the imposing stone façade of the Musée Nissim de Camondo.

Set over four storeys in a splendid villa, the museum reeked of aristocratic grandeur and private affluence.

Cautiously, Miki bought an entrance ticket and went inside on tiptoes.

The simple exterior gave no clue to the excesses of what lay within. The central hallway was floored in black and white mosaics, and adorned with sculptures and potted plants. A glorious sweeping stone staircase rose up to the first floor, an exquisite wrought iron handrail echoing the curve of the stairs.

There were lovely statues and medieval tapestries, giant portraits of imperious-looking aristocrats, and the very finest furniture. There were crystal chandeliers, too, and faded photographs, fauteuils, and bookcases filled with volumes bound in matching red morocco.

Miki closed her eyes and breathed in the smell.

It was a *gaijin* smell, one she had not experienced before. Tinged with musk and dust, it made her think of the pictures she had seen in the coffee-table book from Kinokuniya. It was the Paris she had dreamed of, the one that squared so perfectly with the memories of her *ojiichan*.

Walking softly through the house, Miki felt unworthy and awkward, and wished she had not left the hotel. Still on tiptoes, she made her way through the grand public salons and then up into the private apartments. The grandeur and the luxury were so impressive that Miki felt dizzy.

She feared that she might faint again.

Stepping through into the library, illuminated by the incandescent sunshine of early spring, she steadied herself on the doorframe, and slowed her breathing. The room was a picture of elegance, the walls adorned in oak shelves, each of them arranged with antique leatherbound books.

There was a sense of mystery, as though magic was at work. Calming herself, Miki paced slowly over the parquet until she reached the first window. She turned her back on the room and stared out at the sun breaking through the trees.

A minute passed, perhaps two.

Miki didn't move. She couldn't. It was as though something was rooting her to that spot, just as she had been drawn to visit the museum right then by some inexplicable force.

All of a sudden, a voice startled her.

'Good afternoon, mademoiselle.'

Miki swivelled around.

A tall, suave gentleman was standing two yards away. He was dressed in a cream linen suit, with a red rose pinned to his buttonhole.

'You do not remember me from the bar of the George V?' he asked in Japanese.

'Yes, um, er, yes!' Miki froze like a rabbit caught in blinding headlights.

'The fact that I find you here at Nissim de Camondo, and in the library of all places, suggests what I had already surmised was true – that you are a young lady of impeccable taste.'

Miki blushed and choked, and apologized more sincerely than she had ever apologized before.

'I am sorry to disturb you,' she said after a roll call of apology.

'But it was I who approached you,' replied the *comte* with a smile. He bowed his head a little, as he had learned to do while stationed in Tokyo. 'I should not want to be overly forward,' he said, 'but I wonder whether you would do me the honour of dining with me tonight at the Interalliée.'

Miki clutched her hands to her chest. She apologized again, choked a little more, and gushed an acceptance.

'You are very kind,' she said.

'How did you know that?' the count said. 'After all, you have just met me.'

'Because…'

'Because…?'

'Because you have very clean shoes,' Miki said.

*

LESS THAN A minute after the Comte Hugo de Montfried kissed her hand and excused himself until the evening, Miki was overcome with a sense of absolute terror.

She had accepted the aristocrat's invitation to dine even though the tour group was expecting her to join them for the much-publicized spectacular at the Lido on the Champs-Elysées.

Miki ran out from the Nissim de Camondo Museum in a state of frenzied hysteria. The chance meeting with the count had been the miracle she had wished for, a miracle undoubtedly sent by her ancestors. It was testament that they approved of her obsession with Paris, and of her wish to marry a French aristocrat.

Her head spinning, Miki could think of nothing but her love for her darling Hugo. Chanting his name over and over in her mind, she imagined every detail of his face. Ready to follow him to the end of the earth, she would serve him until her last breath left her chest.

As she shuffled down the street, she thought of the house they would share together on the edge of a brook, a vase of chrysanthemums in the hallway, and delicate touches of Japan all around. And she thought of the children they would have and raise together, little clones of their father – tall, stylish, and exceedingly kind.

Struggling to regain her composure, Miki glanced around hesitantly and spotted greenery nearby – the Parc Monceau. Hurrying over to it, she found herself in a little oasis of tranquillity. It reminded her of a park she had visited as a child near Sendai, taken there by her grandfather in the years before illness took hold.

She sat down on one of the slatted wooden benches and tried to think straight about that evening. The best solution she could come up with was to tell a lie, to say that she was feeling unwell, and then slip out for the dinner once the others had left for the Lido.

No, no, she thought – that could not work.

Nakamura-san had said that the show began at nine p.m., but the count had arranged to arrive at the hotel an hour before that.

Forcing her face into her hands, Miki began to weep.

Her heart was beating fast from love, just as it was pounding from fear of infuriating the chairman of the mighty Angel Flower. Miki may have been regarded as a rebel by Pun-Pun and by her nemesis, Noemi, but she really didn't want to stick out.

The idea of displeasing anyone at all was miserable, but she was ready and willing to endure any amount of condemnation if it meant she might spend an evening in the company of her beloved aristocrat.

Again, she strained to think.

The Comte de Montfried had said he would pass by the George V for a drink in the bar before taking Miki to his club, the Cercle de l'Union Interalliée, on rue du Faubourg Saint-Honoré. Mr. Saito had once told her of it, explaining that it was where all the debutantes were introduced into society at lavish balls. There was no better address in all Paris.

Suddenly, Miki's attention veered from the predicament of the evening to the list of places still to visit. Thumbing through the pages fast, she felt sick in her stomach at seeing so many hundreds of names still to be crossed out.

Shaking, she crumpled the paper in her hands. Then she let out a squeal of angst, disappointment, horror and pain, and she stamped her feet up and down.

At that moment a man approached her.

In his hand was a gold ring.

'I think you dropped this,' he said in French.

219

Miki understood what he meant more from his body language than from his words, which were masked in a thick accent. She shook her head politely.

'No, no, so sorry but it is not mine.'

The man insisted. 'But I am certain it *is* yours,' he replied.

Again, Miki's head shook and, again, the man insisted.

'It is a very pretty ring,' she said.

'So take it, please take it. I won't tell anyone.'

Not wanting to upset the stranger, Miki took the ring and put it on her finger. Still swooning for her *comte*, she imagined it was a wedding ring, sealing their commitment to one another.

'Thank you,' she said. 'You are a very kind man.'

Smoothing out the sheets of paper, she pretended to be busy with her list, in the hope that the stranger would go away.

But he did not.

Instead, he dawdled there, as if waiting for something.

'Will you give me some money?' he asked.

Miki didn't understand. She put her head on its side and sucked in air through her teeth.

'Give?' she said.

'Money,' the man said. 'I want money for the ring.' He rubbed his thumb and forefinger together and jerked up his chin aggressively.

'*Money*?'

'Yes!'

Again, Miki sucked air. She tried to take the ring off her finger so that she could return it.

But it wouldn't come off. It was stuck.

Worried that she had strayed into a realm of Parisian life for which she had not been prepared, she opened her purse and took out ten euros. She passed it to the man.

He took the money, but still he loitered.

'You must give me more than that!' he shouted. 'I want one hundred euros!'

'*One hundred?*'

'Yes! Give it to me now or I will go to the police!'

Miki let out another shriek and began to cry again. She apologized and bowed, and cried all the more.

'Please, I do not want the ring,' she said, begging.

'Then give it back to me!'

'But as you see it is stuck on my finger.'

The man stepped closer until his shadow fell over Miki and the bench – it was cold and haunting, and seemed to smell very bad. His face muscles twisted into a menacing snarl, and he flexed his fingers as though he were about to attack.

Jumping up, Miki ran.

And the stranger ran after her.

Tearing through Parc Monceau, she hurried over to the pond. And the man ran after her, calling out for money or his ring.

Miki's small feet paced fast through a group of ducks and between young mothers out with their prams. She was screaming, pages from her list fluttering away behind her.

The assailant suddenly pulled back.

But Miki was too frightened to stop.

She sprinted on, out of Parc Monceau, to the main road and on into a labyrinth of smaller streets.

Only after another twenty minutes of running did she dare to look around. The stranger wasn't there. He was long gone, but his ring was still on Miki's hand, and it was so tight that the finger was swollen. She stopped in a doorway and tried desperately to pull it off, sucking at it, twisting it, jerking it.

Nothing worked.

All the tugging had added to the pressure, and the finger was now turning blue.

Spotting a café across the street, Miki went in and asked the waiter if she could use the toilet. She was in urgent need of a tap, so that she could hold the finger under cold water to stop the swelling.

'Toilets are for customers only,' the waiter said in an uncompromising voice. 'You have to order something to drink!' He motioned the act of holding a cup to his lips.

Miki pointed to her finger and screwed up her face, indicating great pain. The waiter pointed at a sign. It showed a toilet with a red cross scrawled across it. Miki ordered a cappuccino and, leaving her handbag on the chair, she went into the toilet to soothe her badly throbbing finger in cold water.

She stayed there for twenty minutes, gently turning the ring round and round, until the skin was less sore.

Then, with all her strength, she gripped the band of gold and eased it over the knuckle.

Suddenly, it slipped off, leaving her bruised ring finger the colour of blue-black ink.

Thanking her ancestors for delivering her from agony, Miki went back into the café to enjoy her cappuccino. It had been sunny when she went into the toilet, but rain was now lashing against the windows.

Miki weaved her way between the tables until she got to where her cup of coffee was waiting. She sat down, sipped the cold coffee, and reached for her handbag.

But it was gone.

Leaping up, Miki rushed over to the waiter, who was serving another customer.

'Please! Please!' she exclaimed.

'You will have to wait until I have finished with this gentleman,' the waiter responded.

'But my handbag! My handbag has been stolen!'

The waiter turned. He screwed up his face and shrugged.

'Well, I do not have it,' he said.

'But it has been stolen!' Miki declared, repeating herself.

The waiter shrugged a second time.

'You should have taken it with you,' he said, pointing to a sign of a handbag with a big red cross laid over it.

Miki stamped her feet and waved her fists.

'*Quoi?*' asked the waiter, with upturned hands.

'Police. Please get the police!'

The waiter smiled distantly and shook his head. Then he removed a cloth from his apron and began wiping down a table, as if the idea of a theft was deeply uninteresting.

Miki went back to the table where her cappuccino was still waiting. Pressing a hand to her forehead, she closed her eyes. The suave silhouette of Hugo de Montfried came instantly to mind.

I am sure he will help me, she thought.

Then she remembered the chairman and Pun-Pun, and the other members of the Angel Flower tour group. What was she doing in a café alone without their permission? She reprimanded herself for sneaking away. The theft of her handbag was surely punishment for not doing as she had been told.

And now she would have to admit to the chairman that she had lost her passport, wallet, and all her identification. But worse – much worse – was the fact that the Comte de Montfried's business card had been in the bag as well. Its loss meant that she would never see him again – unless, that is, she managed to elude the others, and meet him for the date.

Miki slumped down on the chair.

After much whimpering she struggled to make a plan. Her head was telling her to retreat to the safety of the George V and to plead with the chairman, begging him to show mercy for her foolishness. But Miki's gut was telling her to sort the problem out for herself.

Placing the gold ring on the table-top beside the cold cappuccino, she cursed. How could she have been so stupid as to take something of such value from a stranger? It was certain to lead to trouble.

As she sat there, trying to work out what to do, the waiter strode up, cloth in hand.

'Do you want a fresh coffee?' he asked.

'I don't have any money,' said Miki. 'I have been robbed and I do not know what to do.'

The waiter's already sour expression soured all the more.

'You have to pay for your coffee,' he said.

'But I don't have any money. All I have is this valuable gold ring. It was given to me by a stranger and it was the start of all my problems.'

Snatching the ring with his claw-like nails, the waiter observed it for a fleeting moment.

'That's not valuable,' he said. 'It's rubbish. Not worth a *centime*!'

Miki put her head in her hands and sobbed.

'You Chinese are all the same,' the waiter barked, 'and you cause too much trouble in our city. You must go now. Get out! *Go! Go! Go!*'

'But it's raining hard.'

The waiter pointed at the door.

'Get out!' he yelled.

*

FOR AN HOUR Miki trudged through the downpour.

She had not been prepared for rain and her sundress was quickly soaked. On an especially high kerb she tripped and the heel came off her shoe, forcing her to limp on through puddles as wide as she was tall.

Three or four times she tried hailing a taxi, but as soon as the cab drivers heard where she wanted to go, they sped away. One of them had shouted: 'They don't accept Chinese hookers at the George V!'

All of a sudden, Miki spotted a little sushi restaurant tucked away on the corner where two narrow streets met. Her eyes lit up. Someone there was sure to take pity on a fellow Japanese. Miki hobbled over to the restaurant and pulled the door open.

A large woman was standing behind the counter.

She had a thick muscular neck and a face that didn't look very Japanese. Greeting the woman, Miki bowed and apologized. She was about to explain, when she felt it necessary to bow again, and apologize one last time before speaking.

And so she did.

Done with pleasantries, she ducked her head down and, feebly, she said:

'I have been robbed and am in need of a little help.'

The woman rapped her knuckles down on the counter aggressively. 'I don't speak Japanese,' she said in French. 'I speak Mandarin!'

'You are not Japanese?' Miki asked, confused.

'*Hah*! No! We are from Beijing!'

'But this is a sushi restaurant, and sushi is Japanese.'

The waitress slammed her fist down.

'I cannot help you! If you have money, you can eat. If you do not have money, you must go or I will call the police!'

Whimpering and weeping, Miki pulled the door open and limped back out into the rain.

Her tears were instantly washed away by the downpour.

Then it began to get dark. Still Miki trudged on, desperately hoping to find the way back to the George V. One sympathetic shopkeeper did give her directions, but she was so confused that she mixed up her left and right and strayed miles out of the way.

Another hour of hobbling, and Miki was far from the centre of Paris. She found herself in an ugly, deprived area. There were children sword-fighting with sticks in the rain, and car alarms sounding, drug addicts shooting up in doorways, stray dogs and high-rise blocks of flats.

A car pulled up slow and kerb-crawled alongside Miki as she walked.

The driver wound down the passenger window.

'*Combien*?' he asked quickly.

'*Combien*?'

'*Oui*.'

'I do not understand. How much for what?'

'For everything?'

Miki still didn't understand, but she knew the man was not a gentleman. He had a big frothy beard and the end of a cigarette screwed into the corner of his mouth.

She limped away at double speed as the car drove on.

Then the rain grew heavier and began falling in sheets. Soaking, and frozen to the bone, Miki sought refuge in the doorway of a boarded-up tenement building. She was shaking and moaning, and was about to collapse when a figure jumped out.

He had a knife in his hand.

Jerking it to Miki's throat, he bawled:

'Give me your money – *all* your money!'

'*I… I…* I do not have money. I was already robbed,' said Miki, stammering in French.

'Give it to me or I'll cut your throat!' the man demanded, as he increased his grip on her neck. The blade was pressed right up to her jugular. She could feel the steel, cold and hard.

Miki got a flash of her grandfather, dancing over the cobblestones, and then of the family home near Sendai, the afternoon sun streaming in through the kitchen window. She struggled to free herself, but the knife pressed all the harder – so much so that Miki feared she was about to die.

Just then, the silhouette of another man turned the corner and began approaching. He was out walking his dog, a pit-bull. Flustered, the assailant clouted his victim on the side of her head with the hilt of the knife and vanished into the shadows.

Miki fell to the ground without the faintest sound.

Not wanting to be associated with the attack, the man with the pit-pull moved briskly on. For more than an hour, Miki lay there in the rain, her face pressed down into the filth.

Then, by chance, a police patrol spotted the huddled figure of a woman lying on the ground. It had been called to deal with a case of domestic battery in a tenement block nearby.

Forty minutes later, Miki was lying on a bed in a corridor at the local hospital. The passageway was illuminated with strip-lighting and stank of industrial disinfectant. There was a constant rush of medical personnel, a sense of despondency and gloom.

Another forty minutes passed, and a doctor with a clipboard strolled up and shone a torch into Miki's eyes. He was young and inexperienced, and hadn't slept in days. Explaining what had happened in French, Miki started to sob uncontrollably.

'You will stay here for the night and we will give you a CAT-scan just in case,' the doctor said. 'After that you should be well enough to go home.' He paused. 'Where is your home?' he asked.

'The George V Hotel,' Miki said.

The doctor rubbed a hand down over his tired eyes.

'God knows what you're doing in this hell-hole then,' he said.

'I was robbed,' Miki replied. 'And then I was attacked.'

'You're lucky to be alive. This is a dangerous part of the city. Don't you know that?'

'I have to go to Louis Vuitton,' Miki answered, her concentration drifting.

'*Louis*?'

'*Vuitton*… I have to buy a coin pouch for my *ojiichan*.'

From: *Paris Syndrome*

Blood for Ink

TWO DAYS AFTER leaving Brighton, Adams and Cochran reached Fleet Street, where Richard Florence was settled comfortably in the chambers. He had spent the weekend drinking his way through a case of vintage port, which had been bequeathed to Cochran by his uncle Henry who was slain the year before, at Waterloo.

It was a damp evening, the rain chilled by a north wind. Too drunk to stand, Florence remained in bed while the other two men took dinner at Mrs. Potts' – roasted veal with baked potatoes, washed down with a bottle of plum wine. They had hardly spoken on the return journey from Brighton. Cochran was worrying about his debts, and the fact that someone was trying to kill him. Beyond that, he was irked that his guest had invited a fellow countryman to stay.

After dinner he set off to deliver a letter to Viscount Fortescue at Camelford House. It explained how the Committee chairman had hired an assassin to do away with Adams and himself.

The two Americans waited up, but Cochran did not return.

Next morning Adams knocked at the bedroom door, but there was no reply. He pushed his head inside but, to his surprise, found Cochran's bed empty and unused. In the small salon, Richard Florence was asleep on the floor, a bottle of port beside his head filled to the brim with cold urine.

Adams waited all morning and into the afternoon, but still Cochran didn't appear. Aware of Sir Geoffrey's proviso, that missing a scheduled session of the narration would forfeit his passage home, he got dressed, put on his coat, and paced up Ludgate Hill in the direction of the Committee.

The peal of bells at St. Paul's got Adams thinking about the English. They were obsessed with the wealth of Timbuctoo, he thought, when it was they who had unmatched prosperity without realizing it.

On the steps of the Committee, Adams found Falkirk.

'Has Mr. Cochran arrived?' he asked quickly.

'No, sir, he's not 'ere.'

'Are you certain?'

'Quite certain, Mr. Adams.'

'What about the chairman?'

'He was inside at six this morning, sir, and in a foul mood he is.'

Stepping across the threshold, Adams removed his coat and made his way up to Cochran's study. The room was warm, the fire prepared by the scullery maid who lodged upstairs in an attic room.

On the desk lay a sheaf of letters tied up with a length of lilac ribbon. Adams picked them up and breathed the scent, *eau de floris*.

'Beattie,' he said aloud, 'how could you have crushed him like that?'

There was a knock at the door.

It was Falkirk.

'Sir Geoffrey is asking for you, sir. He is awaiting you in his study.'

Adams dropped the letters on the desk and a moment later was standing before the chairman.

'I trust Brighton was amusing, Mr. Adams.'

'Very much so.'

'And Mr. Cochran? Where is he today?'

'I have not seen him. He didn't return last night after dinner.'

Caldecott took a pinch of snuff.

'Without Mr. Cochran,' he said, 'you cannot complete your narration, and alas you will not be eligible for your passage home. A crying shame, sir, a crying shame.'

At his home in Soho Square, Sir Joseph Banks was soothing his gums with tincture of cantharides. The medicament was prepared from an odourless liquid, secreted onto the back of the male blister beetle while mating. The pain elicited by the remedy was considerable, but its effectiveness was championed by Banks's house guest, a Bavarian apothecary and physician named Dr. Ludwig von Pfaffmann.

The doctor, whose work had been drawn to Sir Joseph's attention only the year before, had developed a widespread following for his work on curing syphilis using live frogs and quicksilver.

Banks had accompanied his guest to the public dissections held on Albemarle Street the previous week. Both men had a thirst for medicinal knowledge and were concerned with medicinal and scientific research.

In the mornings, Dr. von Pfaffmann would excuse himself after breakfast and retire to his room, where he would engage in an amateur study of the human eye. He was developing a new method of blowing glass into balls in such a way that they might be inserted into the ocular cavities of the blind, with a simulated iris painted onto the front.

After lunch, he and Sir Joseph would ride the streets in an open barouche, even in the rain. Von Pfaffmann believed that forward motion aided the brain, and that precipitation assisted in cooling the heat derived from what he called 'the cranial proclivities'. The doctor insisted that genuine thought could only be achieved while moving faster than walking pace.

Sir Joseph, who had become quickly used to the ways of his distinguished house guest, found his level of conversation unequalled. Mention a random subject, and he could be certain that Dr. von Pfaffmann had done all the background reading on the matter in English, German, Latin and Greek. Quite often, the doctor had himself published the leading theory of the day.

On the afternoon that followed Cochran's disappearance, Banks and Ludwig von Pfaffmann were touring the streets near St. Paul's, when Sir Joseph remembered the Royal African Committee and its singular narration. He called to the driver to repair at once to Old Jewry, in the hope of finding the narration in progress.

As luck would have it, Banks's barouche drew to a halt outside the Committee just as society was arriving. Lowered down into his chair by a footman, Sir Joseph was wheeled by the Bavarian scholar down the long corridor.

At its far end, the magnificent library was already half full.

Robert Adams had spotted Clara Fortescue in the audience. He hastened over to ask if Cochran had visited Camelford House the previous night.

'No, Mr. Adams, I regret to say that he did not,' she replied, touching her hand nervously to her hair. 'My father was at home all evening, and did not receive any visitors at all.'

'Then where could he be?'

Clara shook her head.

'I shall mention it to my father,' she said, 'perhaps Mr. Cochran has written to him as you say.'

Adams turned to look around the room.

'Well I don't know what to do,' he said. 'Without Simon I cannot narrate. Caldecott is looking for any excuse to question my story.'

Clara's anxious expression dissolved.

'I have an idea,' she said with a grin.

She hurried over to Sir Joseph Banks and whispered in his ear. A moment later she rushed back to where Adams was standing.

'Salvation is at hand,' she said, her face lighting up. 'And I can assure you that Sir Geoffrey Caldecott would not dare refuse Sir Joseph the honour of transcribing your tale.'

Sir Joseph Banks was wheeled to the desk at which Cochran had transcribed the previous narrations. A goose-feather quill, ink, and a ream of handwritten sheets were placed before him. Fitting a pair of pince-nez to his nose, he scanned the last page of text.

As a hush fell over the audience, Robert Adams took his place.

'I believe you were describing the taste of freedom, Mr. Adams,' said Banks, the new French teeth causing him to lisp.

'Thank you, Sir Joseph, I had described the feast of enormous eggs, and my arrival at the outskirts of a village known as Wadi Noon.

'I approached from the south, the afternoon sun throwing long shadows over the landscape. As I drew nearer I saw ever more huts, and realized that I had succeeded in crossing the great expanse of desert.

'Overcome with emotion, I thanked the Lord for my salvation. It was then that I noticed smoke rising from one of the crude huts. Without wasting a moment, I advanced towards it.

'A little girl of about five years ran out and set eyes on me. She stopped quite still. It seemed as if we stared at each other for an eternity – the girl terrified at the sight of an unclothed Christian, and I elated at seeing anyone at all.

'After a long while, she filled her lungs and screamed in the most feral and strident manner. An instant later, a man was in the doorway of the hut with a knife in his hand. A moment after that he was running towards me. I held out my hands, ready to embrace another man, a friend. But he was not interested in friendship. Forcing my arms behind my back, he tied them up with a strand of leather.

'He took me over to the doorway of his hut and kicked me to the ground. His wife called all her neighbours to look at the family's new and unexpected prize.

'And that was how I became enslaved once again.

'Late that afternoon, the man dragged me to the middle of Wadi Noon where a slave market was in full swing. Slave owners had come from all over the region, all of them fuelled with greed and high hopes for a good sale.

'My new master stopped to speak to his friends, boasting at how he had come by me so unexpectedly. I took advantage of his palaver and rested beneath an acacia tree. I was sitting there, bemoaning my new situation, when I heard a frail voice.

'In my weakened state I thought it said in a whisper, "Robert? Robert? Is that really you?"

'I looked around.

'There was no one except a haggard-looking slave. I closed my eyes, slipped back to my memories. But the voice came again. "It's me, Robert, do you not recognize me?"

'I turned a second time.

'The slave was closer now, his blue eyes a few inches from mine. I was about to say something, when the man said: "I am Simon Dolbie, ship's mate from the *Charles*."

'Like a pair of frail old men we staggered towards one another and hugged and wept. After a while, Dolbie said: "We thought you were dead."

'"*We?*"

'"Newsham and Clarke, they are alive. Come with me and I shall take you to them."

'As my master was still parleying with another slave owner, I followed my former shipmate to the far side of the broad acacia tree, where our companions were crouching. For a few minutes we forgot our wretched state, rejoicing at the reunion. Each one of us was touched by a sense of absolute delight, the kind we had almost forgotten existed in our cruel world.

'Before I stumbled back to my master, fearing his retribution for going astray, Dolbie spoke out.

'"Our master is here buying slaves," he said. "He's the one with a single eye. Look strong and he may buy you. He knows that Christian slaves are redeemed by the Consul at Mogador, and his longing for easy wealth has led him to acquire as many of us as he can."

'At dusk, my master led me to the patch of dirt where the slave auctions took place. Were I stronger, I would have struck him down and fled, so enraged was I at being forced into servitude once again. Yet I was so feeble that I struggled to stand upright, unable to display any strength at all.

'Dolbie called out to me, urging me to pretend some kind of worth, while he and the other two coaxed their master to take note of me. I must have made for a pathetic sight. But, thanks to Dolbie and my other friends, the one-eyed master clapped twice, the sign he would purchase me. I fell to the ground, weeping in joy at being reunited with my companions.'

Adams paused to allow Sir Joseph's arthritic hand to catch up. The library was silent, except for the sound of the quill scratching inelegantly across the page.

'Pray continue, sir,' said Banks, once he had dipped the nib again. 'My hand is not as sprightly as Mr. Cochran's but I assure you, I have stamina like no other man alive.'

Thanking Sir Joseph, Adams continued:

'During the first weeks of my new captivity,' he said, 'I took advantage of the kindness proffered by my friends. They saw to it that I was fattened up after the hardship of the great Zahara. Each night, Dolbie and the others would share their porridge with me, insisting that I take it, and reminding me that I would do the same for them. As the days passed I grew stronger and, with my strength, came the one overriding desire – to escape.

'Our master was a sullen man, fortunate to enjoy a high standing at Wadi Noon. The other owners of Christian slaves there appeared to look up to him. I discovered that the high esteem in which they held him arose from the fact that he had once torn out a Christian's heart with his bare hands and fed it to the jackals that encircled the village each night.

'There must have been twenty shipwrecked seamen living there. Some of them were withered beyond belief, their eyes sunken, their ribs sharp across their chests. Most of them had resigned themselves to death. Some even looked forward to the event, as if it would release them from appalling servitude.

'Of all the slaves I encountered there, the most pitiful was a woman, named Francesca. A Venetian by birth, she was twenty years of age, although three summers of slavery had given her the appearance of one far older in years. The vessel in which she had been crossing the Mediterranean had been swept onto the African shore in a ferocious gale. The male survivors had all been beheaded on the beach as soon as the Moors discovered them. But, as a woman, Francesca was spared death, and a life of indescribable torment began.

'Her master forced himself upon her in the most vicious and wicked way. He encouraged his brethren to do the same and, with time, she gave birth to a son. Uncertain who had fathered the child and sensible to the fact Francesca had not renounced her faith, the master took the infant out into the desert and snuffed out its fragile life.

'The following week a trader arrived at Wadi Noon. He was tall, big-boned, and wore blue robes and a turban of unusual quality. I was sitting with Dolbie and the other slaves, pausing from our chores, when he came over and greeted us. To our universal surprise, he spoke English fluently. He said his name was Abdul-Malik, the "Servant of God", but that he had been born a Frenchman and was called Maurice Trouin. He had been wrecked twelve years before, on the *Montezuma*, a brigantine bound from Liverpool.

'"Surrender your faith," he said whispering, "and the Moors will regard you as their brother. They will give you a wife and a gun and will grant your freedom."

'"I will *never* renounce my faith," I replied, "even if it were the only way I might escape this hell."

'"Then you are a fool," said the Frenchman, "and so you will die. The sand will drink your blood and the dogs will eat your flesh."

'When he had left, I rallied the others.

'"If only we could get word of our captivity to the consul in Mogador," I said, "we have a chance at redemption."

'Never an optimist, Newsham reminded us we had neither paper nor ink.

'"I have a scrap of paper," said Clarke. "It is small, but we must make do with what we have."

'"But we have no ink," Newsham repeated.

'There was a bent ship's nail on the ground. I picked it up and lanced my forearm.

'"Here is your ink," I said, "and there's no shortage of it!"

'Dolbie took up a stick and snapped it in two to make a nib.

'"What shall I write?" he asked.

'I cleared my throat.

'"Your Excellency," I began, "we are Christians held in servitude at Wadi Noon, desperate in our state. Our ship, the brig *Charles*, was wrecked upon these savage African shores. We ask you by all the ties that bind man to man, by those of kindred blood, and everything you hold dear, to advance the money for our redemption."

'By chance, another trader visited the village at the next full moon. He was overheard to declare he was travelling to the coast. I tended his camel for a week and, in return, he promised to deliver the message to the consul at Mogador.

'A few days passed. Then, one morning, my master's son ordered me to tend his goats. It was Friday, the day we were permitted to rest. I informed him that as it was the Musalman Sabbath, I was not obliged to work.

'"You are a Christian dog" he cried, "and you will toil every day or I shall take your life!"

'I bared my neck.

'"Then kill me now and be quick about it!"

'The man fetched his scimitar and brandished it. The spectre of Death had hung over me for so long that the end would have been a merciful release. So I knelt and waited for the blow, my hands clasped tightly at my chest.

'I closed my eyes.

'Then I heard the blade as it arced through the air and became embedded in my face. The pain was not apparent at first. As fortune would have it, my head was cocked downwards, and so the blade did not sever my eye, but only the meat above and below it. I fell to the ground and was immediately kicked from all sides by a group of Moors who had heard the commotion.

'Once they had beaten me, shattered my ribs and disjointed my shoulder, I was pegged out on the sand and left to die. I soon slipped into delirium, but Newsham, Clarke and Dolbie took it in turns to offer me water, holding a skin to my lips.

'My mind blurred with fever, I asked the ship's mate to take a message to my beloved when I was dead, to say that her name was the last word to pass my lips. He agreed to perform the favour as if he could complete it effortlessly, travel from that forsaken purgatory back to Hudson.

'Three more suns rose, baked me, and cooled to dusk. When it was clear I was about to succumb, my master cut the bindings. He was not without mercy. Newsham and Clarke hurried me into the shade. They fed me water and bowl after bowl of porridge. I told them to keep their own rations for themselves, and for Dolbie. Then it struck me, I hadn't seen Dolbie. I asked most urgently after him. Newsham's face turned pale. A single tear welled in his eye and tumbled down his cheek.

'"Dolbie is dead," he said.

'The next day I woke to find the desert sky had turned scarlet. The Moors were much vexed. My master said it was a sign from the Musalman god, the one they called Allah. He slaughtered a sheep in his name. Clarke and Newsham would not look at me. I wondered if the sky had affected them.

'In the afternoon of the following day, they walked up to our master's black wool tent. I watched them followed by their shadows. Then I understood why they would not look me in the eye. They had decided to relinquish their faith.

'In the evening a fire was kindled and the Moors clustered around. A sharp knife was brought out. My fellow shipmates bared their manhood to the blade, and repeated the vow that professed them as Musalmans.

'The sight of Christians forgoing all they held sacred brought great sorrow to my heart. When they came to me asking for my blessing, I could not look upon them. They held up blankets and other gifts they had been presented by the Moors. Their spirits were high.

"'Robert, join us as Musalmans," said Clarke, "and you shall be rewarded like us."

'My stomach was filled with bile, for I had never witnessed such a loathsome loss of dignity.

'The next morning the Italian woman, Francesca, fell ill. One of the other female slaves attended her. She told me that a torrent of blood flowed from her body. By nightfall, life departed her. I dug a grave for her under an acacia tree. Standing there alone, I recited the twenty-third Psalm.

'Two days after Francesca expired, a Moorish trader arrived at Wadi Noon. My master presented the new converts to him with much relish. They all ate together, while I went to tend the sheep at the edge of the village. Late in the afternoon, the visitor came to where I was sitting, watching over the flock. He asked me in the Moorish tongue if I was still a Christian. I replied that I was.

'It was then that he revealed his true identity. He was the agent of Mr. Joseph Dupuis, British Consul at Mogador. Pulling out a letter from his boot, he passed it to me. I explained that I was unable to read.

"'Then I shall read it to you," he said in English.

"'Wait," I said, "for I must fetch my shipmates."

The agent looked down at the ground. He seemed displeased. Although I was enraged at their conversion, it was my duty as a member of the *Charles'* crew to include them.

'Newsham and Clarke were greatly pleased by the prospect of redemption. They laughed as we walked back to where the agent was waiting. Newsham had received the most schooling and so he asked if he might read the letter.

'Breaking the seal, he ran his eyes over the lines of precise black script.

'"My esteemed friends," he began. "I was most moved and gratified to receive your message this morning. I have frequently heard of the miserable fate of your ship, *Charles*, and have these past months and years endeavoured to obtain information of its crew. I am at once dispatching my most trusted agent, Omar bin Assad, with merchandise and currency with which to effect your immediate release. Yours most sincerely, Joseph Dupuis."

'Clarke fell to his knees and thanked the Lord. Standing close beside him, Newsham let out a shrill wail and began to weep.

'"What is it? What is it, Unis?" asked Clarke.

'"There is a postscript," he said, trembling.

'"What does it say?"

'"I am permitted to redeem only those who are still Christian, and have not forsaken their souls."'

From: *Timbuctoo*

Godspeak

ON THE DOT of five, Harry and Bitu arrived at the school by rickshaw, half-expecting it to be deserted and boarded up.

But to their astonishment, Zap the fixer who could fix the unfixable, was a man of his word.

The school's sign had been replaced by an outsized symbol – the number 6 within a hexagon. The sacred emblem was repeated everywhere – painted on the walls, etched into the windows, and even arranged in flowers out in the garden.

An army of nocturnal cleaners, moonlighting from a nearby power station, had cleaned the school building from top to bottom. The gardens had been landscaped by a platoon of gardeners borrowed from Varanasi's Radisson Hotel. Fountains which hadn't worked in years had been conjured back to life, and banners bearing the buzzwords of Sri Omo-ji were suspended from all the walls, inside and out.

In back rooms dozens of uniformed staff were busy planning projects and prayer sessions, and pretending to send messages to the godman's followers all over the world. In the kitchens dinner was being prepared by a legion of cooks. As for the great hall, it was awash with floral arrangements, giant-sized candles, and incense burners perched on elaborate stands.

Sitting on the floor cross-legged and reverent were more than three hundred orange-clad disciples. Hanging around the neck of each was a garland of pungent *mogra* flowers, and a circular framed photo of Sri Omo-ji, the diameter of a coffee mug.

'What are they doing?' Bitu asked, a hint of trepidation in his voice.

'Praying for the soul of our beloved Sri Omo-ji,' the fixer said cheerily.

'Who *are* they?'

'A handful of the city's homeless… happy to perform round-the-clock prayers in return for clean clothes and a little food. On safety grounds I promised each and every one of them a free health check, too.'

'Health check… *where*?' Bitu asked.

'In the medical centre, down the hall.'

Harry grabbed Zap's hand and shook it very hard.

'How did you do it in such a short time?' he asked, perplexed.

Eyes hidden behind the extra-dark lenses, the fixer replied:

'Wait till you see the MZ.'

'What's that?'

'The Meditation Zone.'

Zap may have exceeded all expectations, but Bitu was fretful.

'There's no stone,' he said.

'Stone?' Harry echoed. 'What stone?'

'The Great Stone.'

'Doesn't matter, Bitu-bhai… he's got everything else.'

The fixer held up a hand.

'Two minutes,' he said.

'For what?'

Leading the way out to the front of the school, Zap pointed at an area of wet cement, then up into the sky. A rock the approximate size and shape of a forty-foot sea container was dangling from the end of a steel cable. Etched on each of the four sides in five-foot-high letters, was the sacred symbol of Sri Omo-ji.

As they watched, it was lowered to earth, along with an exquisite wrought iron bench.

The fixer smoothed a hand down over his handlebar moustache.

'There it is… the Great Stone.'

As if on cue, his phone buzzed with a message from David X David at the Taj Ganges.

'The Americans are on their way.'

Cool as a cucumber, he reached into his pocket, pulled out a miniature air-horn and gave it two long bursts.

'What's that for?' Harry asked.

'All systems go!'

Bitu whacked Harry on the back.

'Quick, go do your godspeak in the auditorium!'

'But what shall I say?'

'Just pretend you're reading from *The Path of Omo!*'

Taking a holdall with the second half of his fee, Zap the fixer hurried out through the back entrance, while Bitu scurried to the bench beside the Great Stone.

As the seat of his jodhpurs touched the wrought iron, he heard feet crunching over freshly raked gravel.

Still battered and bruised, the Americans reached the stone, Rosco P. Schultz III in the lead.

'Your Highness!' he boomed. 'What experiences we've had, and what an honour it is to see you again!'

Stepping forward to the bench, he kissed the maharaja's knuckles, as did the others, each waiting their turn.

The Maharaja of Patiala explained how witnessing the trauma of the crash in Kolkata, His Celestial Highness had experienced their pain.

'Our wounds are healing,' Rosco replied merrily.

'What *is* this place?' Marsha asked in awe.

'The sacred retreat of His Celestial Highness Sri Omo-ji,' the maharaja answered with a stone-cold poker face.

'I wish we'd known of it before,' Marsha blurted out.

'The ashram is regarded as a hallowed ground,' the maharaja answered, 'and only those who His Highness believes have earned it are admitted.'

The Americans appeared crestfallen.

'But we didn't finish the Journey of Sacred Devotion,' said Elaine. 'Does that mean we're not allowed to enter?'

Standing, the maharaja prefaced his reply with an ear-to-ear grin.

'On the contrary my dear lady,' he announced, 'you have all proved yourselves worthy of the highest regard. His

Highness welcomes you to His humble home, and asks that you relax and make yourselves comfortable.'

The group exchanged anxious glances.

'But we don't want to relax!' Rosco declared.

'We want to help the Unloved Children!' another yelled.

'There'll be time for that,' Bitu intoned. 'But first you must perform the sacred ritual of honouring the Great Stone.'

Elaine pushed her way to the front.

'Would you tell us the ritual, Your Highness?' she asked.

Even before the question had left her mouth, the Maharaja of Patiala was demonstrating the curious ceremonial circumambulation of the sacred rock. Walking around it backwards, he pressed both hands to its surface with every other step, and let out a sound resembling the woeful lament of an Arctic wolf howling in the night.

Without a word, the Americans fell into line, copying the ritual as precisely as they could manage. Having circled the Great Stone backwards six times, the Maharaja of Patiala gave thanks to the heavens for His Celestial Highness Sri Omo-ji.

Dutifully, the Americans did the same.

Two thousand miles from the ashram, Two-See the internet maestro in Shenzhen was putting the final touches to a world-class media campaign.

Having received the audio file, he had *The Path of Omo* digitally transcribed in Honolulu, proofread by an impoverished undergraduate at Cambridge, and typeset in

Chennai. Within a matter of hours the godman's spiritual manifesto was for sale on Amazon.

Two-See used the text as the basis of a wide-reaching social media campaign – on Twitter, Instagram, Facebook, Reddit, and on dozens of other platforms. Unlike other media gurus, Two-See relied on a piece of software he'd designed himself which he referred to as XING-92. Cloaked in secrecy, the program enabled Two-See to ensure any message posted went instantly viral, by hacking into a person's social media accounts.

Within minutes of going live, *The Path of Omo* had been seen by millions. A leading inspirator in Los Angeles heralded it as 'An Extraordinary Solution to the Ordinary'. Another claimed 'it was like having a bucket of ice-water thrown over me'.

News of the book went viral.

Posts hyped it from Adelaide to Alaska, as it plugged a gap in the market of literary godspeak.

Having dumped his backpack at the Ganpati Guest House, Marney the Canadian roamed through the telescoping backstreets of ancient Varanasi, and found himself at Manikarnica, the Burning Ghat.

As on every afternoon, the recently deceased were being borne on funeral pyres, the closest male relative stepping up at the appointed moment to crack the skull in order for the soul to be released.

Moved by the scene, and with the lengthening shadows edging towards dusk, Marney strolled solemnly along the waterline, and back to his guest house. Up on the roof terrace he pondered life and death, then sent a message to his best friend back in Toronto, which read:

'India: Light in a World of Darkness.'

Marney posted a selfie from Varanasi on Instagram. Before clicking off his phone, a quote caught his eye:

'He is Light in a World of Darkness.'

Recoiling in wonder, he checked the source and discovered it was linked to His Celestial Highness Sri Omo-ji.

A minute after that, Marney had read his way through the holy man's Wikipedia page – which had gone live eight minutes before. To his delight, he learned the holy man had an ashram in Varanasi, at The Great Stone.

'It's a sign,' Marney said under his breath. 'I must go to him at once.'

When the backwards circumambulation had been completed, and the sacred blessing to Sri Omo-ji made, Rosco P. Schultz III addressed the maharaja on behalf of the group.

'We don't wish to impose, Your Highness,' he said, 'but would it be possible to get a tour of the ashram?'

His stomach churning in trepidation, Bitu dipped his head cordially.

'Of course, I would be more than honoured to show you around,' he said.

Turning, he led the way from the Great Stone, across what had recently been the playground. As they neared the main school building, the door opened and a woman dressed in saffron-orange robes emerged. Like everyone else, she had a photograph of the guru hanging around her neck. Young, pretty, and seductively charming, she greeted the maharaja.

'Excuse me, Your Highness,' she said gently, 'but His Celestial Highness Sri Omo-ji has asked for you to meet Him in the Hall of Unconditional Love. If you would not mind, I would be pleased to give the distinguished visitors a tour of the campus.'

Both feet rooted to the ground, Bitu sensed time stop in freeze-frame. As if observing the situation from above, he marvelled how Zap the fixer had even fixed a guide to appear at the exact moment she was needed.

'Thank you...' the maharaja said, straining to appear solemn.

'*Karnika*, Your Highness.'

'Thank you Karnika... I'll attend His Celestial Highness at once.'

Dressing in the elaborate saffron robes and matching turban which the fixer had left for him in the green room behind the stage, Harry was suffering from a terrible bout of nerves.

He caught a flash of himself about to step out to a packed house at the Blackpool Grand on the night of his monumental fall from grace. On that inauspicious evening the casket had not opened. But, as Harry reflected, the fact that it hadn't had allowed this new reality to take shape, with fresh doors opening in all directions.

The memory of failure was melted by another – the first delicious taste of success. Aged ten, he was standing on a chair performing a sleight-of-hand in the front room of M. K. Thakur. A friend of his father and amateur magician, he'd revealed the first secrets of conjuring, and taught the young Harry Singh everything he knew.

The elation of recollected success was tinged with sorrow, as he recalled how the inimitable M. K. Thakur had quit Blackpool for Bombay. Presenting his pupil with Houdini's literary masterpiece, *Miracle Mongers and their Methods*, he vanished from the magic-obsessed teenager's life.

The sound of a door slamming shut was followed by the sound of feet scurrying over polished linoleum. Bitu appeared backstage, his forehead gleaming with sweat.

'Get onstage, quick!' he hissed.

'Huh?'

'What's wrong with you?'

'Not feeling as right as rain,' Harry replied, befuddled.

'Go on, get through there – the bloody Americans are about to come in!'

'I can't go on with it, Bitu-bhai.'

'What?!'

'You heard me. I'm not a magician. I'm a flop.'

'No one's asking you to be a bloody magician! They don't need tricks. They need *real* magic – love, hope, joy – that kind of stuff!'

Bitu snatched the turban from Harry's hand, and furled it around his friend's head as fast as he could.

'You look *stu-bleedin'-pendous*!' he yelled.

'I'm a fake and a fraud,' Harry moaned dismally. 'And I deserve to go straight to hell.'

Bitu grabbed his friend by the arm.

'One day we'll be laughing about this moment over a good single malt,' he roared. 'Now get out there, and remember you're not Maharaja Malipasse, but His Bloody Celestial Highness Sri Omo-ji – King of the Godmen!'

The Americans were led through into the ashram's gymnasium, in which a female instructor was demonstrating the art of 'yogic flying'.

Bouncing up and down on a trampoline while holding the lotus position, she was transfixed in a meditative state. Decked out in matching tracksuits bearing the Sri Omo-ji logo, half a dozen students were doing their best to follow the teacher's lead.

Karnika opened a door at the far end of the gym.

'And through here is the garden,' she said, 'where we shall see the archery with meditation class.'

Traipsing behind her, the Americans ummed and ahhed at everything they saw, flabbergasted that neither their beloved Sri Omo-ji, nor His Highness the Maharaja, had mentioned the ashram before.

Six archery targets had been set up in the gardens. The devotees, who were known as *punyas*, were taking it in turns to fire at them, blindfolded.

Remarkably, three of them hit the gold.

'His Celestial Highness encourages His disciples to meditate through activities,' Karnika explained as she opened the door to the refectory. 'He believes in beauty through the unification of mind and body.'

Filing into the dining hall, the Americans watched a stream of devotees being served dinner. Rosco pointed at a magnificent stained-glass mobile suspended from the ceiling. Like almost everything else, it was adorned with the number 6 set amid a hexagon.

'That must have taken months to make,' Rosco said.

Swallowing hard, Karnika smoothed a hand back over her long black hair.

'When required, we Indians are expert at getting things done faster than fast,' she said.

Drifting through the billowing saffron curtains into the Hall of Unconditional Love, His Celestial Highness greeted the audience with *namaste*, and slipped dreamily onto a furry white sofa in the middle of the stage.

A technician appeared from nowhere, and adjusted the microphone, before vanishing again. A pair of high-power beams bathed the godman in twin shafts of platinum light.

As Harry gazed down at the devotees – *his* devotees – a door at the back of the hall opened a crack, and the Americans sauntered in.

'His Highness holds a nightly prayer session in here,' Karnika explained in a whisper. 'Sometimes He sits in silence, and on other evenings He speaks for hours and hours, depending on His mood.'

'It's so wonderful to see Him again,' Fred gushed.

'Just being in His presence makes me feel whole,' added Rosco.

'Could we sit and listen to the discourse for a minute or two?' Elaine asked.

Nodding, Karnika led the group to the front of the hall. Self-conscious at being so close to the guru again, the Americans sat cross-legged and peered in wonder at the illuminated stage.

Focused on the middle distance, Harry did his best to forget the audience as his magical training taught him to do. His mind blurring, he thought of growing up in the backstreets of Blackpool, and of his dad beating him for not tidying the bedroom he shared with his brother. Then he thought of the day the health inspector turned up at the butcher shop, and how his mum had cried buckets the day all the furniture had been repossessed. But most of all he thought of the pain that had shadowed his entire life, pain from hiding who he really was.

For ten long minutes Sri Omo-ji just sat there, head pounding, hands trembling in fear. A dozen times he had the first line of an oration in his mouth. But each time, something stopped him – the memory of ridicule on the last night at the Blackpool Grand.

Reclining on the furry white sofa, he saw himself reflected, as though a mirror were facing him at the edge of the stage. He was about to recoil in horror; but as his face muscles tensed to do just that, he heard a voice in his head… the voice of his first magician-teacher, M. K. Thakur.

'A great show is a harmony between audience and performer,' it said, 'in which each loses themselves in their role, drawing strength from one another.'

His blood fortified by a surge of adrenalin, His Celestial Highness took a deep breath, swallowed hard, and began:

'Love is wisdom and wisdom is love. Not the false love of the impure, but the love which causes roses to bloom. The love on the faces of innocent babies. The love that seeks to give but not take. The love uncounted in dollars or rupees, but rather in the communal spirit of tenderness...'

Four hours and five minutes after slipping onto the furry white sofa, His Celestial Highness rose to his feet. He put both hands over his face in a curious new greeting, and drifted back through the saffron-coloured curtains, to where Bitu was waiting for him.

'How did I do?' Harry asked.

'Listen to them clapping! They loved it! And not only the Americans! The homeless people are clapping too – and none of them speak English.'

'Did I go on too long?'

Bitu's face froze.

'*No!*'

'What now?'

'You go through to the staff room and keep out of sight. I'll invite Rosco and the group to stay.'

'Stay here... at the school?'

'At the *ashram*,' Bitu corrected.

'Why?'

'Because it's the best way to reel them in!'

Next morning Bitu woke with a start, the tail end of a nightmare coursing through his slumberous mind.

It had featured an orange laser beam shooting from the Great Stone up to the heavens, and thousands of devotees arriving from all corners of the world.

Once dressed, Bitu went out to the front of the building to inspect the stone. Across the gravel quadrangle, Karnika was at the main gate, chatting with a young man who was wearing a heavy backpack, dangling with camping accessories.

Requesting that he wait outside, she paced over to the Great Stone, where the Maharaja of Patiala was standing, his mind on orange laser beams.

'Good morning Your Highness.'

'Good morning.'

'Sir, that Canadian man over there has come to be a student of His Celestial Highness.'

Bitu looked at her askance.

'He says he saw a quote from Sri Omo-ji.'

'Where?'

'On Instagram, sir.'

'What's his name?'

'Mr. Marney, Your Highness.'

'Bring him over to me.'

The security guard unlocked the gate, wrote the visitor's name on a clipboard, then Karnika led him across to where Bitu was sitting on the bench.

'Hello, I'm Marney… from Toronto,' he said brightly, thrusting out his hand to shake.

Rather affronted at being mistaken for an ordinary member of society, Bitu introduced himself as the Maharaja of Patiala. He extended his right hand to be kissed. Never having encountered royalty before, real or faux, the Canadian bent down and touched his forehead to the hand.

'You want to study under His Celestial Highness?'

'Yes, sir.'

'May I ask why?'

'Because He is Light in a World of Darkness.'

'How do you know that?'

'Because I read it on Instagram.'

'*Really*?'

'Yes, sir.'

'When?'

'Last night.'

Excellent, Bitu thought to himself, the social media guy in Shenzhen has delivered.

'Forgive me, sir,' Marney said, his voice faltering, 'but haven't we met before?'

'I certainly doubt it.'

The Canadian scratched his head.

'I'm sure we have… on the packed train to the Kumbh Mela.'

'Must have been someone who looked like me.'

His line of sight lifting, Marney's gaze fell on a huge awning hanging over the front of the main building, the image of Sri Omo-ji, and the slogan: 'His Celestial Highness Prays for the Unloved Children!'

'That's Harry,' Marney said warmly. 'He was with you on the train. Then I bumped into him at the Kumbh. We were at Mother Mee's *darshan* together.'

Swallowing hard, Bitu beckoned the Canadian to lean in.

'His Highness and I were travelling incognito,' he said quietly. 'Tell no one of meeting us – either at the Kumbh Mela, or on the way there.'

'I understand.'

Relieved, Bitu smiled.

'Tell me, what did you do before coming to India?'

'I was studying electrical engineering – graduated top of my class.'

The .aharaja signalled to Karnika to come over.

'See that Mr. Marney gets breakfast, then take him to the dormitories,' he said.

'At once, Your Highness.'

The Canadian lifted his backpack from the gravel.

'By the way,' Bitu said without turning, 'd'you know anything about laser beams?'

Before the morning was out, the Americans had relocated from the Taj Ganges to the dormitories at the Sri Omo-ji Ashram.

Lavished with full VIP treatment, they were attended by an army of fawning minions. In their rooms they found a variety of key objects awaiting them, laid out neatly on their beds. These included a set of saffron-coloured robes, a framed picture of the guru to wear around their necks, a Sri Omo-ji workbook, and a pair of gloves in a pouch.

Abundantly spacious, the VIP quarters were furnished in orange upholstery, the walls festooned in proverbs and sayings uttered from His Celestial Highness's lips. The bathrooms were exceptionally luxurious, with roll-top tubs, and Italian towels. The only thing missing was a mirror above the sink. In place of it was a life-sized portrait of Sri Omo-ji, captioned with the words 'Embrace the Reflection of the Inner You'.

Changing into his robes, Rosco hung the circular photo frame around his neck, and gave thanks for the life of the guru. Before convening with the others, he washed his hands with a bar of soap engraved with the godman's image, then dried them on an orange towel embroidered with the word 'LOVE', translated into fifty languages.

Down the hall, through a door with a push-button code, Harry and Bitu were running through a list of details.

'Don't know how we're gonna stay on top of it all,' Harry said in a fluster. 'Zap's done wonders, but I'd say we're already out of our league.'

As though unfazed, Bitu swished a hand through the air.

'No problem,' he muttered. 'That girl Karnika's doing a fine job. I've green-lit a list of courses.'

'What courses?'

'Dozens of them... everything from Celestial Pottery With Meditation to Unarmed Combat in the Name of Peace.'

'D'you think she's onto us?' Harry intoned, his voice cold.

'Of course not!' Bitu jeered. 'But if anyone is it's the young Canadian chap who turned up this morning. Saw you on Instagram. Says he knows you.'

'*What?*'

'He was on the train to Allahabad – remember?'

Harry nodded.

'Yeah he was… and he took me to that nutty woman's audience… the one all dressed in white.'

'Should we chuck him out?' Bitu asked.

'No, no. Let's reach out to him… we could get him working for us.'

'I already have,' Bitu answered.

Harry tapped a clenched fist to his chin.

'The big question is how we monetize all this,' he said. 'If we don't get proper funding we'll burn out before we've even begun.'

'Need to hit Rosco P. Schultz III with a wall of love,' Bitu answered. 'Imagine what a show we could lay on with some serious cash!'

'Rosco needs more than love,' Harry said. 'He needs magic!'

At sunset Karnika was called out to the front gate, where half a dozen melancholic Swedes were peering in through the railings.

They explained how they'd heard about His Celestial Highness on Radio Stockholm, and dropped everything to follow the Path. The next thing they knew, they were each presented with a thirty-page contract to sign. The document had been hastily put together by the Maharaja of Patiala, copying and pasting text from a legal site online.

'What's this for?' a Swede named Marek asked.

'Just the usual legal nonsense,' Karnika responded casually.

'It looks very thorough.'

'No more than the legalese stuff you agree to when opening a Gmail account. The difference is that we print it out for you in the name of transparency.'

Marek made a joke in Swedish and his friends laughed long and hard. Then, without delay, he turned to the last page and signed.

The other Scandinavians did the same.

Karnika put her hands over her face in the greeting Sri Omo-ji had demonstrated the night before.

'Welcome to a fragment of Paradise,' she said.

At eight p.m. an announcement was made through miniature speakers mounted into the ceiling of every room.

Everyone was to come to the Hall of Unconditional Love at once, and to bring with them their pouch containing the rubber gloves. His Celestial Highness had a secret to reveal.

Filing in eagerly, the Americans, the Swedes, the sole Canadian, and all the homeless locals took their places – the foreigners pushing their way to the front.

'Can't wait to know what the secret is!' Elaine gushed.

'And I can't wait to find out what these gloves are for,' Rosco said.

Marney, who'd overheard the comments, had a guess:

'Bet you they're both to do with eternal love.'

The house lights slowly dimmed, and the sound of a sperm whale calling for a mate was played, slowed down to half-speed. The hall was infused with the scent of lemongrass – sprayed from ducts in the ceiling.

Fifteen minutes of absolute silence passed.

When the audience could stand the anticipation no longer, His Celestial Highness drifted through the curtains and onto the stage. Gliding to the front, he stood tall, placed his hands over his face, and cried, '*Mamana!*'

Spontaneously, the entire audience echoed the greeting.

The godman launched into an extended monologue about hope, energy, and 'hot love'. Having dictated so much godspeak he found it now rolled off his tongue effortlessly, while he thought about mundane matters, like whether he'd have pizza or curry for a late night snack.

An hour into his oration, Sri Omo-ji paused. His face breaking into a grin, he said:

'Those of us who hold *Mamana* in our hearts have powers above and beyond those of mortal women and men. We walk on this sacred planet with inner ecstasy, and we use our powers with care.'

Staring out at the audience, twin beams of light illuminating him, the guru reached up to his right ear, shaped his hand into a fist and jerked it twice. A white dove fluttered into the rafters. He coughed, regurgitating another dove. After that, he threw a pair of fireballs, the flames tinged blue. And, lastly, he vanished in a puff of smoke, rematerializing at the back of the hall.

As the audience applauded in jubilation, Sri Omo-ji covered his face and exclaimed: '*Mamana!*'

Stepping up onto the stage, he slipped down onto the furry white sofa, and asked the devotees to take the gloves from their pouches and to put them on.

As soon as they did the godman explained that to know hot love they would need to feel pain.

Although ordinary on the exterior, the gloves were designed to give the wearer a taste of the anguish suffered by the Unloved Children. The right glove contained hundreds of miniature needles, while the left was laced with an irritant that made the skin burn.

'We must know pain in order to know joy,' His Celestial Highness said. 'For this reason all *punyas* must wear the Healing Gloves for three hours each day.'

Diving back into another discourse of meaningless godspeak, the spiritual leader rambled on and on. Straining to concentrate, the audience endured the discomfort of the Healing Gloves throughout.

At the end of his extended oration, the living god stood to his feet and vanished – just like that.

Where he'd been standing was a jumbled heap of saffron-orange robes.

From: *Godman*

The Joxican Maze

THE DUNGEONS HOUSED every enemy and miserable dissenter who'd been overheard to slander the good name of King Charlemagne, and spared of execution.

In the permutation 14212/2QWS/A/ČÂ, the jailers were hyenas, and the majority of the prisoners were gilliads, a hybrid of zebra and elk. A truly fearful place, its bleak rock walls were dark from soot, and had somehow soaked up the cries of the inmates kept there for what seemed like an eternity.

Through their adventures, Oliver had not seen Amarath so sorrowful as the moment in which the two of them were thrust into a tiny cell, the wooden floor soaked in blood.

'Fantastic! Thank God we've made it here!' he bellowed, once the hyenas had locked them in.

Amarath looked at him with scorn, as though she was ready to rip out his heart.

'*Fantastic*?!'

'Yeah. It's exactly where we're supposed to be. Have to say, I didn't believe it would work.'

'That *what* would work?'

'All that marching over invisible mountains, and the crazy digging through the abyss.'

'It worked because I was leading!' Amarath snarled. 'And as the leader, I knew exactly where we were going.'

Oliver leaned back against the cell's rock wall.

'Well, as you've no doubt sensed, I'm in the lead now.'

'Damn it for flipping us. It always happens at the worst moment!'

'It happens when it needs to happen,' Oliver replied. 'We both know there's nothing we can do about it – that it's a failsafe so the mission succeeds.'

Amarath peered through the bars at the vaulted corridor, and the torture room beyond. Five or six hyenas wearing leather aprons were sharpening knives.

'Well, you'd better get a move on, or else our laughing friends over there are gonna get in the way of your timeline.'

Oliver didn't reply. Not at first. His breathing shallow, he strained to concentrate, his mind totally focused on the plan.

'It's going to be close,' he said.

*

As CHANCE WOULD have it, Oliver's table was positioned next to the one at which Borbor was seated.

Unsure what to order, he'd been given the house favourite – a Screaming Lizard.

The glass of oily black liquid was prepared from the bile of an albino dwarf lizard. The drink's name derived from the suffering endured by the creature as it was turned from an honourable reptile into a second-rate cocktail.

Oliver took a sip, choked, then slammed the glass down

267

on the table. Wiping a hand over his mouth in revulsion, he retched as though he'd just swallowed a mouthful of poison.

Which, coincidentally, is exactly what he'd done.

More toxic than almost anything else, the bile of the albino dwarf lizard was only made sufferable by the ice cubes. Containing an antidote, they were nine-sided, so they melted at an exact rate.

As the cocktail was consumed, just the right amount of anti-venom was ingested. Despite the fact the poison was deactivated, at least one in five patrons who drank it dropped dead.

Not usually from poison – but from rampant anticipation.

Touched by melancholy, Borbor was in the mood for a chat. Winking at the black liquid, he grimaced.

'That's dangerous stuff,' he said.

Oliver looked over at the lemon-yellow jinn, taking in his great blond pelt of fur, his overly believing eyes, and his innocent expression.

'Wasn't sure what to order,' Oliver mumbled tautly.

'I hear that the lizards scream so loudly they grow legs as they're killed,' Borbor said.

Oliver retched again, a reflux of lizard bile.

'Are you from Grostulas?' he asked.

'No, from Mishmak.'

'Where's that?'

'On the other side of the Great Emerald Desert.'

'Don't know where that is,' Oliver retorted. 'To tell you the truth, I don't know where anything is… except for my own little corner of…'

'Of the Realm?'

Oliver didn't answer.

Instead, he looked out at the sea of creatures, and watched as they challenged the limits of their own imagination.

Limits that were apparently unrestrained.

Two tables away, a pink jinn had imagined the girl of his dreams, who was perched on his lap. Slender as a viper, eyes as large as soup bowls, she had five arms and twice as many hands. When she breathed out, slime-green vapour spewed from her lips.

In the far corner, the tables had been removed to make space for one of the best-known regulars: a carnival jinn with an insatiable thirst for Screaming Lizards.

Shapeless, like an amoeba, he swelled larger and larger the more of the cocktails he guzzled down. Other customers were brought the drinks in glasses, but the carnival jinn was served them by the bucket. The nights that he dropped in were devastating for the albino dwarf lizard population, but excellent for business.

Despite his size and gluttonous behaviour, the jinn was liked by everyone. This was because of his impeccable manners, and the fact that he never refused a favour, no matter what it was.

A few tables away from the corner, a cluster of characters were huddled, pulled from the Grostulas underworld. They were drinking shots of jojopuka juice. In the history of the Members' Bar the record was eleven shots. Stunned into a state of apoplexy, the leader of the group downed a ninth glass, before collapsing.

In his stupor, he imagined he was being trampled by a striped rhinoceros from the Dominion of Smoo.

Within a moment, he was.

'What an odd place this is!' Borbor snapped all of a sudden. 'Think of someone or something and they materialize right in front of you. I've already been visited by my employer, Mr. Ot, some old school chums, and a rather enraged blacksmith. Thankfully, I managed to get him to disappear by reversing the imagination.'

Scanning the Members' Bar, Oliver took in the wild and varied assortment of members and their imaginings.

'How d'you do that... reverse the imagination?' he asked.

The lemon-yellow jinn took a sip of his juice.

'By thinking of rotten apples.'

There was a pause in the conversation, as Oliver tried to make sense of the comment.

'I'm going to Zonus!' Borbor announced energetically. 'I've been called to appear there by the Order of Concilus itself.'

'Just came from Zonus.'

Borbor's eyes widened.

'*Really*? How was it?'

'Absolutely insane.'

'You mean insanely fabulous?'

Tilting his head a little to the side, Oliver gave the question thought.

'No. Not fabulously anything,' he responded. 'Just insane.'

'And where are you going?'

'Anywhere... as far away as I can get from Zonus.'

Borbor took another sip of his cocktail, a second glass of stagnant postulak juice.

'Do you like smorop pods?' he asked.

At that moment, a thunderous commotion on the floor above shook the frescoed ceiling.

'Sounds as though someone's imagined the mother of all jinn,' said Borbor.

Glancing towards the door, Oliver breathed in sharply. He could feel them in his bones – the chameleon guard.

'They're coming,' he whispered in trepidation.

'Who are?'

'The Invisible Ones,' he said.

*

THE MAIN MATTER of concern for Epsilius was where to construct the trap.

Having pondered the question long and hard, he came to the conclusion there was no point in selecting anywhere that Nequissimus might know.

That was the problem.

The great jinn knew the Realm better than anyone, or anything. Moving effortlessly across frontiers between one dominion and the next, he prided himself on the ability to navigate even its most secret haunts.

But for all the genius of Nequissimus, there was ample equal in the intellect of Epsilius.

As he saw it, the answer was not to construct a trap in the existing Realm, but to fashion a new dominion from scratch.

A dominion that would be unknown to the great jinn.

When it came to creating new dominions, the rules and regulations were extensive and intertwined. So bogged down were they in red tape that almost no new dominions were ever successfully registered.

There was, however, a breed of creatures not only adept in handling the paperwork, but in designing dominions as well. Residing in the little-appreciated Kingdom of Gooorg-Papat, they were rat-like and meek. They called themselves 'vœkkaq', but everyone else knew them as 'the Builders'.

Of all of them, there was none more expert than Spatrid.

He'd devoted his life to the art of the joxican maze.

*

AFTER THREE DAYS of sharpening, and of howling, the hyenas had got the knives as they needed them to be.

The newest prisoners were chained and blindfolded, and dragged from their cell. Despite being in the lead, Oliver was fearful – a point that Amarath sensed.

All he could think of was the permutation in the Arctic Mountains where he'd messed up and caused the mission to fail. Because of that, he and Amarath were where they were. The Arctic Mountains had been proof that, even with constant preparation, things could, and did, go wrong.

Amarath was the first to be lifted onto the torture table.

The embodiment of calm, she didn't wriggle or protest. Inside, however, she was in turmoil, desperately afraid Oliver would mess up again.

Once on the trestle table, the chains were removed, and Amarath was strapped in, bound so tight her hands and feet went blue. Nearby, chained and crouching, Oliver watched as the knives were sharpened one last time.

Anyone else in his position may have called out, but he did not. He was waiting for the exact moment, as had been prescribed to him.

As always in the Seventh Dungeon, the jailers took it in turns to work away at the prisoner until execution had been achieved.

In the old days they had dispatched their victims more speedily, but that was regarded as far too lenient. After all, why end life swiftly, when the process could be spaced out over time?

The first hyena stepped forward, his leather apron dark with dried blood, a knife in either paw.

Amarath flinched.

Oliver winced.

The jailer leaned over the prisoner, both blades lowering towards her face.

Amarath was struggling now, unable to help herself from doing so.

The tip of the first blade pressed down onto her cheek, pricking through just enough to release a single drop of blood.

Then, raising the second knife above its head, the hyena paused.

Cackling, he plunged it downwards at Amarath's left eye.

What happened next was indescribably unlikely. But, it

being permutation 14212/2QWS/A/ČÂ, it was exactly what was expected, and required.

The chains and leather bindings turned to water and drained away.

The knives morphed into swallows, which fluttered up into the beams.

And the hyena jailers transmuted into grapes, tumbling to the floor.

Reeling, Amarath lay outstretched on the trestle table.

'Really didn't believe that would work,' Oliver said, leaping to his feet.

'Thanks for having confidence I'd be OK!' snapped Amarath.

*

Rustling leaves heralded the invisible force as it swept through Grostulas, and into the Central Saloon.

Within a minute of their arrival, the chameleon guard had made mincemeat of the place. Every table and chair had been upturned, and the customers were tossed down onto the floor, their cocktail glasses smashed.

His face slammed against the back wall, the landlord was quizzed about the fugitive from Zonus. Given no choice, he revealed the way to the Members' Bar.

The guards bounded down the stone stairs, and used brute force for their password.

Like a shamanic rattle, the rustling of leaves swept in.

Both ears trained to the sound, Oliver sensed his muscles

pumping. As they did so, his brain streamed in thought, an infinite stream of words.

Millions of them.

Coursing, surging, vaulting, leaping through the limits of his mind. Without Oliver actually thinking, the words themselves crunched away at a solution.

'*The Book of Methuselam*,' he mumbled, bewildered. 'I can feel it.'

Like everyone else in the bar, the pink jinn had turned to the door, the girl of his dreams slipping off his lap onto the ground.

'This is not good,' uttered Borbor blankly.

As the rudimentary remark left his mouth, the chameleon guard surged into the Members' Bar.

Along with the rustling of leaves came energy, warmth, and a sense that no amount of opposing force could protect the prey from their terror.

At lightning speed, the guards swept through the room, their skins camouflaging to the backdrop of debauchery.

Oliver crouched down on the floor behind the lemon-yellow jinn, his breathing shallow, his bloodstream charged with adrenalin. As his muscles readied themselves for battle, the sound of the rustling ebbed away – replaced by a rhythmic droning in his head.

The mumbling of words.

Like the indistinct communication of bees in a hive, they were at work.

At work creating a strategy.

A strategy by which Oliver could escape.

As the invisible guards tore through the bar, the plan was seeded deep in Oliver's subconscious.

At that precise moment, as he was peering out from behind the lemon-yellow jinn, an unexpected occurrence took place.

An occurrence that surprised Oliver but, apparently, no one else. Unlike him, they had all witnessed it before.

Every inch of empty space was suddenly filled with live eels.

Air eels.

Their long, silvery forms gliding in all directions, pressed against one another in a monumental school of slippery snake-like fish.

Plaguing great swathes of the Realm, they appeared and disappeared at random.

In more normal circumstances, air eels were regarded as vermin. But, in this one instance, they were a blessing more valued than any other.

The reason was that the chameleon guard could camouflage themselves perfectly against anything.

Anything, that is, except for air eels.

All of a sudden the soldiers' scaly outlines were clearly visible.

Seizing the moment, Oliver leapt over the tables, the eels parting easily as he pushed through them. His face slippery in their slime, he weaved a route between the upturned tables, so as to avoid the guards.

Their malachite swords hacking tempestuously at the elongated fish, they drenched the Members' Bar in eel blood.

A half-filled glass of stagnant postulak juice balanced on his palm, Borbor squinted to make out what was taking place. He watched as Oliver clambered fast over tables and chairs, as the guards slashed at him.

Then, launching himself through the eels, Oliver sprang headlong at the carnival jinn.

A moment later, the eels vanished, gone as instantly as they had come. Without them, the chameleon guard were invisible once more. But no amount of camouflage could answer the question facing each one.

What had happened to the fugitive, Oliver Quinn?

*

A WELL-DOCUMENTED CONDUIT linked the paradise island of Sofulatt with the Kingdom of Gooorg-Papat – where the expert architects of joxican mazes were found.

When it came to their work, the Builders were fair, but regarded the correct payment to be of paramount importance. It wasn't a question of having to stump up a high price, so much as one of acquiring the preferred currency.

Refusing conventional forms of payment, they insisted upon some of the most obscure elements in existence – elements that tended to be worthless to everyone else.

The direct conduit from the island of Sofulatt to the Kingdom of Gooorg-Papat was affected by complex centrifugal rearrangement. Although quite harmless to the populations of either kingdom, it affected visitors from other regions – subjecting them to temporary modification.

The actual form of the change depended on who was travelling through the conduit, and when their journey was made. It ranged from an affliction of sores, to alterations in skin colour, to differences in bodily dimension. In some cases, the conduit had been known to inflict far more unusual and disturbing effects.

Aware of the risks, Epsilius had not had occasion to use the conduit before. A diehard gambler at heart, he'd always longed to try his luck – buoyed by the fact that in most circumstances the effects were temporary.

Dusting the sand from his feet, the celebrated Jinn Hunter murmured a short prayer, and strode up to the conduit – the outline of a door halfway down the beach.

Opening it, he stepped inside.

To his surprise, there was none of the razzmatazz that often accompanied conduits.

No whistling sounds.

No flashing lights.

Or spectral vision.

Not even the scent of juliap juice – which, more often than not, was a form of conduit lubrication.

Instead, Epsilius found himself on a hillside, all covered by wortle weeds, peppered with grazing creatures resembling the muddle of a billy-goat and a mountain lion.

From the moment he stepped through the conduit and into the Kingdom of Gooorg-Papat, Epsilius grasped something was awry.

When he raised his right foot to walk, his left foot moved. And when he touched a hand to the left side of his face, his right one made the movement.

Winking his left eye had the opposite reaction than intended. It was as though the left and right sides of his body had been flipped along the vertical axis.

Despite the rearrangement, Epsilius had no trouble in tracking down Spatrid, the most celebrated Builder of all, and the preeminent architect of joxican mazes.

As with all the other Builders, he lived in a nest made from shreds of zulak bark, on the damp side of the Slow Bleak Cave.

As chance would have it, the cave was a stone's throw from the conduit. A passing vœkkaq child was more than willing to show Epsilius the way.

Even before the Jinn Hunter had called out the Builder's name, Spatrid was standing before him.

'The conduit seems to have rearranged me from left to right and right to left,' Epsilius said, once the two had introduced themselves.

Spatrid grinned subserviently.

'It happens when the moons are full and the scent of glum-glue has blown in from beyond the mountains,' the Builder replied. 'Have no fear… within a little while the sensation will fade.'

'How long is "a little while"?'

'Just when you're getting used to right being left.'

Epsilius shook his head, left to right.

It moved right to left.

'I'm here because I need something from you,' he said.

The Builder slunk down, his elongated snout picking up the faint scent of glum-glue on the air.

'Tell me.'

'A joxican maze. I need a joxican maze.'

Spatrid ground his back teeth – a vœkkaqian expression of perturbed surprise.

'There's a lot of paperwork for those,' the Builder said. 'Mountains of it. Things are not what they used to be and, Zonus…' his face froze. 'As I'm sure you're aware, the powers at Zonus are against the registration of new dominions.'

Epsilius raised his left hand. The right one motioned towards the Builder.

'I've heard that you are without equal,' he said, 'especially in the art of designing joxican mazes.'

'There's the registration to be dealt with, too,' Spatrid said, 'a sea of forms and an ocean of officialdom.'

'I am willing to pay the price,' said the Jinn Hunter.

The Builder sniffed the air again, his long nostrils distended with pleasure.

'We can prepare the maze,' he whispered in a cold, flat voice. 'But we'll require payment in our preferred currency.'

'Tell me what you need, and I will do my best to get it,' Epsilius answered.

The Builder licked a paw and groomed back his whiskers.

'I'll give you a list.'

'A list of ingredients for the maze?'

Spatrid blinked a 'no'.

'A list of what the payment must include,' he said.

*

SOFTENING AS IT dissipated, the dazzling light gave way to dark, and to the commotion of a city.

Exhausted from the Seventh Dungeon, Amarath begged for a little time to regroup.

Oliver balked.

'We've got to get the gryal,' he snapped. 'Time's against us. You know it as well as me!'

'I know, I know,' Amarath groaned. 'But...'

'No buts! It's not far. Should be over there.'

Pointing to the distance, Oliver realized he hadn't given thought to where they were, or where 'over there' was.

As soon as the question was raised, the answer flashed through his mind in neon lights.

Chicago

20th June 1893

*

THE DAWN SKY was alive with lightning, cascading down on the palace domes.

There was a distinct sense the Kingdom of Imagined Souls was no longer safe.

Oliver's mind was still buzzing with words streaming from *The Book of Methuselam*. A sequence that had given protection against the chameleon guard, whispering instructions on how to escape.

The regulars in the Members' Bar had all assumed that

281

the school of air eels had appeared at random, as they were known to do throughout the Realm.

But they'd been wrong.

For it was the whispered words of *Methuselam* that had coaxed Oliver to imagine the eels into existence. Against their backdrop, the guards had become visible, allowing their prey to make his way over to where the carnival jinn was sprawling.

As the guards' malachite blades slashed left and right, Oliver threw himself at the jinn. Like everything else thrust towards it, he became embedded in the creature's amoeba-like form.

Perplexed at how he'd known to act so decisively, Oliver kept still, despite the fact that all kinds of objects were swishing around in the voluminous beetroot-red bubble.

A bubble apparently unbound by the customary rules of physics.

As unexplainable as the space itself, was how such a variety of objects and life had become lodged in there.

Among them was:

An army of terracotta giants.

A herd of indigo unicorns from the Archipelago of Scrox.

A ship with junk sails fashioned from whale bones.

A pair of conjoined bortle twins.

A bottle containing the zest from a gostid fruit.

A shack made from mashed-up elephant hair.

The nest of a lame Roc bird.

A pin upon which was balancing a spinning crocular seed.

And, half a school of air eels.

The difference between Oliver and everything else trapped inside the carnival jinn was that he knew the way out.

The words had whispered the secret:

'To escape, you leave the exact way you entered.'

Once the chameleon guard had swept out, certain their quarry had fled, the carnival jinn had decided to call it a night. He'd ambled home to his cave, on the outskirts of Grostulas.

Imagining a quartet of myoxulan singers into existence, he lay down and fell into a deep sleep, soothed by their discordant tones.

On hearing the hushed strains of what was regarded by myoxulans – but few others – as fabulously pleasing music, Oliver prepared to escape. Squatting with fists clenched, chin pressed down against his chest, he leapt backwards with all his strength.

Against a rip-roaring frenzy of sound and a blur of red, Oliver flew up and out, and found himself on the stone floor of a cave.

The myoxulan singers were on one side of him.

They were playing living zím instruments, bred for the purpose in a forest beyond the Koolapsh Mountains.

On the other side, snuggled down in a matted nest of fruzulak grass, was the carnival jinn. Snoring hard, he was dreaming of an age when his species had been more appreciated.

Striding over to the cave opening, Oliver peered out.

Absolute stillness.

Leaving his saviour to sleep in the comfort of the music, he went outside. Disorientated, he sat down on a smooth rock, and did his best to take stock of the situation.

Before long, he was thinking of Uncle Sinan and the life he'd always known. He thought of the carpet shop, and of his fantasies, of his obsessive need for patterns, and of the dragon's eye in the basement.

His mind abounded with an array of crystal fortresses and Prism cells, of labyrinths, albino dwarfs, living furniture, air eels, and rogue jinn.

'How can any of it make sense?' he asked himself. 'It's absurd. So absurd it must be a dream.'

Plunging his head into his hands, Oliver wondered what to do. He would have to escape from the Kingdom of Imagined Souls, or else the Invisible Ones would get him. They were out there, searching for him.

He could feel them.

It was as though his veins were running not with blood but with letters and syllables, from *The Book of Methuselam*. Like a thief cracking a safe, they were working on a solution. Trying every combination in the background of his mind.

As the words crunched away, Oliver considered the Realm itself. He pondered if it could really exist as it had been described. How could it? After all, the human world in which he'd been born and raised was hermetically sealed.

A unit in itself.

A land where fact and fantasy were separated.

A place of order and regulation.

A domain in which everything was governed by the rigid laws of physics and nature. Laws laid down by great scientists through centuries of scholarship.

His face pressed against his palms, Oliver considered all the maths and the physics he'd ever learned.

Classes.

Examinations.

Mind-numbing theories and laws committed to memory.

All of a sudden, a kindly face slipped into his mind.

Aged and familiar, the head to which it was attached was crowned in a profuse crop of grey hair, its moustache ample, the eyes tired and watery.

The more Oliver considered the face, the more detail he perceived. He may never have seen it in the flesh, but there was nothing about it he couldn't imagine. As he sat there on the rock, face pressed in hands, Oliver began to feel someone watching him.

Slowly, he raised his head, eyes blinking.

Beside him, on the edge of the rock, an elderly figure was sitting in silence. A mass of grey hair covering his head, a grand moustache hanging above his upper lip. He appeared to be in quiet reflection, wide-eyed and quizzical.

Oliver choked.

'I don't believe it!' he exclaimed. 'Or rather, I wouldn't believe it, if I wasn't here.'

'And where exactly is *here*?' asked the man in a studious tone.

'You are… *we* are… in the Kingdom of Imagined Souls.'

'Are we really?'

'Yes.'

The figure frowned. Not angrily, but out of genuine interest.

'And where exactly would that be?'

Oliver swept a hand back through his hair.

'In the Realm,' he said.

Albert Einstein smoothed both eyebrows back.

'I must admit I'm intrigued,' he replied. 'Intrigued at what exactly that could be, and how I got here.'

'I can answer a little of both,' said Oliver. 'The Realm is the real world. Or, rather, it's the whole – of which our world is the smallest and most meaningless splinter. As for how you got here… I confess I'm guilty…'

'*Guilty?*'

'Yes.'

'How?'

'For imagining you here.'

Einstein grinned in a childish way, as though amused by a playground prank.

'The Kingdom of Imagined Souls?'

'That's right. You see, all you have to do is to imagine hard enough and the person appears.'

'So if I were to imagine someone… Plato, for instance,' Einstein asked, 'would he materialize for me?'

'I'm not sure if the imagined can imagine,' Oliver replied. 'But you could give it a try.'

The old man's wrinkled lids drooped down, quivered hard, before his eyes opened once again.

Einstein seemed disappointed.

'No Plato,' he said.

'So sorry,' Oliver countered.

'It was worth a go,' said Einstein as he looked around. 'Perhaps you'd do me a little favour, and tell me more about this... this *Realm*.'

'I can tell you what I myself have been told,' Oliver said. 'It doesn't make sense. In fact, that's the striking thing about it. Most of it's nonsense. But it's reality. Or, rather, it's *a* reality.'

'Sounds intriguing,' said the physicist. 'Please go on.'

'Well, like I said, it is entirely,' Oliver explained. 'A place in which every conceivable permutation of possibility coexists. Imagine it – a multiverse of every possible event, all existing on top of itself. Not just the possibilities of humanity, but those of all life forms, and even jinn.'

Einstein frowned.

'*Jinn?*'

'The *other* life form. You know... genies... like from *The Arabian Nights*.'

'Oh, believe me, I have had experience of them.'

'You have?'

'Oh yes,' Einstein replied. 'But I imagine we all have, although most hardly realize it.'

'The jinn are the reason I am here,' said Oliver. 'It's because of them that we're both here.'

'And why is that?'

'Because the most evil jinn in existence has escaped.'

'And who would that be?'

'He's known as Nequissimus.'

'Escaped from where?'

'From the Prism. The most secure of jails.'

Einstein frowned, his mind wrestling to understand.

'What can you tell me about the structure of the *Realm*?'

'Not very much. Only that there are eleven dimensions, and that everything is linked by conduits. Imagine it – absolutely every detail and inconsequential fragment, linked to everything else. I realize it sounds preposterous.'

'Not at all,' Einstein replied at once. 'It sounds plausible. In fact, to my ears, it sounds fantastically so!'

'I'm sorry I dragged you here,' Oliver muttered. 'It was selfish of me. You're the one man ever to have lived who, I imagine, could make sense of it all.'

The physicist smoothed his eyebrows back again.

'Don't think for a moment I've got all the answers,' he said. 'I'm not sure that I have any. But what I know is that the world we humans inhabit is the smallest tip of a fingernail on a vast and intertwined creature of ultimate possibility. We are less than nothing, although most of the time we like to imagine we're everything.'

'The world, *our* world, is being ravaged by Nequissimus,' Oliver broke in. 'So is the entire Realm. There's no hope until he's been caught and caged once again in the great prison.'

'And who'll do that?' Einstein asked.

'The Jinn Hunters will,' Oliver said.

From: *Jinn Hunter: Book Two – The Jinnslayer*

On the Trail of Bogart

BLAINE COVERED THE half-mile from Mers Sultan at a slow, methodical pace.

His mind was on the hardback envelope tucked away in his breast pocket, as much as it was on the mental freeze-frame of Mortimer Wu lying there, all lifeless and drenched in blood.

He planned to head back to Ghita's apartment and to open the envelope there. But the closer he got to the building, the more he wondered about her.

All of a sudden, Blaine thought of his grandfather.

He was sitting on his porch slurping iced tea through his gleaming white dentures.

'Don't trust her!' the old man barked. 'That girl's nothing but trouble!'

So Blaine crossed the street and threaded his way through Derb Omar. The textile merchants were closing up for the night, packing away the great bolts of cloth, donkey carts hauling off the mountains of discarded packaging. He passed the Rialto, and Le Petit Poucet, and was about to drop in on monsieur Raffi when he heard footsteps behind him.

They were coming fast, in a sprint.

Blaine turned sharply.

A plump, dark man in a thick winter coat was running straight towards him, his right hand outstretched, the fingers clutching the hilt of a knife.

Without thinking, Blaine ran – like he had never run before.

Up Mohammed V, and then doubling back fast in the adjacent street.

The figure followed, and was closing in.

Blaine made a left turn back onto the main drag, then darted down the dimly lit Passage Gallinari, a stone's throw from the Marché Central.

He charged down to the end, to where the hookers gathered when it rained. The footsteps had paused at the passage entrance, as though unsure which way to go.

Suddenly Blaine felt a hand grab the collar of his coat. It yanked him back hard towards a doorway, catching him off balance.

He fell, panting, cursing, hands protecting his head.

'Stay down there!' said a voice. 'I think you've escaped him.'

Blaine looked up. He got to his feet.

'Saed?' he stuttered, still panting from the run. 'What are you doing here?'

'Saving you. That's what I am doing,' he said.

Up on the fourth floor, Blaine took the shoeshine boy through the wardrobe into Ghita's secret world. He might not have trusted her, but options were limited. And she had trusted him with a key.

Once inside, he went straight over to the counter, poured himself a Grey Goose, and slugged it back in one.

'Why does she hide…?' asked Saed, dazed by the luxury.

'It's something about proving herself to her father.' Blaine paused, poured another vodka. 'If you ask me, she's a complete nutcase.'

He sat on the couch, fingertips pressed together at his chin.

'I don't understand what's happening,' he said. 'Who was that guy – a mugger?'

Saed helped himself to a neat Grey Goose, then another.

'An assassin. But not one from Casa,' he said casually.

Blaine looked up.

'You think he killed the backpacker?'

'Yes.'

'And what does he want?'

'I do not know. But he thinks you have it.'

'Have what?'

'The thing he wants.'

The shoeshine boy's ever-ready smile melted away.

'I need to ask something from you… a favour,' he said.

Blaine felt a tinge of apprehension in the pit of his stomach, as though a demand for funds was about to be forthcoming.

'A favour?' he repeated in a slow, dry voice.

'This looks like a safe place – a secret safe place,' Saed said.

'Yeah…'

'Could you keep something for me, for a few days?'

291

The American breathed a sigh of relief.

'Sure… although I'm a guest of Ghita's sofa, an invited guest.'

Saed pulled up his T-shirt and unzipped a money-belt. Inside it were a collection of random credit cards, foreign currency bills, and an envelope with what looked like Chinese handwriting on the front.

'Will you keep this envelope for me?' he asked. 'The police stop me very often…'

'You don't have to explain.'

Blaine took the envelope and slipped it into his satchel.

The sight of it reminded him of the treasure trail that had ended at Bar Atomic. He went over to his coat, pulled out the dirt-speckled envelope and opened it.

There was another postcard inside.

It bore the black-and-white image of a sleek, open-topped limousine. Rising up behind it was the Shell Petroleum headquarters at the top of the old Avenue de France.

As with the first postcard, the reverse side was blank. And, as before, Blaine peeled back the photograph, revealing Bogie's spidery hand.

'I want to find this building,' said Blaine, having glanced at the text. Saed waved a hand towards the window.

'It's just down there, two blocks away.'

At that moment, the door opened, and Ghita slipped through the cupboard into the apartment. She was surprised to see the shoeshine boy, who was lying outstretched on the couch.

'He's my saviour,' said Blaine quickly. 'Saved me from an assassin.'

'It sounds as though you've had a colourful afternoon,' she said, walking over to the kitchen and putting down her purse. She took in the half-empty bottle of Grey Goose, raised an eyebrow and looked at her wristwatch.

'While you've been drowning your sorrows,' she said, 'I have been getting information. I've discovered where the commissioner drinks, and the exact location of Club Souterrain.'

Saed waved a hand towards the window a second time.

'It is under the Marché Central,' he said. 'But the entrance is at the Hotel Touring.'

'That sounds complicated,' Ghita said.

'It is more complicated,' said Saed. 'You see, there's a passcode. It changes every night.'

'I thought you were too young to go inside.'

'Yes, I am.'

Blaine sipped his vodka pensively.

'How would you get the code?' he asked.

'I can get it for you,' said the boy in an easy voice. 'I know the person to ask.'

'And will the commissioner be there?'

Saed tapped his watch.

'Of course he will,' he said.

At a quarter to twelve Blaine crept from the apartment building, past the Marché Central, to the Hotel Touring. His wallet was weighed down with Ghita's spending money, his hair gelled back, and his slim frame squeezed into a borrowed tuxedo, sourced at short notice by Saed.

A throwback to the glory days, Hotel Touring was a favourite with working women who appreciated its hourly rate, and with backpackers who were willing to endure the lice in the name of economy.

Saed was waiting inside the door. He led Blaine down a twisted iron staircase into the maze of subterranean tunnels that crisscross old Casablanca.

'You got the code?' Blaine asked.

'Yes. It's CIGOGNE. The French word for "stork".'

'When I'm inside, what do I do?'

'Order a bottle of Scotch. Something expensive. Don't ask how much it is. It's better to seem like you can afford it, whatever it costs. Ask for a table near the bar. Tip the doorman as you go in, and the manager who takes you to your table. And when you get in there, ask him to introduce you to the commissioner.'

'Why shall I say I want to meet him?'

Saed stepped around a pair of dead rats.

'Say you want to check the price of Alphabonds,' he said.

'*Alphabonds?*'

'Government bonds. The money of the underworld. Untraceable and as good as cash.'

'What happens if the police commissioner doesn't turn up?'

The shoeshine boy pushed open a reinforced door at the bottom of the staircase. He seemed anxious.

'He'll come,' he said. 'He always comes.'

They walked down a slender tunnel, the walls lined in rusted iron sheets. It was illuminated by bare low-watt bulbs and stank of industrial pesticide.

'I can't believe there's anything down here at all,' said Blaine.

Saed stuck out his hand.

'This is as far as I can go,' he said.

'You're leaving me *here*?'

'Keep going down there and turn right at the end.'

'And what then?'

'Then you will be at the door.'

Blaine peered down the corridor. He half wondered whether it was a trap.

'It doesn't look safe,' he said.

Saed didn't reply. He had gone.

'Bastard!' spat Blaine.

He took a deep breath, wiped a hand hard over his face, and quickened his step towards the secret door of Club Souterrain.

A moment before he reached the end of the tunnel, he heard footsteps and conversation. It sounded like a pair of men approaching – deep voices and city shoes.

Panicking, Blaine ducked into a side tunnel and hid in the shadows. Slowing his breathing, he caught a single snapshot of the men as they passed. One was tall, the other short, both well dressed in suits and ties.

When they were gone, Blaine jumped out, and hurried the last few yards to where he expected the club's entrance to be.

But there wasn't a door, just a dead end.

That's impossible, he thought. They couldn't have vanished like that.

He searched the iron-panelled walls for a hidden doorway, but there wasn't one. Blaine was about to turn back, when he noticed a faint ribbon of light at the edge of one of the panels.

At first he assumed it to be a reflection. But, looking more carefully, he saw that the light was coming from behind. He put his ear to the iron and listened hard. There was a trace of sound, little more than an indistinct whisper of vibration.

He looked for a handle or a catch, but he couldn't find one. So he knocked gently… once, then again.

A moment passed, and the panel opened inwards very slowly.

Blaine stepped into a small, square chamber.

Lit more brightly than the corridor, it smelled of perfume and cigarette smoke. Each of the walls was covered in a full-length mirror, a perpetual reflection.

A hatch in one of the mirrors opened at eye level, and a doorman's face hung in the shadow behind.

'*Oui, monsieur?*' he said in a sour tone.

'The Club,' Blaine said, faltering. 'Souterrain.'

'*Oui?*'

'Um, er… *CIGOGNE.*'

The word was followed by a *click*, the sound of a lock snapping back, and well-oiled hinges pressing against themselves.

The mirrored door opened. Blaine stepped forward into a small vestibule.

It was dark, hot, and ended in a curtain of crushed black satin. But it was the noise that was most surprising – the wild, rollicking noise.

A doorman held a hand in invitation towards the curtain. '*Bienvenue, monsieur*,' he said.

Blaine pushed the black satin to the side, and found himself in a realm worthy of his own far-fetched fantasy.

A cavernous salon spread out before him, packed with immaculate waiters and guests. Filled with conversation, with laughter, and with a haze of cigarette smoke, it was lit by a dozen crystal chandeliers.

At one end, the gaming tables were in full swing – roulette, baccarat, poker and blackjack. At the other, a group of attendants in white jackets were preparing drinks, a blur of cocktail flasks shaking Martinis at the bar.

In the middle of it all, the outsized hands of a female pianist were gently caressing the keys of a vintage grand. An Argentine from the good side of Buenos Aires, she was big-boned and overly hirsute, and she swaggered boisterously as she played.

Impeccable in a white tuxedo jacket and tie, a manager appeared as if by magic.

'*Bonsoir, monsieur*.'

'Good evening. I would like a table. A table for two.'

'At once, monsieur. Please come with me.'

Blaine followed the white tuxedo as it weaved between the clusters of lounge chairs, upholstered in pink velvet with gold piping down the sides.

Crossing the room, he thought of Bogart sitting languidly at the bar, head in hands, cigarette screwed into the corner of his mouth. He felt as though he had actually travelled back in time. And, rather than fearing the situation, he was calmed by it.

The manager motioned to a cluster of chairs set around a low table a few yards from the bar. Blaine dug in his pocket and pulled out a large bill, folded small in anticipation of the moment. It disappeared into the manager's pocket so fast that the American was left wondering whether he had given it at all.

'I'd like a bottle of Scotch,' he said. 'A single malt.'

'Certainly monsieur. I can offer you a bottle of Glenlivet, twenty-five years old, with a hint of oak.'

'That will do fine.' Blaine paused, then beckoned the manager a little closer. 'I am hoping to invite the police commissioner to join me for a drink.'

'Of course, monsieur. I shall extend the invitation at once.'

The pianist blew a kiss to a haggard man at the bar, and began to play 'Blue Moon'.

A waiter glided up, a silver salver borne high on an upturned palm. He put the whisky, the ice, and soda siphon on the table, and waited for instructions.

'No ice, and a splash of soda, please.'

Blaine took the glass, held it to the light. Touching it to his lips, he tasted the oak.

A woman approached. She was dressed in a long flowing gown, Chinese silk ruched at the sides, with precariously high stilettos.

'Would you like a little company, monsieur?' she said.

'Er, not right now, I'm expecting a friend.'

As if on cue the manager returned.

Beside him was a uniformed officer – six foot two, broad at the shoulders, with a walrus moustache and the kind of face that prompted small children to scream.

'I should like to present the commissioner of police.'

In one motion, Blaine introduced himself, invited the officer to sit, and slipped the manager another neatly folded bill.

'Could I offer you a whisky?' he asked, pouring a triple.

The officer took the glass, clinked it to Blaine's, and downed half the liquid. He licked his lips.

'It's good,' he said with a grin. 'Very good.'

Blaine refilled his glass, replacing small-talk with drink.

Within five minutes, half the bottle was gone, and the commissioner seemed drowsy.

Blaine seized the moment.

'I'm new in Casablanca,' he said awkwardly. 'And I'm interested in getting my hands on some Alphabonds.'

The officer sipped his drink thoughtfully.

'How many do you want?'

'It depends on the price.' He drew breath. 'How much *is* the going price?'

'A thousand dirhams each, more or less. But I am surprised that they would interest a man like you.'

Blaine cocked his head expectantly.

'Why?'

'Because you are an American, are you not?'

'How did you guess?'

The commissioner lit a cigar, inspected the end, and thought for a moment.

'Because whether he be in Casablanca, Paris, or Timbuktu,' he said without looking up, 'an American sticks out. He doesn't blend in. Why not? Because he can't.'

Blaine may have debated the point, but he knew there was truth in it. The officer was right – while Americans liked to think they are experts in social camouflage, the only place they are capable of blending in is at home.

A few minutes of silence slipped by.

The commissioner sucked on his cigar, and the hookers paraded, one by one, their gowns brushing the gold piping of the chairs. The pianist began playing an old Edith Piaf number, her large, brusque hands vigorous on the keys.

When the number was halfway through, Blaine touched a hand to his jaw.

'I heard that an Asian tourist was killed at the Hotel Marrakech,' he said absently.

'He's lying in the morgue now,' the officer replied with equal disinterest. 'Throat cut clean in two.'

'I wonder who did it.'

'A gangster, a lowlife,' said the commissioner. 'We caught him. He confessed after a thorough interrogation.'

'Oh,' said Blaine timidly, 'that is good news, isn't it? What's your plan for him?'

The commissioner nodded, sucked long and hard, exhaled, then sipped his Scotch.

'When he's been tried and found guilty, he will be taken to the most secure prison in the kingdom,' he said.

'*Will he?*' Blaine asked with interest. 'And where exactly would that be?'

'In the mountains. The prison there is reserved for the worst offenders.'

'Like that Globalcom boss... what was his name? Let me think.'

'Omary,' the commissioner said in a flash. 'Yes, he's been taken there, too. A lot he has to answer for. He will never get out alive.'

'Out of interest,' said Blaine indifferently, 'where exactly in the mountains is the prison located?'

The commissioner drew a breath to speak a name. The word moved up through his vocal cords and onto his tongue. But, just before it emerged into the world, an immensely large man sidled up and kissed the commissioner on the cheeks.

The two men hugged, and embraced again.

'This is my old friend Dr. Weisemann from Hamburg,' said the officer with considerable delight. 'He has a business making ball-bearings for motor cars.'

Blaine extended his hand, waved to the waiter for another glass and another bottle of single malt. As he did so, Dr. Weisemann's ample backside made landfall on the pink velvet.

The conversation turned to secret Swiss cabarets, and then to German prostitutes. Blaine glanced at his watch. He tried time and again to steer the conversation back to the subject of remote mountain jails, but without any success. After all, Teutonic whoring was so much more appealing to his audience than the ins and outs of the Moroccan penal system.

At two-fifteen, the commissioner stood up, thanked his American host courteously for the drinks, hugged the German, then staggered away towards the door.

A protracted silence followed, after which Dr. Weisemann fluttered a set of distended fingers at the girls clustered near the bar.

'Which one are you going to take?' he asked.

'Oh, er… I'm really not interested in them,' said Blaine.

'How can that be?' Weisemann's eyes widened. 'Is it not ladies you admire?'

'No… I mean, yes, I do like ladies, just not right now, just not tonight.'

Ghita was still awake when Blaine arrived back at her secret apartment. She was sitting on the sofa in a bathrobe, her hair pinned up on the crown of her head.

'Please don't judge how I look,' was the first thing she said.

'I'm not judging you,' Blaine replied tenderly.

'Did you get the information… did you find out where they're holding my father?'

'In the mountains. They're keeping him in the mountains.'

'Which mountains? The Atlas or the Rif?'

Blaine pulled his bow tie loose.

'He didn't say. I'm so sorry.'

Ghita began to weep. She covered her eyes with her hand.

'I don't know what to do,' she sobbed.

There was a knock at the door.

'Are you expecting someone?' Blaine asked.

'No... no one except for you knows I am here. No one except for...'

'Saed.'

Ghita unlocked the door and the shoeshine boy stepped in as if he owned the place.

'How was Club Souterrain?'

'Well, the good news is that they've caught a guy who admitted to killing the backpacker.'

'And the *bad* news?'

'That I couldn't find out where Ghita's father is being held – just that it's in the mountains.'

'Which mountains?'

Blaine shrugged.

'Dunno.'

Ghita started sobbing again.

'I have an idea,' said Saed. 'An idea that may work.'

'What is it?'

'I'll ask my girlfriend.'

'You've got a girlfriend?' Ghita and Blaine exclaimed both at once.

'Yes, of course I do. She's older than me, and she works for the commissioner at the main police station.'

'Why didn't you tell us this before? It could have saved a lot of time,' Ghita said witheringly.

'Not to mention a lot of drinking,' murmured Blaine.

Saed filled himself a tumbler of neat Grey Goose and took a long, satisfying gulp.

'You are very lucky,' he said.

'How's that?'

'Because she owes me a big favour – a favour I have been waiting to use for a very long time.'

For three days and nights it rained.

It wasn't mild European splish-splash rain, but a full African downpour. The city was flooded right away, the old French drains clogged with decades' worth of dirt and grime. A number of *bidonvilles*, shantytowns, were washed clean away, leaving the impoverished residents homeless and bereft.

Up the hill in Anfa, Casablanca's *nouveaux riches* were moaning about what they imagined to be the terrible inconvenience of it all. They sat indoors, cancelling their golf games, and flicking through imported magazines.

Down near the port, one of the last remaining Indian traders was bailing the rainwater from his shop. His family had come to Casablanca back in '28, lured by the promises of the French, and by the prospect of a land untouched by low-cost Indian wares. His name was Ankush Singh and while he himself had never visited the land of his ancestors, he knew it through the stories his grandfather used to tell.

As he chucked out another bucket of dingy grey water, he spotted a pair of sensible, well-made shoes standing at the kerb. They led to slender ankles, and up to fine legs, a pretty dress and, eventually, to a lovely face.

Putting down the bucket, Ankush Singh looked at the girl.

Unable to remember the last time beauty of any kind had visited his premises, he wanted to savour the moment.

'Someone told me that you are a pawn dealer,' she said.

'Yes, I am, but business is a little slow at the moment,' the shopkeeper replied. 'The rain's driven my customers away and there's some flooding down there in the back.'

'Could I come in for a moment?'

'Of course you may.'

Ghita stepped inside, drying her feet on the mat.

'I am rather embarrassed to be here like this,' she said.

Ankush Singh patted his hands on his shirt.

'And why is that?'

'Because I am from a family of means,' she replied. 'My father has run into some trouble and our assets have been seized. I have begged my friends for a loan, but they have all forsaken me in my moment of need.'

'I don't loan money,' Ankush Singh explained. 'But I can give you money in return for an object of value.'

Ghita pulled a tissue from the sleeve of her dress and pinched it to her nose.

'I've sold most of my clothes – practically gave them away. The rest are at our family home and the police have sealed it shut.' She fumbled with the clasp of her necklace, a gold

305

locket, encrusted with diamonds and sapphires. 'This is all I have left,' she said.

Ankush Singh inspected the jewellery with a loupe.

'It's excellent work,' he said. 'Looks stolen to me.'

Ghita stamped her foot.

'How dare you? I am no thief!'

The shopkeeper leant over the counter. He took Ghita's hand in his and turned it over.

'Your palm is as soft as silk,' he said gently. 'You have never done a day's work in your life, have you?'

Ghita blushed.

'I don't need to work,' she said defensively.

The shopkeeper stepped away from the counter and motioned to a chair.

'Please do sit down. May I offer you some tea?'

Before Ghita could refuse, the shopkeeper had lit a burner and was brewing the pot.

'I don't know why, but you look familiar,' he said, looking at her side on. 'Have you come in here before?'

'No, no, never.'

'Are you sure?'

Ghita blushed again.

'I am certain,' she said icily.

'Then maybe your brother or sister.'

'I am an only child.'

The shopkeeper spooned some loose tea into the pot, dropped in a sprig of mint, and a chunk of sugar the size of his fist. He stirred and, as he stirred, he frowned.

'Who is your father?' he asked.

'His name is Hicham Omary. He owns the telecommunications company Globalcom.'

'I knew someone of that name when I was a child,' said Ankush Singh. 'He had a deep scar on his cheek from wrestling with me out there in the dirt.'

Ghita looked up.

'My father has a scar on his cheek,' she said.

'Is it curved at the end?'

'Yes... yes, it is.'

Ankush Singh poured the tea into a pair of small Chinese-made glasses.

'He was always lecturing us about his Berber heritage. He was *so* proud of it. In every game we played, and every fight we fought, he was a Berber warrior protecting his homeland.'

'That's my father,' said Ghita with half a smile.

The shopkeeper reached out and touched her hand.

'I will help you in any way I can,' he said.

Ghita handed him the locket.

'Then would you lend me a little money in return for this?'

Ankush Singh dug a hand down into his underwear and took out a cloth bag filled with banknotes. He passed it to her with his right hand. And, with his left, he returned the necklace to her.

'To help the daughter of an old friend is an honour,' he said.

During a break between downpours, Blaine walked along Boulevard Mohammed V in the direction of the Casa Voyageurs railway station.

The main thoroughfare of French-built Casablanca, the street was once the preserve of the most fashionable shops, cafés and restaurants. For a company to have a headquarters there was a statement of influence and power.

But, despite the new tramway and a coat of fresh whitewash, most of the buildings were in a wretched state, symbols of the despised days of the French Protectorate.

Put up back in '34, the Shell Building stood in pride of place at a little crossroads, once named after General Patton. Like everything else with a French title, it had been subsequently renamed. In the postcard there had been a prim new streetlight there, the kerb around it striped in black and white.

Weaving between the parked cars and the mounds of soaking garbage, Blaine made his way to the exact spot where the open-topped limousine had stood in the photograph. A Rolls-Royce Silver Ghost, its liveried driver was holding a door open for a lady in a wide-brimmed sun hat.

Unsure quite what to do, Blaine went inside.

The building was empty and was gutted of its original contents and fixtures. A guardian emerged from the shadows. He had been feeding milky bread to a nest of puppies.

'*C'est fermé*,' he said. 'This building closed.'

The American held up a hand.

'I was hoping something might have been left for me.'

The guardian winced.

'*Quand*? When?'

'About seventy years ago.'

Blaine realized how foolish the sentence sounded before he had even spoken it. He passed the guardian the postcard. Holding it into the light, he moved it close to his eyes. And, after a long wait, he seemed to smile to himself.

'This picture... very old,' he said. 'Cars different now.' He motioned to the passing traffic. 'Small, ugly.' He drew a breath. 'This one... beautiful!'

'I am hoping that an envelope or something might have been left for me,' said Blaine.

'Your name?'

'Oh, it wouldn't be in my name. If anything, it would be in the name of Mr. Bogart.' He took a step back. 'Monsieur BEAU-GART,' he said, enunciating. 'He was an American gentleman.'

'Your father?'

'No, not exactly.'

'Oh.'

The guardian appeared a little displeased.

'Well, yes, kinda,' Blaine corrected. 'My father.'

A big toothless smile welled up on the guardian's face.

'Father, good,' he said.

'Well, do you know if anything was left for him – for my father, Mr. Bogart?'

The guardian shook his head and went back to the pups.

'*Non, monsieur*,' he said as he went. '*Il n'y a rien ici pour votre père.*'

At Café Berry, across from the Shell Building, Blaine sucked down a black coffee and waved a hand through the suffocating smoke.

The waiter hadn't asked whether he wanted it in a glass or a cup, but had served it in a glass – a sign that he was looking more like a local. After all, most Moroccan men take their coffee in a glass, especially those who while away their lives in run-down Art Deco cafés.

For fifteen minutes Blaine stared at the postcard without looking up once. He studied every detail, every speck. And he read and reread Bogie's spidery scrawl.

When he finally did look up, he noticed an elderly lady. She was watching him. The only woman in the entire café, her large, meaty frame was stuffed into a flowery dress. Her hands were muscular and seemed somehow familiar. But Blaine was bad with faces and even worse with names.

He glanced down at the postcard, and then up again.

The woman was still looking at him. She grinned anxiously, stubbed out a cigarette and moved over towards him, parting the empty tables with her legs.

'How are you?' she said in a rather hoarse voice.

'Fine thank you, and you?'

'Oh, you know… I'm surviving.'

There was an uneasy pause. Blaine took a sip of coffee and swallowed.

'Do I know you?' he asked.

'Last night… I was playing.'

'*Playing?*'

'The piano.'

The American caught a flash of the Club Souterrain and an aftertaste of single malt.

'Of course. The pianist.'

The woman fluttered her strong, masculine fingers.

'Yes, the pianist,' she said.

'Please join me,' Blaine replied.

The pianist introduced herself as Rosario. Then she wasted no time in revealing her background. She had come from Buenos Aires decades before, and had put down roots in Casablanca – roots that had taken hold.

'What brought you here?' asked Blaine with genuine interest.

Rosario looked sheepish.

'A surgeon's knife,' she said.

'A...?'

'A knife.'

The pianist touched a thumb to her pearl earring.

'Gender reassignment,' she said.

'Oh,' Blaine replied, wondering whether to deliver it as a question or an exclamation.

Rosario ordered a coffee. It came in a glass as well.

'Back in the seventies,' she said, lighting a cigarette, 'Casa had the only reliable clinic in the world offering The Operation.'

'Which operation?'

'You know...'

'Do I?'

Rosario jabbed a thumb between the American's legs and made a scissors motion.

'Excuse me?'

'I know, I know,' Rosario continued, 'even then it was a little shocking, and a little sordid.'

Blaine didn't want to appear impolite, but he couldn't think of anything to say.

'That sounds painful,' he mumbled after a long pause.

The Argentine pianist stubbed out her cigarette and tapped a fresh one from a soft pack. She lit it with a match.

'It was agony,' she said.

'Was it legal?'

She giggled frivolously.

'Of course not,' she responded mischievously. 'But this is Casablanca, a city with far less on the surface than there is underground.'

'And why did you stay here, and not go back to Argentina?'

'I fell in love,' the pianist said. 'Hopelessly and stupidly in love. When I woke up to realize he was a rotten egg, it was far too late. You know how it is. Life traps you.'

'Oh, believe me, I know all about getting trapped,' said Blaine.

'Well, I am guessing you have not come to Casablanca for gender reassignment,' the pianist replied.

Blaine might have smiled, but he did not.

'I have come in search of Bogart,' he said.

'As in Humphrey?'

'Yes.'

'A little before my time.'

Blaine pulled out the postcard.

'I'm living in the past,' he said. 'Following clues. This one led me to the Shell Building across the street.'

'I hear it's going to be turned into a boutique hotel,' said Rosario. 'But if you believe that, you'll believe anything.' She held the writing to the light and squinted. 'My eyes are showing their age,' she said. 'But it looks like it says "Les Cafés du Brésil", that's a little shop on the corner of the Central Market. It's been there for ever.'

Blaine's eyes lit up. He shook Rosario's hand, pressed a couple of coins to the tabletop, and stood up.

'I'll see you around,' he said as if distracted.

'At the club?'

'Maybe.'

The Argentine pianist pointed to a building adjacent to the café.

'That's where I live,' she said. 'The fifth floor. I'm always ready for a little conversation, or to take a stroll down memory lane.'

A pair of hobnail boots clattered down the slim corridor before coming to an abrupt halt outside Cell No. 3.

The guard pulled the inspection hatch back with his claw-like fingernails, blinding the prisoner with a stream of low-watt light. He stood there for some time. Omary could hear him breathing, as though he were making up his mind what to say.

'You were on the television,' the guard growled in a slow cold voice. 'Seems like you are very rich.'

'I am a prisoner,' said Omary. 'And that's all I am.'

The guard flicked a switch to the right of the door, bathing the cell in blinding light.

'You could buy yourself a little luxury,' he said. 'Better food, a blanket, even a chair.'

Squatting at the back of his cell, Omary crept forward on hands and knees, until his mouth was an inch from the door.

He could smell the guard.

'Bribe my way into a world of luxury?' he said incredulously. 'How dare you?! I'd rather rot to death in here than demean myself by paying you off.'

The inspection hatch slammed shut and the light vanished.

Then the thud of the boots came again, more deafening this time. It was followed by a gushing sound in the distance.

More boots, steel keys rattling, blinding light, and a bucket of ice-cold water was flung into the cell.

The sales assistant at Les Cafés du Brésil had slipped a hardbacked envelope across the counter, identical to the one hidden in Bar Atomic's toilet. It smelt of roasted coffee, having lain undisturbed for decades in a drawer at the back of the shop. The clerk showed no surprise that it was being collected at long last.

A little later, when Blaine opened it up at Baba Cool, he found a third postcard – bearing the image of a snake charmer standing in front of an ancient minaret. As before, he separated the card from the photograph, and found a line and a half of Bogart's almost impenetrable scrawl.

Directions, which began at a place called 'Koutoubia'.

As he sat there pondering the clues and what they might lead to, Ghita arrived.

'I thought I'd find you here,' she said.

Blaine showed off the postcard and explained where he had found it.

'I don't understand how clues could have been left unnoticed for so long,' he said.

Ghita ordered a *nous-nous*.

'We're not a young country,' she replied, 'not like your America. Here in Morocco something has to be over a thousand years in age to be considered properly old.'

'But Casablanca's far newer than that.'

'I know,' Ghita replied. 'And that's why it's an embarrassment to most Moroccans, and the reason why they're happy to rip down the buildings without a second thought.'

'But they're jewels... Art Deco jewels.'

'They may be to you. But to the locals they're ugly, like a monstrous eyesore from the sixties... An eyesore created by colonial oppressors.'

Blaine put the card away and, as he did so, his eyes lit up.

'Did you know that Casablanca was once the gender reassignment centre of the universe?' he said with a smile.

'Gender...?'

'*Reassignment.*'

'I don't understand,' Ghita said.

'Sex change... it's where all the early sex changes were done. I met a guy – I mean a woman – called Rosario, who had her tackle chopped off here forty years ago.'

'That's disgusting.'

'No it's not.'

'Then what is it?'

Blaine thought hard.

'It's a cry for help,' he said.

There was a thunderous roar of applause from the back of Baba Cool, and all the tired old men hiding from their wives cheered. Some waved their fists in the air; others slapped their friends on the back.

'What's going on?'

The waiter, who was distributing fresh ashtrays, cocked his head back towards the oversized screen.

'One-Zero to Morocco.'

'Who are they playing?'

Disbelieving that anyone could be unaware of the match, the waiter replied:

'Algeria, monsieur. Our most bitter rival.'

Five minutes later, Morocco's old adversary equalized and, a moment after that, Saed hurried in, a cardboard box in his hands. He was hawking baseball caps with the Moroccan flag glued unevenly to the front.

'I've sold fifty this afternoon,' he said. 'I got them from a Chinese store in Derb Omar.' He put down the box. 'I'm the champion of champions.'

'Because you're good at selling hats?' said Ghita.

'No, not that. Because I've found out where they're holding your father.'

Ghita froze, her eyes filling instantly with tears.

'*Where...* where is he?'

316

'In a prison high in the mountains.'

'We knew that already.'

Saed took out a scrap of newspaper. There was something scribbled on the back.

'You read it,' he said, passing it to Ghita.

'Why don't you?'

'I don't read much. Been too busy selling hats to learn.'

'It's the name of the jail – beyond the Gorge of Ziz.'

'Where's that?'

'A long way.'

Blaine held up his hands.

'Wait a minute,' he said. 'What's your plan... to turn up and ask sweetly for them to hand your father over?'

'I'll plead with the guards,' said Ghita. 'I'll beg them.'

'And you really think that'll work?'

Saed put a second scrap of paper on the table. It was larger than the first, and looked as though it had been torn from a child's exercise book.

'I think this will help,' he said.

Ghita looked at the thick, unruly Arabic script.

'It says: *Abdelkarim Hamoudi the goldsmith will repay the favour owed by his grandfather. The password is the name of The Prophet's steed.*'

'The Night Journey,' said Saed. 'The Prophet ascended to Heaven on a horse with wings...'

'It was called Buraq,' Ghita said.

Another chorus of cheering erupted at the back.

'What is the favour the goldsmith is willing to repay?' Ghita asked.

'Am I missing something here?' asked Blaine. '*Who* is the goldsmith?'

Saed seemed unusually serious for a moment.

'When my father died he left me nothing,' he said. 'Nothing, that is, except for three favours that were owed to him. The first was a favour owed from a fisherman down in Agadir. The second was one owed by a doctor in Oujda. And the third, it was owed by a man up in Tangier.'

'But surely you can't call in a favour if the person it's owed to has died,' Blaine said.

'Of course you can,' Ghita replied. 'Or at least you can here in Morocco. This is a medieval country, you see – a place where the repayment of a favour is an almost sacred duty.'

'A duty of blood,' Saed added. 'The man in Tangier knows that. I found out that the cousin of his wife is related to a man who works as a guard at the prison. If I demand the favour to be repaid he will help. He has no choice.'

'Even if it's breaking the law?' asked Blaine.

'Of course. You see, repaying a favour... having the burden removed from a family's shoulders, is a great blessing.'

Saed reached over and touched Ghita's sleeve with his hand.

'I want to help you,' he said.

'But why?'

The boy grinned mischievously.

'Because when you have saved your father perhaps you will remember me.'

Ghita leaned forward and pressed her lips to the shoeshine boy's cheek.

'You may be filthy and rough on the outside, but you have a heart of gold,' she said.

The American rolled his eyes.

'How are you gonna get to the mountains?'

'You would have to drive,' said Saed.

'But you don't have a car.'

'I think I know where to get one,' Ghita said.

From: *Casablanca Blues*

Mittle-Mittle

THERE WAS ONCE a kingdom in the Horn of Africa where all the men were brave, and all the women were beautiful.

Surrounded by desert, it was a land of great abundance and verdure. The grass was the colour of crushed emeralds, the flowers dazzling pinks, reds and blues, and the air crystal clear.

At one end of the land there was a mountain capped all year round with blinding white snow and, at the other, a forest impenetrable and dark – the Forest of Empty Souls.

There was no king, because the people had found over centuries that they did better without a leader. The last king had passed away without issue, and it was then that the citizens decided they didn't have any need of a monarch at all.

When there was a matter to be dealt with or decided, they went to a pool in the palace, a pool filled with toads. And, with great reverence, they consulted the toads.

Although no one in the kingdom could speak the language of the toads, they found that the creatures seemed to understand what they were being asked. Through croaking and twitches of their wart-covered bodies, the amphibians managed to make their feelings known.

Now, in the kingdom there was a special shrine. There was no religion as such, yet the shrine was worshipped night and day, and revered like nothing else.

A thousand and one steps crafted from porphyry led up to the central chamber. Each morning and each night it was rinsed with tears gathered from the populace.

As there was no sadness, or very little indeed, the people grew a special kind of onion, the mere hint of which made their eyes stream with tears. Enormous fields of these onions were grown by the farmers, for the sole purpose of rinsing the steps of the sacred shrine. The women would take it in turns weeping into miniature silver buckets, which were taken ceremoniously to the steps at dusk and at dawn.

As for the shrine, the interior walls were fashioned from pure gold, embossed with the images of toads at play. Deep inside, beyond a golden screen of filigree, lay a simple chamber. And in the chamber was a plinth, on which stood a cedarwood box the colour of walnuts, all cracked with age.

No one in the kingdom had ever seen the contents of the box. It's not that they didn't want to, rather that they were so fearful that no one had ever dared to open it.

From time to time children, as they drifted to sleep, would ask their mothers what was in the shrine.

The answer was always the same:

'There is a box, my dear.'

'But what's in it?'

Every mother in the land always gave the same reply:

'Never you mind. Go to sleep now and leave it at that.'

One day, a boy of about eight or nine found that he couldn't stop thinking about the box.

His name was Mittle-Mittle, which meant 'good-hearted' in the language of the kingdom. He begged and begged, and he begged and begged, but his mother refused to reveal anything more than she knew – that in the sacred shrine was a box, a box the colour of walnuts, all cracked with age.

Disgruntled at getting a less than satisfactory answer to his question, Mittle-Mittle decided to venture to the shrine and have a look for himself.

The next morning, when all the other little boys were huddled over their desks in school, Mittle-Mittle slipped unnoticed through the streets, passed the Toad Palace, and scampered up the great long staircase, just as it had been deluged in a rinsing of fresh tears.

The guards didn't notice the boy because they wore special helmets which made seeing anything shorter than themselves very difficult indeed.

With care and on tiptoes, Mittle-Mittle zigzagged his way through the gold-walled chambers, until he came to the room in which the box was kept.

At that very moment, his mother was chopping onions and blinking into a silver bucket, quite unaware that her favourite son was up to no good. But the last thing on Mittle-Mittle's mind was his mother, and the part she played in the tradition of the land.

As he entered the chamber in which the box was kept, the boy wiped a hand down over his mouth and glanced around carefully, making certain he wasn't about to be caught. No one seemed to be watching, and so, very quietly, he crept forwards until he was standing beside the box.

The keyhole was in line with his lips.

Reaching up, he prised the lid open, his small fingers forcing the hinges apart.

He craned forwards, straining on tiptoes, holding his breath.

'Oh,' said Mittle-Mittle in a whisper. 'I see.'

A few inches away in the box, laid on a bed of dusty green felt, was a nail.

It was rusty, bent at one end, and appeared to be very old. Without thinking, Mittle-Mittle snatched up the nail.

Leaving the lid of the box wide open, he hurried away backwards, so that if anyone saw him they would imagine he was arriving rather than on his way out.

In his bedroom that night, Mittle-Mittle made a careful inspection of the nail. But, after a considerable amount of examination, even with a scratched magnifying glass, he came to the conclusion that there was nothing unusual about it at all.

As he regarded it again, his mother slipped in to kiss him goodnight. Her face was fraught with worry, her eyes red from weeping.

'A terrible thing has happened,' she said.

Mittle-Mittle asked her what.

'The sacred box in the sacred shrine has been opened, and its contents have been stolen! The entire kingdom is in disarray. Every home is being searched by the guards, and every woman is weeping a little extra, to rinse the sacred steps that have been so unpardonably defiled.'

'But how can the guards find what is missing if they don't know what was in the box in the first place?'

Mittle-Mittle's mother frowned.

'They will know,' she said decisively. 'Believe me, they will know.'

When his mother had tucked him in bed and was gone, the boy opened the window a crack. He was about to toss the nail out, when he had an idea. He had often heard his father talk of a wise man that lived in the dark, impenetrable Forest of Empty Souls – a wise man who wore an amulet made from a dodo's skull.

The wise man would know why there was an ordinary nail kept in the box.

Slipping on his clothes, Mittle-Mittle climbed through the window, the old nail clutched tight in his palm. He hurried through the empty streets until he was at the edge of town.

A little further, and he found himself at the forest.

Most other boys might have felt a pang of fear in their gut, but Mittle-Mittle wasn't fearful of anything at all. Slinking between the trees, he snaked his way towards the middle of the forest where he expected the wise man to live.

Meanwhile, in the town, the guards were searching from house to house, questioning one family after another. Eventually they arrived at Mittle-Mittle's home. The boy's father opened the door to them courteously, inviting them in. A moment later, their son's empty bed was discovered, the window open.

Mittle-Mittle's parents were dragged away to the cells.

Deep in the Forest of Empty Souls, an elderly man was huddled over a fire at the base of a towering green winter oak. With eyes closed, he was murmuring incantations, scribbling figures in the air with the tip of one finger.

Around his neck was an amulet fashioned from a dodo's skull.

Mittle-Mittle watched from a distance.

For the first time in his life, he sensed fear. It was not so much a fear of the wise man, as a fear of something he didn't understand. Why would the people of the land in which he lived keep an old rusty nail in a box, and protect it from one generation to the next?

Very slowly, with sure footsteps over moss, the boy approached the wise man. As he drew nearer, Mittle-Mittle could feel the heat of the flames on his face.

'Excuse me,' he said when he was close.

The wise man froze. He opened an eye. Then the other.

'And who are you?' he asked.

'I am Mittle-Mittle.'

'And what do you want?'

'I want to know why the people of our kingdom keep an old rusty nail in a box, guarding it day and night, and washing the steps to its shrine with tears.'

The boy held up the nail and, as he did so, the old man smiled, his teeth reflecting the firelight.

'Come and sit beside me,' he said, 'and I shall tell you.'

The boy sat down on the soft green moss. As soon as he was comfortable, the wise man began to talk...

TAHIR SHAH

The Tale of the Rusty Nail

THERE WAS ONCE a tyrannical emperor in Ethiopia who spent his days counting the sacks of treasure in his many vaults.

They were piled from floor to ceiling in rows of a hundred and one – each of them bursting with rubies and emeralds, diamonds and gold.

Each year, as his wealth doubled once and then again through taxes and foreign wars, the people grew eager for change. Their sons slaughtered in battle, their precious savings confiscated to satisfy their ruler's insatiable greed, they sought a secret way by which to end his run of tyranny.

The problem was that the emperor rarely left his palace, a vast marble structure twenty storeys high, set on the banks of the sprawling River Walaqa, a tributary of the Blue Nile. The kingdom had been plundered to construct the palace, and to fill its magazines with treasure. And, with such poverty surrounding him, the emperor had no interest in ever leaving the luxurious quarters of his home.

So, instead, he reclined in his gardens, or in his grand salons, and allowed his retinue of servants to drop peeled grapes into his mouth, one at a time.

Every so often the secret police caught a group of citizens conspiring against their emperor. The conspirators would be dragged away, hung, drawn and quartered in the main square.

Then their heads were skewered onto spikes as a warning to others.

Now, in this land there lived a small boy, about your age. He had never known his parents because they had been imprisoned in the Slate Tower, which lay on an island in the middle of the River Walaqa. Their crime was daring to question out loud why their emperor required so many sacks of loot when beyond his palace walls there wasn't enough food to eat. So the boy lived with his aunt, a fresh-faced woman with a limp, who was very good to him.

His name was Rintin, and he was the cleverest boy in his school. He never said much, but when he did say something others listened, because what he said tended to be very clever indeed.

One day, Rintin was on his way back from school when he saw his elderly neighbour in chains, being led towards the gallows in the main square. On that day there were so many others in line to be hanged that the neighbour was forced to crouch down and wait his turn.

Nimbly, Rintin hurried over to the old man, greeted him, and said:

'I will save you, I promise, I will save you.'

The wizened old man smiled at seeing the boy, then held up his wrists, weighed down with manacles.

'Keep away from me dear Rintin,' he said softly, 'before they take you too.'

The boy charged off into the back streets, and stopped at the first house he could find. A little girl was playing with her doll outside.

'Tell your parents to go to the palace gates at dusk,' he said. 'The emperor is going to make an announcement. Your parents must spread the word.'

Clutching her doll, the little girl ran into the house.

As for Rintin, he ran on through the streets, warning everyone he passed to gather at the palace at dusk. Once he had reached the end of the town, he made his way to the banks of the river.

With the palace itself so heavily guarded, the only way to observe it unnoticed was from the water.

Borrowing a canoe from a fisherman, he pushed out and paddled his way into the middle, halfway between the palace and the Slate Tower, in which his parents were imprisoned.

Turning his back on the island, Rintin looked carefully at the pleasure dome of the emperor. He scanned the walls, taking in every detail, questioning why it was as it was.

Now, the lad's cleverness derived from the fact that he observed very keenly. Almost nothing ever escaped his attention. He knew, for example, when a storm was approaching because he could sense the trembling of the leaves. And he could tell when his aunt was unhappy because her handkerchief smelled very faintly of salt from her tears.

Rintin's gaze moved over the blocks of marble, looking for gaps, or for an unguarded window amongst the sheering white walls. The stones were flush together, joined in a zigzag edge so that nothing could ever prise them apart.

All afternoon, the boy gazed at the palace.

As the shadows lengthened, he felt a pang of worry, after all the townspeople would be making their way to the gates to hear the announcement. No one would dare stay away, for the emperor was very strict indeed about announcements.

An hour before dusk, Rintin paddled the canoe a little closer to the wall, which was now deep in chill shadow. Approaching, he noticed something strange. Where the walls disappeared at the waterline, there was a knotted mesh of reeds.

The palace was, it seemed, constructed on a kind of giant woven raft, one made from bulrushes. It was incredible that such a mighty structure could sit securely as it did on a foundation so flimsy and feeble.

Scanning the zigzag lines between the blocks of stone, Rintin noticed that there was an unevenness near the waterline. A piece of marble had been wedged into a crack where the zigzag joins were broken, and a definite force was being exerted upon it. But stranger still was the fact that a fragment of wood, no bigger than a matchbox, had been hammered into place beside the sliver of marble.

The wood was held in place with a nail – a bent, brown, rusty nail.

Touching a finger to his chin in contemplation, Rintin made a series of calculations.

By his reckoning, the entire palace was being held by this single nail.

How extraordinary, he thought, that the emperor's mighty seat of power was so precariously in the balance, and all because a craftsman had cut a corner he imagined no one would ever spot.

Paddling his canoe over to the nail, Rintin knocked it up and down with his oar until it was loose. Then, taking a deep breath, he pulled it away from the wood.

Nothing happened.

Not at first, anyway.

A minute passed. And another. The boy cupped a hand to his right ear. He had heard something – a faintest undertone of sound. He gasped, grabbed the oar, and paddled away as fast as he could.

A moment later, there was a deafening noise as the zigzag joins began to part, and the palace began to fall.

Deep in his treasure vaults, the emperor was counting the sacks, ordering them to be rearranged in a new way.

All of a sudden he heard the sound of masonry collapsing in the distance.

'What's that?!' he thundered.

His vizier swiped a hand through the air and oozed reassurance.

'Surely it's nothing, Your Importantness,' he whispered unctuously. 'But I will…'

Before he had time to finish his sentence, the floor of the treasure vault disappeared clean away beneath them.

The vizier, the emperor, and all the precious treasure were plunged into the now choppy waters of the River Walaqa.

Spying their monarch struggling for his life, the guards fled, the palace nothing more than rubble around them.

With the sun touching the horizon, the townspeople flocked to the imperial gate.

Rintin clapped his hands and addressed them.

'You are free!' he yelled. 'And never again will you be prisoners!'

He held up the rusty nail, with a bend at one end.

'This nail is a symbol that even the worst despot can be brought down in the simplest way. The great power is power that hangs by a thread.'

The crowd cheered.

Then a wizened old man pushed to the front.

Rintin recognized him as his neighbour, saved from the gallows in the nick of time.

'This boy has saved us,' the man exclaimed, 'and so I vote that we make him our king!'

There were more cheers, and Rintin was carried at shoulder height through the streets. The emperor's launch took him across to the island where he was reunited with his parents.

In due course Rintin was indeed made the king and he ruled for many years.

He married the little girl with the doll, and had six sons, each one wiser and more handsome than the last.

On his desk he kept an orb, and a walnut-coloured box.

And in the box he kept the nail.

After a great many years, King Rintin breathed his last, his beloved queen and many sons clustered around his bed.

The royal family and their kingdom mourned the loss. And, according to his wishes, they buried their monarch in a simple grave on the island where the Slate Tower once stood.

In a letter left to his children, King Rintin decreed that the son with the keenest power of observation should follow him as ruler of the land.

'But how shall we decide which that is?' asked the queen.

The lord chamberlain, who was reading the letter aloud, motioned to the page.

'"The one of you who can glimpse a secret level in a story,' he read, 'will take my orb, my sacred wooden box, and my throne."'

There was a pause as the sons eyed each other anxiously. The eldest took a step forwards.

'Secret level,' he spluttered. 'Story… *what* story?!'

The lord chamberlain broke the wax seal on a second envelope, and removed several sheets of paper, written in the king's own hand.

'This story,' he said.

The six sons eyed one another again.

'Read it to us,' they all said at once.

And so the lord chamberlain did…

The Shop That Sold Truth

A LIFETIME AGO, in Upper Egypt, there lived a farmer and his wife.

They had very little money, and every month they grew a little more impoverished until, one day, the farmer could stand it no more.

'Tomorrow I am going to the town,' he said, 'where I am going to sell the last of our possessions, so that we can have one good meal before the landlord ousts us from his land.'

'But what will we do after that?' asked his wife.

'We will throw ourselves into the hands of fate,' the farmer replied.

And so the next day, he piled the kitchen table, the chairs, the bedstead and the pots and pans onto the cart, and pulled them himself into the town, a handful of miles away.

By dusk, all the possessions were sold, and the farmer had a pocket jingling with coins.

He was about to go to the market to buy some food to take home, when he noticed a rather grand shop at one corner of the town square. Not having seen it before, he approached it cautiously, and pressed his face up to the window.

The walls inside were lined with tall glass jars. Each one had a label but was quite empty of contents. His curiosity piqued, the farmer dusted himself down and pushed open the door.

The unfilled jars were a little larger than they had appeared from the outside, their labels written neatly in gold script. And it was the labels that caught the farmer's eye. Although he had left school well before his time, he had learned to read, and he read the labels one by one.

'Wisdom, Hope, Perception, Deceit, Truth, Goodwill, Remorse, Bravery, Melancholy...' he frowned and, as he did so, a hunchbacked salesclerk appeared.

'Can I help you, sir?' he enquired in an even tone.

The farmer jumped back.

'I noticed the jars through the window,' he spluttered, 'and was so intrigued that I simply had to come in.'

The clerk dusted a hair from his shoulder.

'And what, may I ask, was it that you found so intriguing?'

The farmer pointed to the empty jars.

'Those,' he said.

The hunchbacked clerk narrowed his eyes.

'And...?' he hissed. 'What is so strange about them?'

'Well, er, how can you sell Wisdom, or Truth... or whatever?' he said. 'The jars are empty. It's as plain as day.'

The clerk, who was growing impatient, cracked his knuckles.

'Whoever said that qualities had a colour or a texture?' he asked angrily.

'But whoever said they could be bought and sold?' the farmer replied.

'Who said they could not?'

The farmer blinked.

'I don't believe it.'

'Why not?'

'Because I fancy you're a trickster, who's set up shop to dupe God-fearing men like me.'

The clerk stepped over to the door and pushed it open.

'It was you who came in here uninvited,' he said calmly.

The farmer was about to stride out, but something caused him to pause.

He slid the tip of his tongue over his upper lip.

'You think I can't afford your wares,' he said. 'Well, I've got money.'

He pulled out a pocket full of coins.

'So what is it you would like to buy?' asked the clerk.

The farmer scanned an eye over the shelves.

'Well, it depends how much they cost,' he said.

'They are all priced differently and sold in small bottles of their own,' the clerk replied. 'The most expensive is Wisdom, and the least is Shyness.'

'Why would anyone want Shyness?' the farmer asked.

'You would be surprised, sir.'

'Well, for a handful of coins, could I get a selection? You know, so I can test some of them out.'

The clerk was about to refuse, when he was overcome with goodwill. He glanced up at the goodwill jar, fearing its stopper was loose.

'Very well,' he said, 'after all, I am about to close for the night.'

Five minutes later, the farmer found himself clutching a sackcloth bag in which were jangling six miniature bottles.

Just before he left the shop, the clerk gave a caution:

'Although they are magical,' he said, 'you have only purchased samples of my wares, and in this size the effect of each bottle lasts only a single day.'

It was dark by the time the farmer returned home. His wife was standing outside the shack and she was weeping.

'We can't go in,' she said. 'The landlord has thrown us out. I hope you made us enough money so that at least we can eat.'

Her husband pulled the sackcloth bag out from behind his back.

'I bought something far better than food,' he said.

His wife looked at him expectantly.

'I bought these little bottles.'

'We need more than liquid, we need *food*.'

'But they don't contain liquid.'

The farmer's eyes were wide.

'Then what's in them?' asked the woman, snatching one and holding it up to the moon.

'It's empty!' she scowled.

'They all are,' the farmer explained. 'And that's the point.'

The next thing the farmer knew, a clenched fist had hit him between the eyes. His wife's fury knew no bounds. As he came to his senses, he thought of something.

Picking up the little bottle that his wife had thrown on the ground, he uncorked it, and held the rim to his pursed lips. He felt something strange enter his mouth, something intangible and warm.

'You've ruined us,' said his wife, as she began to weep again.

The farmer stood up.

'My dear, dear woman,' he replied, 'please forgive me. I can never find the words to apologize enough. You deserve a far better man than I, and so I will take leave of you and return only when I have made something of myself.'

'Good riddance to you!' barked the old woman.

But her husband had already gone.

On the ground where he had been standing was a tiny bottle. Squinting, and holding it to the full moon as she had done before, she read the handwritten label – *Remorse*.

Within a day, the farmer had crossed the fields and reached the edge of the neighbouring town. He met a fisherman beside a stream, approached him and said:

'Hello friend, do forgive me for disturbing you. Oh, how very sorry I am. Truly, I really mean it.'

Struck by the stranger's politeness, the fisherman offered him some grilled fish for lunch. The two men became instant friends and, before he knew it, the farmer was invited to stay in the fisherman's home.

That night, he reflected on the day's events and how the course of his life had changed. His mind wandering, he opened the bag and pulled out the first bottle he could find.

The label read, *Bravery*.

'Hmmm,' thought the farmer to himself. 'I'd like to be brave.' And, without giving it too much thought at all, he prised out the cork and sucked down the bottle's contents.

That night, while the fisherman and his family slept, a band of thieves broke into the house, each one armed with a scimitar. They came in over the roof, and in through the windows, moving in complete silence.

Then they sprang.

The fisherman and his family were roused from their beds, tied up and relieved of all that they owned.

In the clamour of the attack, no one noticed the farmer sleeping in the kitchen beside the fire. Hearing a commotion, he crept stealthily into the sleeping quarters, armed with a cleaver. And, hardly knowing how he did it, he took the attackers by surprise.

Within less time than it takes to tell, he fought them all at once, and disarmed them all in a feat of unbridled bravery. Minutes later, the band of thieves lay dead, their bodies dismembered on the floor of the fisherman's home.

News of the farmer's bravery spread.

The corpses were taken into the town's main square, where they were hung up for all to see. A passer-by recognized them as the most feared bandits in the realm, with a handsome reward on their heads.

Before he knew it, the farmer was being received in the royal palace, where he was decorated by the king, and rewarded with six bags of gold. Hardly able to believe his luck, he bought an ornate carriage and fine clothes for himself.

Then he set off back to his village to be reunited with his wife.

Unaccustomed to luxury of any kind, the farmer ordered the coach driver to pull up at dusk on the banks of a brook. He selected a spot beneath a sprawling neem tree, protected from the wind by an outcrop of rocks.

'We will camp here for the night,' he said, 'and set off at dawn.'

The moon full above him, the farmer found himself unable to sleep. And, eventually, his mind turned to the little bottles he had left.

Opening his sackcloth bag, he removed the remaining bottles and held them up to the moon for light. But his water bottle had leaked some of its precious fluid and the writing on the labels had been smudged.

As much as he squinted, he was unable to read a word.

'I should open them all and release their contents into the air,' he thought aloud, 'after all, they could contain harmful elements.'

But something niggled at him and, before he could reason with himself, he had snatched one of the bottles out, pulled away the stopper, and drunk down its contents.

A few minutes passed and the farmer began to sense something. He could hear a distant sound, like the clatter of hooves galloping far away. He looked to the right, then the left, and realized that the sound was coming from the base of the neem tree.

He leant down, cupped a hand to his ear.

A procession of ants was marching across a root, exposed above the surface of the ground. The farmer watched as they made their way across a stretch of barren land beside the brook, and down a hole no wider than his thumb.

The bizarre thing was that he could hear them walking, and talking as well, and he could understand exactly what they said. He could hear the sound of fish, too, swimming through the nearby water, and a nest of magpies up in the highest branches of the tree.

But that was not all.

The farmer walked over to the coachman, who was asleep on the grass. Without quite knowing how, he knew that the man had an eye condition that would very soon make him blind. And he knew that the carriage he drove was stolen, the yellow lacquer having been painted over the red livery of the king.

With his heightened perception, the farmer felt truly alive, for the first time. He thought of all the possibilities, all the things he could do with such a gift.

But then something caught his attention.

The ants.

He overheard one complaining to another.

'What a nuisance it is that we have to dig this mine shaft,' said the first.

'And that there are these great big yellow blocks of metal hindering our way,' said the other.

'If only someone would move them for us,' the first replied.

Wasting no time, the farmer started digging.

Within an hour he had unearthed forty bars of gold, the pure metal glinting in the moon's light.

'I'm rich!' he exclaimed. 'Richer than in my wildest dreams!'

The coachman was woken by the farmer's outcry. He sat upright, rubbed his eyes, and screamed.

'I'm blind! I can't see a thing!'

Loading the treasure into the carriage, the farmer helped the old coachman aboard as well. Then, fearing that the people of his own town would recognize him as the impoverished farmer that he was, he rode on and on until he came to the next kingdom.

Once there, he rented a fine mansion for himself, found wealthy new friends, and set himself up as a member of the landed gentry.

As the weeks slipped away, and as his funds were invested, the farmer became the wealthiest man in the land.

Then, one morning, he remembered his wife.

In all the excitement of his new life he had quite forgotten about her or, rather, had suppressed all thought of her because he was having such a good time.

Changing back into less opulent clothing, he set off in a simple cart to find her.

A few days later, he found her in the town near to where their farm had stood. A few feet away from where she was squatting, hand outstretched, was the shop that had sold the farmer the glass bottles so many weeks before.

But the shop was abandoned, all the windows smashed, the door hanging off its hinges.

'Dear wife,' said the farmer, approaching the huddled figure. 'I have returned and, as I promised, I have made something of myself.'

The old woman glanced up, squinted, and slipped back into the shade. She was imagining things again.

'It's me, your husband!' cried the farmer.

Within a week or two, the couple were installed in their mansion. And as the days went by the farmer's wife grew increasingly used to the lavish lifestyle that instant wealth can bring. She spent a fortune on fine dresses for herself, and was soon bossing her husband around as she had always done.

As for himself, the farmer spent more and more of his time in leisure until, one morning, he remembered the three remaining bottles. He asked one of the servants where his old sackcloth bag had been kept. It was brought to him on a golden salver, rose petals sprinkled around the edges.

The farmer opened the bag and removed the bottles. The labels were far too smudged to read.

'Do I dare?' he asked himself.

There was the sound of his wife barking him orders from the salon downstairs. Grimacing, he summoned his courage, opened one of the bottles and quaffed down its contents.

As before, nothing happened at first.

The farmer's wife asked for a purse of gold, so that she might buy herself a jewel-encrusted necklace. Her husband opened his safe and was about to hand over the coins, when he felt a shiver down his spine.

'If I give her this money,' he thought to himself, 'she's going to ask for some more, and then even more, and very soon we'll be broke.'

So he put the money back in the safe and shook his head. His wife protested, but he walked through into another room, where he started thinking.

For the first time in his life, the farmer had clarity of thought, the kind of which he never imagined was possible. He could think of solutions to the most complex problems in science, in everyday life, and the arts.

On a single day – the day on which the *Wisdom* was effective – the farmer came up with solutions to a thousand things.

He worked out how to solve the kingdom's terrible water shortage, and where to mine the abundant deposits of gold. He settled marital disputes and invented new machines, designed a new city from the ground up, and cured the king of the illness that was about to claim his life.

Before he knew it, the kingdom was wealthier than any other, and the farmer was celebrated as a visionary of the rarest kind. Realizing that his people no longer wished him to lead them, the king abdicated, naming the farmer as his successor.

A little time passed, and the new king's initial genius quickly wore thin.

There were lines of people queuing around the palace, all waiting for an audience – for their king to provide a solution to their woes.

The farmer sent agents across the known world to find the shop clerk who had sold him the potions.

But each one came back empty-handed.

In a moment of desperation he reached into the bag and fished out one of the two last bottles. He had no idea what was in it, but felt sure it would give him the boost he so badly needed.

Unscrewing the stopper, he sucked down the invisible contents, and prepared for what was to come.

An hour passed and the farmer's wife – now the queen – shuffled in. She insisted on an increase in her allowance, and demanded a new crown.

The farmer king smiled tautly. Then, clapping his hands, he ordered the royal guards to take the queen to the tower.

'I have always despised you!' he exclaimed. 'And will now never have to listen to your moaning again!'

As the guards marched the queen away, the farmer king called his household staff to attention.

'I am doing away with you all,' he cried, 'because I know that you have been stealing from me, and are spying on me, and I hate every one of you!'

After that, he sent a message to the neighbouring king declaring war, on the grounds that the next kingdom was using too much air. And then he roamed the streets in his royal carriage, as his soldiers arrested every third man and woman for plotting against him.

A mutiny ensued.

By the end of the night, the farmer king had been overthrown by his people – all because he had drunk the miniature bottle once labelled *Deceit*.

Stripped of his medals and dressed in rags, he was taken to a small cell below the one in which his own wife was still imprisoned. The cell door was slammed, and the key turned in the lock.

The most wretched of all the cells, its walls were masked in dried blood and filth.

'They'll hang you at sunrise,' said the toothless jailer through the bars as he strode off.

The farmer king crouched down, put his head in his hands, and wept.

'That's enough noise!' bawled the jailer from a distance. 'Any more and I'll come in and thrash you!'

Wiping away his tears, the prisoner coaxed himself to be strong. But his pitiful situation was too much to take. The farmer was about to break down in tears again, when he remembered that around his waist was a belt into which the last miniature bottle had been sewn.

Taking a deep breath and squaring his shoulders feebly, he said to himself:

'Well, what could be worse than what's promised to me – a gallows at dawn?'

He unpicked the stitches, opened the bottle, and drank down its contents.

A little time slipped away, and the farmer found himself feeling quite good. In fact, given his circumstances, he felt marvellous, as if there was everything to live for.

Jumping to his feet, he began scoping out plans for the near future, enthused about the little time he had left. The last grains of sand may have been running through the hourglass, but each one gave rise for hope.

Scanning the grimy whitewashed walls of the cell, the farmer noticed something scribbled high up around the room, in the few inches where the walls and ceiling met. He had missed it before, while lying on the floor in a crumpled heap.

Peering up keenly, the farmer king turned pauper found himself reading what looked like a tale...

From: *Scorpion Soup*

Oculosis

One night, after a long day at Mount Sinai, the surgeon went home, put on his French linen pyjamas, and poured himself a glass of Hautes-Côtes de Beaune. Having taken a gulp and swilled the precious liquid around his mouth, he turned on the television.

After flicking channels for a moment, he reached BBC America. There was a special bulletin from the English countryside where oculosis had taken hold, and where poultry was now being slaughtered en masse.

A reporter was standing outside the Half Moon Public House in the market town of Shaftesbury. Amadeus Kaine recognized it at once. He had stayed nearby on honeymoon, in a thatched cottage off the high street. It was the one happy memory he had of being with Francine.

The reporter said that oculosis was spreading across Europe like a plague, and was now threatening hundreds of thousands of people. She likened it to the Black Death in the way it was reducing a functioning system to outright anarchy.

Switching the television off, Kaine changed back into his regular clothes and put on his overcoat. He was frustrated, his hands moving fast with the buttons and then with the leather laces of his brogues. The frustration arose from the

347

sense of grave responsibility. As he saw it, he was in a land of imbeciles, and was the one man alive with a functioning brain. Certain that oculosis could be treated without surgery, he was adamant that it was merely a matter of making the right connections.

Leave it to the masses though, and there wasn't a hope in hell.

Amadeus Kaine went downstairs. Greeting the doorman, he asked him about the vacation he was planning to take with his elderly wife, before sweeping out into the street. A minute later he was walking north on Park Avenue, his mind on one thing alone.

Green eyes.

The addict beneath Pont Alexandre III had for a short while changed his psychology in the most fundamental way. For a few fleeting hours he had been Einstein, or Aristotle, Da Vinci, Newton, Beethoven or Shakespeare – or the whole lot of them rolled into one.

But by the time he came to terms with the genius at his fingertips, the power was beginning to fade.

He knew it was wrong, but Kaine needed the power back.

Without it there was no hope of ever thrashing the scourge of oculosis. The human race would be resigned to living in darkness for eternity. It was a future that was no more than a few wretched steps away.

But where to find green eyes?

The eye surgeon had considered going online, making a date with a call girl, filtering the results by eye colour. It was an ingenious idea, but one which would have taken too long to set up.

He needed green eyes right away.

As for a preference in gender or age, he didn't really have one. He wasn't going to eat the eyes for some bizarre sexual turn-on, or for psychopathic thrills. His need was far more elemental. It was about the effect of certain amino acids on the mind.

All he could think about was the colour. The deeper the shade of green, the better.

In the left pocket of his overcoat was a small wooden box. His fingers caressed it as he walked. Hidden inside was a pair of curved slivers of glass. They had been the first he ever made, and were the only objects connected to eye surgery that Kaine kept in his apartment.

The streets were almost deserted.

Terrified by the thought of contracting oculosis, most New Yorkers had bolted themselves up at home. Dozens of stores had closed up or had employed armed security to guard the doors. A few had even gone so far as to supply their employees with ski masks and protective suits.

Turning right onto East 86th Street, Kaine was surprised to find the Fairway open for business as usual. The alternative supermarket was the one general source of food he trusted, although it carried next to nothing in obscure cuisine.

Outside, a couple of employees were packing up the fruit and veg. Both of them were sporting cheap plastic overalls and what appeared to be swimming goggles. They seemed drained and confused, and were huffing and puffing in the cold. Making his way past them slowly, the surgeon struggled to get a glimpse of the colour of their eyes.

Both had dark brown.

Striding on into the store, Kaine walked casually to the back. It was brighter there. He pretended to be searching for Marmite, a British brand of yeast extract. Three more sales staff helped him, all women with yet more brown eyes, all of them hidden behind identical swimming goggles.

Suddenly, he noticed a young man with a limp, pulling a shopping cart behind him.

Kaine looked around slowly.

Blue-grey eyes. He cursed. Damn New Yorkers, he thought, when you wanted them to deliver on something they always came up short.

For twenty minutes he stalked the aisles and counters. At last he spotted a woman who was mumbling to herself. She had mousy brown hair and was well below average height, with a pale face, reddish cheeks, and delightful olive-green eyes. She must have been thirty, but she looked younger.

Kaine glanced into her basket and frowned.

She had no idea of what to eat, he thought, despite the fact she was shopping at the Fairway. Still mumbling, she glanced at him as she passed.

'I see you like Marmite,' he said.

The woman blushed.

'I lived in England. I know it's an acquired taste, but I guess I acquired it, along with a love for English weather and hot buttered scones.'

'I adore it – Marmite, I mean,' said the doctor.

He took half a step forward so that the woman could see a large jar of it in his own basket. She was attracted to him – he could feel it by the way she leaned in and looked down.

'You have the most beautiful eyes,' he said.

'Thank you.'

'It must sound like a pickup line, but I assure you I'm not at the Fairway just before midnight on the prowl.' He let out half a laugh.

'You look as though you just got home from work.'

'That's right. I did.'

'What do you do?' she asked, as if hardly caring.

'I'm a surgeon, an eye surgeon.'

The woman appeared almost frightened.

'It's awful, what's happening with the illness… with Oc…'

'*Oculosis.*'

'Yes,' she paused, blushed again, and held out a small, pale hand.

'I'm Marcie,' she said.

'Good to meet you, Marcie. My name is Amadeus Kaine.'

Within an hour of leaving the Fairway, Marcie was dead, her neck snapped like that of the addict beneath Pont Alexandre. She hadn't suspected a thing, not even when the surgeon had nudged up close as they walked. Choosing his moment, he waited until they were under scaffolding between Lexington and Park Avenue. Then, quickly, he slipped behind her and separated the second and third cervical vertebrae.

Jerking his victim into a doorway beneath the scaffolding, he pulled on the yellow rubber washing-up gloves he had bought at the store, then sucked out Marcie's eyes and swallowed them whole. Removing the glass eyes from the box, he forced them nimbly into place. No one alive could quell ocular blood-flow or insert glass eyes as expertly as he.

Almost at once Amadeus Kaine could think with total clarity.

It was as though he had been a zombie just moments before. Churning away at lightning speed, his mind processed everything his eyes showed him.

He looked down at the smooth concrete beneath his feet, and wondered why the city didn't ripple it gently so that people wouldn't slip in the winter months. And the scaffolding poles – why weren't they covered with a phosphorescent paint so that they were more conspicuous in the dark? But there was no time to solve all New York's problems right then.

Kaine had problems of his own to deal with.

Quickly, he stuffed Marcie's purse into his coat pocket, and threw her body into the workmen's dumpster, covering it with rubble. Then, taking a cab down to Mount Sinai, he entered the hospital through a back door.

Once there, he made sure to ask the clerk on duty whether his ID had been found, so that he would be remembered in case an alibi were required.

By 2.25 a.m. he was back home, his mind racing as it had never raced before. Unable to sleep, he paced up and down counting numbers on his fingers and reciting the alphabet backwards. He was gripped by a sense of euphoria, as though the world were a paradise, a realm untouched by the shortcomings of man.

As for taking the life of another innocent victim, he didn't feel bad about it in the least. In truth, Kaine hardly gave it a passing thought. Marcie had made a small sacrifice, allowing him a burst of unmitigated genius – genius that could now be harnessed for the good of all mankind.

The eye surgeon spent the remainder of the night with his fingertips pressed together, sitting forward in a cabriole chair. He went back through every memory and printed word he had ever read – piecing together a treasure trail of clues that would help solve the riddle of viral oculosis.

The next morning, after no sleep, Kaine discarded Marcie's purse in a garbage bin near the East River, and then he made his way back down to Mount Sinai for another session of surgery.

Peering into the eyes of the morning's first patient, he suddenly had a flash of inspiration, and found himself regarding oculosis in an entirely new light. As the surgical team stood round awaiting orders, Amadeus Kaine burst out laughing.

'Is everything OK, doctor?' asked a nurse hesitantly.

'I don't believe it.'

'What?'

'That I've been so stupid, so damned blind.'

The nurse looked over at the anaesthetist and shrugged.

Kaine completed the operation in ten minutes, restoring the patient's sight in both eyes.

'We're done here,' he said, pulling away his mask.

'Already?'

'Yes, nurse, *already.*'

'But…'

'I thought of a more efficient method.'

'Just like that?'

'Yes, nurse, just like that.'

By lunchtime, Kaine's breakthrough was headline news on all the networks. The eye surgeon was mobbed as he left Mount Sinai that afternoon, a swarm of reporters rushing up with microphones. Standing just outside the hospital, he was immediately engulfed.

'Is it true that you've beaten oculosis, doctor?' shouted a reporter in a Mexican accent.

'Is oculosis a thing of the past?' yelled another.

Kaine pinched a thumb and forefinger to the cuff-link on his right wrist and took a sharp breath.

'Don't jump to conclusions,' he said. 'All I've done is to develop a kind of shortcut treatment.'

'What does it mean for all the sufferers across America?'

'It means that other surgeons can use the technique and make a real difference.'

A journalist pushed his way to the front. He was wearing an old raincoat and a trilby, and had a digital recorder in his hand.

'Can you tell readers of the *New York Times* why oculosis struck?'

Kaine held out a hand.

'I believe that this disease is just the first in a multitude of afflictions that will be visited on the American population in the coming decades,' he said.

'But why us? Is it related to the War on Terror? Is it a new threat dreamt up by al-Qaeda?'

'Look at us,' shouted Amadeus Kaine. 'We live in a mechanized, industrialized society. We use machines to do everything, and we think that we can create food by the same mass industrialization. It's lunacy. We've become detached from the earth of our ancestors, and oculosis is nature reminding us of that.'

Early that evening, Kaine went to his office and leafed through the pile of unopened mail. He couldn't imagine going back to the old routine of neurotic VIP patients and despotic dictators with their feeble anxieties and invented woes. They were sapping his strength, and wasting a brilliant career.

He turned on the lights in the lab and checked his stock of glass rods. Mrs. Phelps might have driven him half mad, but she was good at keeping stock levels in order. There must have been enough glass to make fifty glass eyes, with pigments for any imaginable shade of iris.

Removing his jacket, the surgeon swapped it for his old lab coat. Then he set about conjuring the most perfect pair of glass eyes. Choosing the colour with care, a delicate Limoges blue, he set to work warming the gather under the flame.

Any colour would have been fine, so long as it wasn't green.

At 9.20 p.m. the surgeon slept for three hours, waking in a calm, rested frame of mind. The effect of Marcie's eyes was already on the wane. It was as though he was building up a kind of tolerance. He thought back to the first human eye, the one in the very first pie, and how long its effect had lasted.

As Kaine pondered it, there was a distinct possibility that green eyes had a far shorter impact than other colours, but they released such a charge of enlightenment that they were worth the extra trouble.

Soon after midnight, he placed the newly made glass eyes, a pair of surgical gloves, and a Kaine Excisor in a dark-blue daypack. Then he turned off the lights and made his way down to the street.

For the next three hours he roamed Manhattan, dodging the vigilante gangs that were now prowling the streets.

Buoyed by adrenalin, he felt strangely light-headed. At the same time he saw the world around him with an astonishing sense of clarity.

There were flashbacks, too.

He could remember climbing trees down in Brooklyn with Bill McMarsh, and chugging down a bottle of stolen whisky with him in Central Park. How old were they then? He squinted into the memory – fourteen, fifteen?

He walked northward on Park Avenue until he reached 125th Street. There were vigilantes everywhere, battling the legions of petty thieves and muggers. The pungent stink of oily smoke from burning cars hung low over the streets, and the ubiquitous squeal of car alarms was punctuated from time to time by hysterical screams.

Amadeus Kaine turned left and hurried down Martin Luther King Jr. Boulevard. In his mind he was counting the squares of a chessboard, multiplying each one by six and a half. As he did so, he found himself sucked deep into another world, a world that had become his reality.

In the dozens of blocks that passed beneath his feet, he registered almost nothing at all. He was normally so utterly fastidious, such a connoisseur of the insignificant. But on the night of the long walk north it was memory that constructed the architecture of his thoughts.

He thought about his mother and his father.

They had been good people – well-mannered and quite unnecessarily kind. But Kaine had never really understood them. Given good educations and sufficient resources, neither had bothered to push themselves, to excel. They had been mediocre people. And the one thing the eye surgeon despised was mediocrity. Most of all, it angered the son that the parents had not had obituaries when they died.

In his mind, every man and woman over thirty should aspire to have a long obituary – preferably in the *New York Times*. Not to be featured in its hallowed pages was, in his mind, to be a loser, a wretched and humiliated subject of contempt.

It was like having never lived at all.

As he walked, Kaine remembered reading of an Afghan family in which, at birth, a child's name was added in pencil to the family tree. Only if that infant achieved real success in adulthood was the name over-written in ink. If he was a disappointment, the name was quietly erased from the lineage and his existence was forgotten.

Amadeus Kaine crossed Second Avenue and cursed the mediocrity of it all. There was nothing of any merit for dozens of blocks, only wastrels and profligates. Consuming their eyes was certainly no loss.

As he walked, he considered how he was doing humanity a grand service. Through his own inimitable brand of genius he had discovered a kind of portal to a new existence. It was one that he imagined must have been known to the ancients, but had been lost knowledge for centuries. Through a stroke of luck, revealed in part by the deranged antics of the Supreme Leader Vladimir Drusnev, he had happened upon the one hope left. Without it, mankind was surely destined for a miserable future, one of darkness and futility.

Thanking the universe for sending him to the supreme leader, Kaine began counting again. This time it was multiples of nine. Very soon he had passed five thousand. Then, all of a sudden, he spotted a large convenience store across the street. A towering sentry stood to the left of the door. Stretched between his hands was the shaft of an axe, and over his face was a wool balaclava.

Doing his best to nod a greeting, Kaine pushed past into the store, the daypack slung casually over his shoulder.

Inside it was bright, with security cameras in every corner. The back area was devoted to a large display of hard liquor, arranged in a kind of cage, along with the cigarettes and the sales clerk. He had an angry face that seemed to express how sick he was of working nights in what wasn't far off a war zone.

He watched the eye surgeon keenly as he moved up and down the aisles.

'You gonna buy somethin'?!' he yelled.

'I'm looking,' said Kaine.

'What for?'

'For a particular product.'

'What?!'

'It's got a greenish cover.'

The clerk screwed up his face and jerked a thumb towards the door.

'Get out of here!'

Kaine felt his back warm with fury, but he coaxed himself to stay calm. He made his way past the freezer packed with ready meals and was soon at the door. Pushing it open a little wider than he had needed to do, he made way for a wino on his way in. Reeling from side to side, the wino found that the rectangular doorway posed him a severe spatial challenge.

In the fraction of a second as the drunk moved from darkness into the bright fluorescent interior, Kaine looked into his eyes.

He couldn't believe it.

Another stroke of luck.

Dilated from drink, the irises were a deep moss-green.

The doctor went out and waited across the street. No one entered or exited the store for fifteen minutes. Squinting from the shadows, he could see the drunk chit-chatting to the clerk, as though they were friends.

Another five minutes slipped by, and the wino lurched out through the door, past the guard. Under his arm was an oversized brown paper bag. Swaying down the street, he paused to steady himself against a wall. Then he threw up before continuing a little faster in the direction of the Harlem River Park.

Amadeus Kaine followed at a discreet distance.

He had not been to the park before. It was an agreeable enough place and, despite the darkness, the half-moon gave satisfactory light. Gradually, it broke through an oval aperture in the clouds.

Dr. Kaine couldn't get over his good fortune. After all, only two per cent of the American population had green eyes. But, as he pondered it, perhaps it wasn't luck at all.

He had begun to believe that it was through a heightened sensitivity, as much as by luck alone, that he had encountered the drunk. Turning the idea around in his mind, he realized that he had known the man had green eyes even before he had set eyes on his face. He had sensed their existence instinctively, in the same way that menstruating women have been known to sense the existence of snakes.

The drunk flopped down on the first bench he came to, screwed off the top of the vodka bottle, and put the rim to his parched lips. He took a good long gulp, then another, and a third. He burped, coughed, and spat into the dark.

The surgeon moved in slowly, covering the space between himself and the bench with measured circumspection. He didn't want to rush things. Experience had taught him that drunks react unfavourably to quick movement. They can't process speed.

Sliding forward in a kind of slow-mo, Kaine reeled about as if also drunk. It was a plan designed to put the wino at ease.

'Good evening to ya!' said the man, a veil of the Emerald Isle shadowing his words.

'Hello, how are you?' said the doctor.

'Not bad, meself. Missing home and just out for a little wander.'

'You're from…'

'From Galway – from out west.'

'A fine part of the world,' said Kaine. 'Land of Poitin.'

'You know the Emerald Nectar?'

'Oh, yes, had it when I was travelling through Connemara.'

'You've been to Connemara?'

The surgeon looked at the drunk, his eyes locking onto his.

'Oh yes,' he said in a calm, even voice. 'I know it quite well.'

The wino held the bottle in Kaine's direction.

'Go on, have a sip,' he said.

'I would, but I think I saw a cop over there.'

The drunk Irishman jerked upright, as though someone had plugged him into an electrical socket.

'Where? Where is 'e then?'

'I saw him heading this way,' Kaine said. 'I know, why don't we go over there into the trees? We can have a nice little drink there. What do you think?'

'Yes!' exclaimed the drunk mischievously. 'A splendid idea!'

The eye surgeon thrust a hand under the man's arm and guided him off the bench and into the darkness. Within a minute or two they were standing between a young elm tree and a bush. Again, the wino offered the bottle's rim. And this time, Kaine took a swig. He choked.

'That's good stuff,' he said.

'I'd say so meself,' whispered the drunk.

And they were the last words he ever said.

In the privacy of the park, Kaine used his Excisor to suck out the Irishman's eyes, having broken his neck. He was salivating heavily but he forced himself to wait. Inspired by his victim's delight in alcohol, he had the idea of enjoying the eyes with a little aperitif.

Stowing them in his little wooden box, and positioning the glass prosthetics in the Irishman's face, Kaine pushed the body as forcefully as he could into the bush. It made very little sound as it went.

Then, congratulating himself, the eye surgeon retreated to the comfort of his apartment. He walked ten blocks south, down to 119th Street with Lexington. And from there he took a cab to the Upper East Side. It amazed him that in a city collapsing from the effect of oculosis, yellow cabs were still running.

By the time the driver pulled over just north of 775 Park Avenue, Kaine was hyperventilating, shaking, babbling, like an opium addict chasing the dragon. The last thing he wanted was to make a clumsy entrance into the prestigious address, and so he stood outside for more than a minute composing himself.

Relaxing his back muscles, he whipped out his mobile phone. It may have been the middle of the night, but everyone knew him to be an important surgeon – one who had just had a breakthrough in the war against oculosis.

Pressing the phone to his cheek, he hurried through the lobby, giving advice to an imaginary surgeon on the other end.

The doorman looked up from his newspaper and nodded.

Two minutes later Kaine was inside his apartment up on the sixth floor. Removing his overcoat and brogues, he put on a Prelude by Bach, and washed his hands three times, with different soaps.

Then, and only then, did he take out a bottle of Armagnac. It was a fine one, from the house of Nismes-Delclou – the 1905 vintage. He had kept it for years, imagining it with a prune and hare pie. But why save it any longer, now that the perfect hors d'oeuvre was about to be served?

Pouring a little of the amber liqueur, he moved it around the sides of the glass, breathing it in. But didn't taste it. Not yet. He wanted the little snack to be perfect in every way.

In the kitchen he transferred the green eyes onto a silver saucer. He had bought it in a Prague flea market a decade before. They looked serene there, as though the metal receptacle had been awaiting them all its life.

Kaine wondered whether the eyes ought to be warmed. He considered poaching them, or heating them gently in the oven. No, no – heat would damage the delicate capillaries. And besides, he couldn't wait.

He speed-counted to nine hundred in multiples of three.

Taking the silver dish through into the sitting room, he slid it onto the coffee table. Then he placed the glass in front of it and a little to the right.

He counted to sixty.

Unable to wait a moment longer, he licked his lips and ate the eyes one at a time, before taking a long, satisfying sip of Armagnac.

Leaning back in his chair, the surgeon allowed the sense of ecstasy to cascade over him. It was like being baptized in the waters of immortality, or being pulled into the bosom of nature.

How could he ever be satisfied by the food of mortals again?

From: *Eye Spy*

The Garuda Mask

THE CITATION TOUCHED down at Namlea Airport on Buru Island at 6.29 p.m. the next day. After the luggage had been unloaded, Will consulted the CODEX. The machine hadn't yet provided a clue about the final component.

'We've come all this way,' he said vacantly, 'and I have no idea why.'

'Have you tried BURU?' suggested Emma.

'Yeah, but it didn't work.'

Chaudhury cleared his throat,

'Might I suggest CAVIAR?'

Tapping in the word, Will shook his head.

In her pocket, Emma's fingers fondled the rosary.

'Alina, try A-L-I-N-A,' she whispered.

As soon as the name was entered, the CODEX's mechanism came alive.

The display showed a grid reference and the word:

G-A-R-U-D-A-M-A-S-K.

Following the coordinates, they arrived next morning at a desolate beach on the southern coast of Buru Island. The sand was pure white, rough to the touch and peppered with fragments of coral-pink seashell.

Fifty yards from the waves, separated by a perfect beach, lay the jungle. Will could hear it loud and clear, a cacophony of birdsong and vibrating insect wings.

Their bare feet disappearing into the sand as they walked, the three travellers made their way down to the water's edge.

Will looked out to sea, paused, and got down on his knees, Emma and Chaudhury standing behind him. Opening the CODEX, he observed the display. Then he checked the iPhone and, after it, Hannibal's cloth-backed map.

'Think I've made a mistake,' he said. 'The grid reference isn't here on the beach.'

'Then where is it?' asked Emma.

Will motioned to the water.

'About two miles that way.'

'Perhaps we ought to double check it, sir,' urged Chaudhury.

'Have already – twice.'

'Hannibal must have got his bearings off,' said Emma.

She looked at the others, realizing how unlikely that would be.

As the three of them stood there, staring out at the waves, a hollowed-out wooden canoe made its way silently around the cove. Two men were paddling in time with each other, the sweat on their bare shoulders glistening, home-made oars in their hands.

One of them looked like a local. He was thin and sinewy, his body the product of its environment. The other was a foreigner – as out of place as his companion was at ease. Balding, he had wire-rimmed glasses, and a thick meaty body all covered in sores.

Will, Emma and Chaudhury watched as the pair jumped out in the shallows and rammed the canoe up onto the sand.

Reaching back into the canoe, the local pulled out half a dozen fish, hooked together at the mouth. As soon as he spotted other people, the foreigner made his way over to where they were standing.

'Can't remember the last time I saw gringos down here!' he called, his voice a heavy southern drawl. 'You here for big game fishing?'

Will introduced himself.

'Not exactly,' he said.

'Frank Pittzer, with a double "T". Happy to show you around, or help you get a boat.'

'That's good of you,' said Emma.

'If you can keep up you're welcome for a cocktail.'

'Where's the bar?'

Pittzer jabbed a thumb at the undergrowth.

'In there. 'Bout three miles.'

'Is there a hotel?'

'*Hotel?* You crazy?! I live with the tribe.'

'*Tribe?*' echoed Chaudhury dispiritedly.

'That's right. The Garuda.'

Pittzer's home was a shack he had built himself from thick staves of black Java bamboo, dried palm fronds laid on top. It was offset from the centre of the village, and had an improvised terrace tacked onto the front.

'I'm an anthropologist by trade,' he said, pouring bamboo cups of home-brew. 'Been here three years now.'

'What're you researching?'

'The Garuda customs.'

'And do they have any curious ones?' asked Emma. 'You know, any freaky stuff…?'

'They have sin-eaters,' said Pittzer, 'and you don't get much freakier than that.'

'What are they?'

'In every village there's the shaman who'll swallow the sins of the guilty… for a price.'

'How does that work?'

'Means you can swear, fornicate, drink till you drop, or even kill – and have your sins completely absolved. Hell, it's even better than a confession booth in church.'

'I could imagine that catching on back home,' said Will.

Pittzer pointed to a hunched figure walking between a nearby row of huts. His face was peppered in pustules, the skin on his back gnarled and burned. His right hand was missing entirely.

'That's him,' he said.

'Jesus Christ.'

'All that from swallowing a few sins?'

Pittzer slugged down a cup of home-made firewater and burped.

'Who said it was a few sins?' he said.

In the silence which followed, Will tried to work out why Hannibal had sent them to a remote island in a forgotten archipelago.

'Do they believe in God?' he asked all of a sudden.

'They put their faith in Mar-ram-ap.'

'What's that?'

'The Great Being, the Balance of the World.'

'Do they worship him?'

'It's beyond worship,' said Pittzer. 'The Garuda are utterly preoccupied with him. They regard him as their communal father, the husband to their wives, their teacher, priest – an all-powerful deity.'

'How do they worship him?'

'They believe he's around them, but they feel his presence most strongly in the temple at Mulam-ya.'

'Where's that?'

'That way... up in the hinterland.'

Pittzer poured another round of drinks.

'Most people have never been to the temple, and certainly never inside.'

'Why not?'

'Because it's filled with giant hornets. Get stung and even the sin-eater can't help you.'

'So what do they do if they can't worship at the temple?'

'They worship an icon instead – say it represents the power of Mar-ram-ap. You find it everywhere in the village: carved into the doors, on the altars in homes, tattooed on chests and backs.'

'How does it look?'

'It's kind of rectangular, and almost looks like a monogram of an F and an H.' Pittzer pulled back his sleeve. 'Got one done as a way of blending in.'

As soon as Will saw the symbol, he knew they were in the right place. When Pittzer stepped out to greet the tribal chief, Will leaned over to Emma.

'Not an F and an H, but an H and an F,' he said.

*

1925

Laid out on the floor of a grand longhouse, the building camouflaged in dense foliage, was a banquet fit for a god.

There were roasted piglets, giant-sized lobsters, grilled Borneo shark, and banana platter leaves adorned with exotic fruit – papaya, mangosteen and rambutan.

Seated on a carved wooden throne looking down at it all with disinterest, was Hannibal. He was wearing a feather headdress, his body smeared in war-paint.

A scantily clad maiden scooped out the eye of the shark and dropped it into his mouth. At the same moment, a second maiden entered the longhouse and set about massaging the explorer's shoulders.

All the while, members of the tribe trooped past the longhouse, bowing down as they neared the door. Some of them bore gifts of food, others offered simple objects whittled from coconut shells.

When Hannibal could eat no more, the remains of the feast were bustled away, to be distributed among the destitute.

As soon as the last platter had gone, a straight-backed man ascended the steps into the longhouse. He was barefoot, wearing what appeared to have once been tweed trousers, his chest clothed in a fibrous shirt.

'The chief has requested the honour of an audience with you, sir.'

Hannibal opened one eye, yawned, and pulled himself upright.

'Very well, send him in, Chaudhury.'

Cowering, a tribal warrior crawled into the longhouse, his face a mask of worry. So fearful was he of the Englishman, that he dared not make eye contact with him.

Reclining back on his throne, Hannibal greeted the chief in the Garuda tongue and motioned for him to approach. The tribal chief crouched low on the floor, a short distance from the base of the throne.

As was the tradition, silence prevailed until the Mar-ram-ap, the Great Being, was ready for the palaver to begin.

'Yes, my chief,' Hannibal said at length in Garuda. 'What is your concern?'

Averting his eyes, his face flushed with fear, the chief replied:

'Oh Great Being, Exalted One, forgive me for troubling you with the trepidations of mortal men, but there is a matter I wish to address.'

Hannibal Fogg gazed listlessly out at the jungle.

'Speak!'

Cowering like a dog kicked hard in the belly, the chief stammered:

'Oh Supreme One, in the time of the ancestors, when the ocean swallowed our world, we moved to higher ground. And now, there have been omens that the Great Wave will once again devour us.'

Hannibal listened, his face expressionless. After all, it would not have been appropriate for a deity to show emotion.

After a prolonged hush, he asked what exact omens had been seen in the village.

The chief's eyes widened with terror.

'A pig was born without any feet,' he said, 'and a chicken was found to have two hearts.'

The Great Being remained remote and emotionless. Eventually he replied in a deep voice:

'To protect against the danger,' he said, 'you will build a temple in the hinterland according to precise plans which shall be provided. One single deviation and...'

The chief looked up, making eye contact with the Great Being for the very first time. Such was his sense of anticipation that his heart missed a beat.

'...and the end of the world shall befall you!' boomed Hannibal Fogg.

*

Pittzer led the way through the jungle into the island's hinterland, his machete chopping vines and foliage as he went.

Will, Emma and Chaudhury followed behind in single file, moving clumsily through the tangled undergrowth.

It took two more hours to reach the rocky promontory on which the temple had been built.

There was a sense life had stood still there for decades, since the stone blocks had been heaved up from the makeshift quarry below.

By the time they reached the sanctuary, they were all drenched in perspiration, their backs covered in sweat beads. Climbing up onto the outcrop, they got a clear view over the jungle and out to sea.

Pittzer halted short of the temple itself – which was another thirty feet up a sheering granite bluff.

'This is where I leave you,' he said.

'Are you frightened?'

'You bet I am,' the anthropologist crowed. 'This is forbidden ground. Don't forget,' he said, turning, 'it's protected by hornets.'

Will touched Emma on the shoulder.

'You and Chaudhury go back with him,' he said. 'I'm doing this one alone.'

'Are you crazy? Of course we're coming!'

'I'm immune to insect stings,' Will explained. 'Don't know why, but I am.'

Emma sighed.

'I'm sure we'll be fine.'

'No,' said Will firmly. 'You've both gotta leave me. I'll see you back at the village when I'm done.'

Leaning forward, Emma hugged him, crushing his ribs.

'You take care,' she said.

'Holler if you need us, sir,' added Chaudhury.

A minute or two later, Will's boots were searching for footholds among the rocks, his fingers digging into leverage points as he scaled the bluff.

The humidity didn't make the task any easier. Stifling his breathing, it caused his head to spin. He got a flash of his great-aunts sitting in their comfy chairs back in Oakland, breathing in the scent of honeysuckle. Then, pulling himself up the last few feet, he saw his dorm room in SFSU. He had almost forgotten the life left far behind.

Cloaked in a screen of palms, the temple's ash-grey walls were overgrown in vines. Twisted and contorted, they doubled back on themselves – layers upon layers. A great monument of stone, the construction must have been fifty feet high. The rear was lost in foliage, the front bathed in stems of yellow and red heliconia flowers.

Cautiously, Will made his way towards the portal.

Set in the middle, at chest height, was the sacred sign of the Garuda tribe – a symbol known to him as the monogram of Hannibal Fogg.

A little lower down, offset to the side, was a second symbol: a rectangular box bisected by a line – the Egyptian hieroglyph for 'house'.

Glancing at the back of his hand, Will looked at the lapis lazuli ring Hannibal had left him. Working out what to do, he nudged it to the hieroglyph on the door.

Nothing happened at first...

But then, very gradually, the great portal began to draw back, against a rasping sound of stone on stone.

Wedging a rock in place so that the door could not be sealed behind him, Will stepped inside.

The temple had a long, tapered hall, a wooden roof and polished stone floor. At the narrow end was a raised altar, crafted from a vast slab of pumice.

But it was the walls which caught Will's attention.

Set into them, on either side of the nave, was a series of impressive stained glass windows, through which jungle sunlight streamed.

Moving down the nave, Will took in the scenes one at a time.

The first depicted a church – not in the jungle but lodged at the top of a precipice. Beside it was a double helix: the Ladder of Mithras. The next window showed the Hands of God, set against a backdrop of human symbolism. The third portrayed the Tumi dagger of the Incas and, the fourth, the Orisha Stone.

Will turned to the opposite side of the nave, where the symbols continued.

As he stepped over to focus on the detail of the Prayer Wheel of Kublai Khan, the temple filled with butterflies – thousands of them, cascading out from fissures in the walls.

Lost in a blizzard of multi-coloured wings, Will caught a glimpse of the blue diamond depicted in stained glass.

Beyond it was a last panel.

Surrounded by Prussian-blue waves was a mask fashioned in the shape of a magnificent bird.

Another step forward and the butterflies vanished.

Approaching the altar, Will wondered whether they had existed at all.

Ascending a flight of white marble steps, he reached the altar itself.

Lying on the surface of the volcanic rock was a cylindrical tube, crafted from silver.

Taking it in both hands, Will twisted it, scrutinizing the strange repeating pattern etched into the surface. For some reason it reminded him of his parents' funeral, and of the first time he had looked into Emma's eyes.

Prising off the end, he found a letter.

It was written in English in a familiar hand.

> *My dear William, were there more time, I would regale you with tales of how, by strange coincidence, I have become regarded as a deity in the eyes of the Garuda tribe.*
>
> *But, alas, time is of the essence.*
>
> *I must ask you to read the directions on the reverse of this letter only once you have fled this shrine.*
>
> *Leave at once!*

The reason is simple: to prevent the wrong person from appropriating this amulet in the decades that separate us, the tribesmen down in the village believe – quite rightly – that, by entering the Temple of the Great Being Mar-ram-ap, they will release a swarm of Vespa mandarinina, *the giant Asian hornet.*

Although wary of the fact that, like all males of our line, you will most likely be immune to their sting, I would imagine that encountering the swarm would be exceedingly unpleasant.

By the time you have spent a little time regarding the artwork between here and the door, opened this cylindrical container and read thus far, the hornets will have woken from their slumber.

So, grasp the letter, and run like the wind!
Affectionately yours,
Hannibal

Will's ears filled with the sound of insect wings.

Not a drowsy summer meadow bumble-bee buzzing, but a ferocious orchestra of raw terror.

He swivelled round.

Careering at him from all directions were tens of thousands of giant hornets, the size of golf balls. The temple was filled with them.

Overcome with a sense of panic, Will tossed the cylinder to the floor, grabbed the letter and fled.

The hornets followed.

He scrambled back down the rocks into the undergrowth, through the twisting vines and over fallen trees. Tripping, regaining his balance, charging, arms flailing.

The buzzing grew louder.

And louder.

Then, as he clambered over a tree stump, the first of the hornets made contact with his flesh.

It was like being slugged with a cricket bat. The first sting was quickly followed by another… and another… and by twenty more. He screamed out in pain as he ran.

Miraculously, the swarm vanished.

His head twitching left and right in shock, Will crumpled into a ball at the foot of a coconut palm.

A full hour passed before his breathing calmed.

Once near the village, he pulled out the letter, turned it over, and read:

> *I do hope the suffering was not too terrible, William. As you have no doubt already learned, there was once a city located a little due south of the beach, submerged by an earthquake in antiquity. The ruins lie deep under the ocean. Despite numerous attempts, and having employed my own aquatic breathing mechanism, I have been unable to dive down to a sufficient depth. My efforts have been*

hampered by toxic levels of hydrogen sulphide, released from the sea floor by volcanic action.

If my calculations are correct, there will be a small window of time in which the sacred Garuda Mask may be retrieved from the seabed. The ocean will be drawn, allowing approximately 21 minutes and 15 seconds to enter the submerged city, retrieve the mask, and make an escape, before the ruins are destroyed forever by the full force of a tsunami.

As ever, I have attempted to pave the way with a little preparation, but much rests on your own skill, William.

The experience you have gained thus far should, I hope, stand you in good stead for this, the greatest challenge of all. There is one last piece of equipment I am sending you. Set the CODEX to the saddest date you know and follow the instructions.

HGF

At dawn next morning, Frank Pittzer left his shack armed with a machete.

He strode off into the jungle. To anyone who might have seen him it would have appeared he was heading off for the call of nature. But tucked under his shirt was an Iridium satellite phone.

Ducking down behind a tree, he switched it on and waited for the unit to fire up. Eventually, the screen came alive, its yellowy-green display reflecting over Pittzer's face. Selecting a number from the contacts list, he flipped up the antenna and waited for the satellites to log on.

A minute later he was connected with a secretive agency in the Balkans, with an enduring preoccupation with the Alexander Mechanism and Hannibal Fogg.

'Code reference?' asked a female operator.

'Nine-two-four-Alpha-Delta-Foxtrot.'

'Confirm: Nine-two-four-Alpha-Delta-Foxtrot.'

'Code reference confirmed.'

'Setting code?'

'GARUDA: that's Golf-Alpha-Romeo-Uniform-Delta-Alpha.'

The operator repeated the code word.

'Setting code confirmed.'

'Thank you, Garuda, I shall connect you now...'

Will stood near the water, bare feet sinking into the wet sand. He had been there for an hour, eyes on the horizon.

'So do I just wait until the Red Sea parts?' he said brusquely when Emma came over.

'Frank's grilled some fish with Chaudhury. Come join us,' she said.

'But what if the water rolls back? I've got to be ready.'

Putting her arm around Will's shoulder, Emma twirled him one-eighty to face the trees.

'He'd have sent you a sign.'

'How can you be so sure?'

Emma did a double take.

'We're talking about Hannibal Fogg, are we not?'

Pittzer skewered a chunk of sea bream and dropped it onto a banana leaf.

'It's called *ikan panggang*. Watch out for the bones, they're like needles.'

'Thanks.'

'How 'bout you…?'

'*Chaudhury*.'

'Don't you have a first name?'

'Everyone just calls him "Chaudhury",' said Will.

Pittzer grinned.

'Doesn't he have a tongue of his own?'

The manservant licked his upper lip timidly.

'My first name… it's Mihir.'

'Well, Mihir, it's time you lightened up, let your hair down.'

Chaudhury looked over at Will, then at Pittzer.

'I think that might be a little inappropriate,' he said stiffly.

'Tell me, Frank,' Will asked, 'have you ever heard of the Garuda Mask?'

Pittzer looked up.

'Sure I have. The tribe are obsessed with it.'

'What do they say?'

'That it's made from dark green jade, and that it was worn by the King of the Underworld.' He paused, took a bite of fish, and added: 'They believe it's conjured from what they call water magic.'

'Meaning?'

'Meaning it can bring the dead back to life.'

'Where is it?' asked Emma.

'Out there somewhere – under the waves.'

'In the ocean?'

Pittzer skewered another chunk of sea bream.

'In the city under the waves,' he said.

That evening, Will sat alone, away from the others, trying to make sense of all the loose ends. Above him, the stars were more dazzling than on any night he could remember, millions and millions of them, like salt sprinkled over a blackboard.

He thought about his great-aunts, and the way they quarrelled about nothing at all. And he thought about the woman he had seen mugged on Market Street. After that, he wondered how exactly the Alexander Mechanism might have worked.

But most of all, he pondered how his life had changed – stretched from a narrow line into full bandwidth. Gazing up at the Big Dipper, he thanked the universe, and said a prayer for his parents. Their death had been the most painful time of his life.

His saddest day.

How could Will have forgotten the last line of Hannibal's message?

Running over to the CODEX, he tapped in a date: 29th April 2005 – the day his parents had perished.

The gears began to turn, grinding in a way they had not moved before. The CODEX was growing warmer. Will could feel it, even through the leather case.

Squinting in the darkness, he read a set of instructions as they rolled into view, letter by letter.

Although apparently not in code, they still didn't make sense.

But then, as Will pondered it, in Hannibal's cloak-and-dagger world, very little made any sense at all.

As London's Big Ben chimed four, a tattered manila envelope was carried unceremoniously upstairs, in a grotesquely modern building half a mile from the Houses of Parliament. Following a series of curious alerts, the envelope had been dispatched from a secretive classified unit located in the vaults beneath the Home Office.

On the outside were stencilled the words 'TOP SECRET'.

Five minutes after reaching the department, the envelope was on the desk of the home secretary. She had just finished a long and painful meeting on anti-terrorism. Sipping a cup of Guatemalan blend, she cursed the day she had entered government.

'What's that?' the home secretary asked her secretary.

'It was sent up from Classified Storage A.'

A silver letter opener sliced the envelope down the side.

Inside was a single sheet of white paper. Folded three times, it appeared to be very old indeed.

Sipping her coffee without looking up, the home secretary read the typewritten text.

TAHIR SHAH

4th March 1912

To whom it may concern:

The government has a continuing duty to track
the components of the Alexander Mechanism and,
to that end, an appropriate apparatus has been
long established. If this letter is brought to the
attention of a departmental head, it most probably
indicates that a descendant of Hannibal Fogg is
working to reassemble the components.

   Government is advised to strive to make certain
that the Mechanism is not reconfigured. Should it
be so, the political balance of the Empire will be
de-stabilised in the most spectacular way.

   I leave it to you to understand the importance of
the situation at hand, and to act accordingly.

   Faithfully yours,

G. K. L.

*

WILL WAS AWAKE long before dawn.

   By the time the first rays of sunlight had broken
through the jungle, he had made a series of fires down the
beach, using kindling and driftwood. From ground level
they looked quite random. There were more than a dozen
of them, the damp wood spitting sparks up into the cool
morning air.

'What are you doing?' Emma called, stumbling down onto the beach.

'Signalling.'

'Signalling *who*?'

Will glanced at his iPhone. Slipping it away confidently, he held his ear out to the sky.

'For that…'

'What?'

'Listen.'

Emma strained to concentrate. Her ears picked up the roar of the waves and the chatter of cockatoos in the high branches of the forest.

But there was another sound, too.

It was so faint it was almost inaudible, a hum… like the background noise a refrigerator makes, the kind you never quite hear because it's always there.

As she listened, the humming grew louder.

Every second it was twice as loud again, until it sounded like one of the hornets up at the temple.

Craning their necks back, they both scoured the sky.

'Don't see anything.'

'*There!*'

Will pointed at a dot way out over the horizon, where water became sky.

A minute later, the silver fuselage of an immense aircraft, a C-130 Hercules, had come into sight as it banked into the morning light.

'They've seen the signal,' said Will. 'Thank God for that.'

Emma clapped her hands.

'What's going on?!'

Will didn't reply. Instead, he ran forwards until his ankles were in the ocean, his face following the plane.

Another couple of minutes and the Hercules had made a full three-sixty. It was out over the sea again. The pilot eased the throttle back. The propellers slowed, and the cargo door at the rear dropped down.

No more than a speck, an object was falling through the clear air, plunging fast in the direction of the water.

'What the...?'

'Wait and see,' cried Will.

Halfway between the aircraft and the waves, a trio of parachutes deployed, blinding white canopies billowing outwards as they caught the wind.

Dangling below them, an enormous wooden crate was swinging to and fro.

'It's gonna land on the beach!' bawled Emma.

The crate descended rapidly, colliding into the sand fifty feet from where they were standing.

Will ran forwards, cut away the parachutes and gathered them up. Then he marched over to the crate, flipped up what looked like the cover to a fuse-box and punched in an eight-digit numerical code:

29-04-19-98.

In sequence, a dozen explosive bolts fired.

The front of the crate was blown clean away.

Following Will, Emma peered in.

Lost in shadows was a vehicle.

At the front was a raised silver radiator, crowned by the Spirit of Ecstasy figurine.

Beyond a giant-sized engine were dual yoke-style controls, a back row of seats and, after them, an extremely large sealed box made from oiled bridle leather.

As far as Will could make out, there were no wheels at all. Instead, the vehicle's underside was enveloped in a farrago of brass pipes, furling up over the bodywork and into the engine.

Emma's hand brushed over the Spirit of Ecstasy.

'Is it a Rolls-Royce?' she asked incredulously.

'Of course it is,' Will replied at once.

'I get the feeling Hannibal approved of nothing else.'

Will looked Emma in the eye.

'It's not any old Rolls,' he said. 'It's one of a kind.'

The home secretary had forgotten about the letter brought up from Classified Storage A. Putting it down to colonial hysteria from another age, she had asked her secretary to 'take it along the hall', a euphemism for having it destroyed. By five o'clock on the day it was opened, the envelope and its contents had been shredded and then incinerated.

Three days passed.

The home secretary arrived early for work, Big Ben striking eight in the distance. So accustomed was she to the chimes, she didn't hear them at all.

Through the morning she worked on a speech due to be delivered on international terrorism in Brussels the next week. Writing had never been her strong point. She was sitting at her desk with an online thesaurus open, trying to find yet another synonym for the word 'evil', when there was a rap at the door.

'Come in.'

The door opened. Her secretary was standing there.

'What is it, Flo?'

'A car's arrived for you.'

'From where?'

'From the MOD.'

By a quarter to nine, the home secretary was sitting in the upstairs briefing room at 10 Downing Street. She was wondering why an armoured vehicle had been sent to drive her the short distance, and why soldiers had been posted outside the prime minister's residence.

At five minutes to ten, four senior officers entered, along with the prime minister and a handful of her closest staff. There was none of the usual joviality, no laughter or smiles.

The prime minister took a seat at the head of the table. She looked drawn, as if she hadn't slept in days.

'This is an emergency COBRA meeting,' she announced in a cold voice. 'Let the record state who is present: Myself, Rear Admiral Phipps, General Sir John Whiteman, General Hackman-Jones, Group Leader Lambert, the Home Secretary, and the Ministers for Terrorism and Defence, in addition to my private security team.'

The prime minister took a sip of mineral water and cleared her throat.

'Thank you all for coming at such short notice,' she said. 'I would not have bothered you, believe me, but this is a matter of national security – one which affects us all. We are regarding it as "Critical". Now, I would be grateful if, Sir John, you might fill us in on the current situation.'

Rising to his feet, General Sir John Whiteman stiffened his back and thrust out his chest, allowing the rows of medal ribbons to catch the light.

'Thank you, Prime Minister,' he said in a stony voice. 'What I am about to tell you is classified at the highest level. Although scarcely believable, it's apparently completely true. About a century ago the British government learned that an ancient machine, known as the "Alexander Mechanism", had been created in antiquity for the purpose of unifying mankind with God.

'The machine was supposedly the reason Alexander the Great was able to conquer the known world without defeat. In the aftermath of his death, it was essentially defused, specific pieces having been removed and concealed. As we understand it, those who hid it hoped that sometime far in the future the various components would be reinstated when humanity was sufficiently ready.'

The general leaned back on his heels, taking in the politicians one by one. Hailing from a long line of soldiers, he despised civilians.

'That is where we come to Hannibal Fogg,' he said.

The prime minister winced.

'Hannibal *who*?'

'Hannibal Fogg. He was an explorer, an author, and a linguist too. At the turn of the last century, Fogg was understood to be searching for the components. He seemed to have believed that the business of reuniting the Alexander Mechanism was an ancestral duty. We did our best to discredit him, asserting he was a spy. We arrested him and purged his published work. Despite our best efforts, in the years since his disappearance, Fogg attracted an almost cult following.'

The general swallowed hard.

'There's even a Hannibal Fogg Society on the internet,' he said. 'As well as blogs devoted to his life and work. It's incredible, of course, because we have spent millions doing all we could to make Fogg out to be a fictional character and a hoax.'

'He sounds like a crackpot,' said the minister of defence.

'Perhaps. It's hard to be sure. What is certain though is that Fogg came very close to his goal.'

'To reconfiguring the machine... the Alexander Mechanism?'

'Precisely.'

'Forgive me, General,' the home secretary called out, 'but what matter is this Mechanism to us?'

The officer looked at her sternly.

'If the Mechanism is restarted,' he said, his eyes glaring, 'then the political balance of the world may well be destabilized in the most spectacular way.'

Remembering the letter she had received from the classified archives, the home secretary hoped no one would bring it up.

'What's the current situation?' the prime minister asked.

'It seems that Hannibal Fogg left information which would allow his descendant to locate the components and return them to the machine.'

'What descendant?'

General Sir John Whiteman glanced at the dossier open in front of him.

'Fogg's great-great-grandson,' he said. 'His name is William Fogg.'

One of the prime minister's advisers raised a hand.

'Is he British?'

'No,' said the general, 'I regret to say he's American.'

'Then why don't we let them deal with it in Washington?'

General Sir John wrung his hands together anxiously.

'I trust we are all in agreement that this is a rather British affair and ought to be handled by us.'

'So what to do?'

'Prime Minister,' said the general, 'I suggest sending in CRU, the Covert Reconnaissance Regiment.'

'With what objective?'

'Either to capture or destroy the Mechanism.'

The prime minister frowned.

'Do we know where it is?'

'We shall find it.'

'How?'

'By following Mr. Fogg Jr. We have been tracking him for weeks. He's been bouncing around like a rubber ball.'

'*So*?'

'As we understand it, he's about to get his hands on the last of the components.'

'What does that mean, General?'

'It means, Prime Minister, that it's only a matter of time before Fogg has what he needs to restart the Mechanism.'

'How long?'

'We can't be certain.'

'How long do you need to mobilize the Covert Reconnaissance Unit?'

'Three hours at most.'

'Where are they?'

'At their base at Akrotiri.'

The prime minister stood up, her eyes trained on the desk blotter squared before her. Slowly, she looked up, scanned the room, pushed back her shoulders, and replied:

'Have them ready to deploy when Fogg appears to be nearing the Mechanism. Do you understand?'

General Sir John Whiteman nodded.

'Yes, Prime Minister.'

The Rolls-Royce slipped out onto the sand on its own hydraulic pallet. Set against the jungle backdrop, it looked like an invention from another world.

The vehicle was dominated by a V-12, 14-litre Falcon aviation engine, built at Rolls-Royce's fighter aircraft factory.

As he walked around the car, Will understood how his great-great-grandfather had been lauded as a deity by the Garuda tribe. They must have been utterly amazed by him.

Having heard the C-130, Chaudhury came running out from the undergrowth, his arms up in the air, his head thrown back in laughter.

Pittzer shot out from the undergrowth, too, and tore across the beach. Not because of the Rolls but because of the tribe.

'They're not happy!' he cried. 'Not happy at all!'

'What's wrong?'

The anthropologist took in the vehicle and threw up his hands.

'There's disorder in their heaven!' he shouted. 'The sacred amulets have been defiled and they're mad as hell.'

'Are they coming down here to cut our throats?'

'Quite the opposite,' Pittzer replied, wide-eyed. 'They're running up to the hills.'

'Whatever for?' Emma asked.

'The shaman's telling them there's going to be a "wave-mountain".'

Will looked round.

'A tsunami?!'

'Yeah…'

'Chaudhury, help me get our luggage into this contraption.'

'But it doesn't even have wheels!' Pittzer bellowed.

'When did a boat need wheels?' said Emma.

Will cleared his throat.

'Almost right,' he said. 'Except this isn't a boat.'

Taking the right yoke in his hand, he pushed the ignition button. Instantly, the aviation engine groaned, but didn't turn over.

'Looks like your battery's dead.'

Pittzer hurried back across the beach, heading for the jungle.

'See you later. I've got to calm things down or else I'm screwed.'

The Indian manservant from Cooch Behar lifted the cowling and fell back at the sheer size of the machine. Searching the mass of intertwined pipes and vents for the carburettor, he adjusted it. His family had owned more Rolls-Royces than he cared to remember. The vehicles were favoured for tiger shoots because of their suspension and the size of their running boards.

Having tightened the carburettor's springs, Chaudhury furled the engine's cowling back down.

'Would you try the ignition again, sir?'

Will got in and pressed the starter button on the dash. Nothing happened at first. Then, after a delay, the Falcon engine turned over once, then again, and again, belching out clouds of dense, oily smoke.

Steadily, the cushion inflated with air and the Rolls-Royce rose up off the sand.

'It's a hovercraft!' yelled Chaudhury triumphantly, his voice barely audible. 'It's a Rolls-Royce hovercraft!'

Emma's line of sight ranged beyond the car, down to the ocean.

'That's funny,' she shouted above the thunderous wall of noise.

'What is?'

'The tide's going out.'

'So what?'

'Well it's almost high tide. So it's supposed to be coming in.'

She walked down to the water. As she advanced, the ocean retreated.

Will looked round.

'What the…?'

'I believe it's called drawback, sir,' said Chaudhury. 'It precedes a…'

'A tsunami!'

Will sprinted down the beach.

'Quick! We have to get the stuff!'

A siren blasted loud and shrill above the noise of the Falcon engine. Will jerked round.

Chaudhury was racing the Rolls hover-car across the sand.

When he and the luggage were aboard, Will took the controls and steered the vehicle round one-eighty. Aiming at the horizon, they shot forwards across the beach and onto the flats where the ocean had so recently been.

Having walked far out into the wasteland, Emma was picking up shells, marvelling at the secret world that had been revealed. She heard the engine behind her and turned.

'Quick! Get in!' Will roared, struggling to apply the brakes.

The vehicle glided to a halt, its voluminous rubber air cushion deflating just long enough for Emma to get aboard. Will forced the accelerator down and the hovercraft surged forwards, the engine deafening beyond belief.

On the dash, a panel of gauges and dials rotated into place. The central instrument was the largest. Its digital display seemed to be winding backwards.

'What's that?'

'It appears to be a timer, sir,' said Chaudhury. 'It's set at twenty-one minutes.'

'It's counting down,' said Will.

As the hovercraft shot forwards towards the horizon at breakneck speed, the ocean retreated even more.

On the coral reef below, rainbow fish, crabs and other sea life floundered about in the mud.

As the water pulled back, the outline of a ruined city emerged.

'How the hell are we going to find a jade mask in all of that?' shouted Will above the noise of the engine. 'It's like searching for a needle in a haystack.'

'Think we may be in luck,' countered Emma.

Leaning in, she tapped a small dial on the dash.

'What's that?'

'I may be way wrong, but it looks like an FMMLU.'

'Huh?'

'A Ferro-Magnesium Magnetometer Location Unit.'

Will and Chaudhury looked at Emma in disbelief.

'And what good's that going to do us?'

'It'll locate a concentration of the isotope in nephrite, the appropriate form of jade,' she said.

Spotting a giant boulder straight ahead, Will jarred the yoke to the right. The vehicle banked sharply, missing the rock by inches.

Will thrust the pedal to the metal.

'I took enough chemistry to know you have to have some kind of index value for…'

'For the ferro-magnesium… the value of nephrite?'

'Yeah… something like that.'

Emma pinched a forefinger and thumb to the end of her nose.

'Its valence is eight.'

'How d'you know that?'

Emma jabbed a hand at a neat brass plaque fixed to the dash.

'Because it's written right there,' she said.

Following the shaman, the tribe had climbed up to the Temple of the Great Being.

Pittzer had remained down in the village, where he pulled out the satellite phone.

Once again, he underwent the security screening, before being patched through.

'Rogers here.'

'Rogers, this is Pittzer. Target Exposed! Repeat Target Exposed!'

There was silence the other end.

'OK Pittzer, be advised to monitor Target. Report back on SGF. Channel 6 at 1700 hours.'

Chaudhury set the FMMLU to digit eight on the atomic scale.

'Is it giving a reading?' Will asked.

'It appears to be in tracking mode, sir.'

'Tracking the jade concentration?'

'Yes, sir.'

Will glanced at the timer.

'Well it had better damn well hurry up. We've only got fifteen minutes until the tsunami hits.'

Thrusting the control yoke to the left, he skirted around the western edge of the city.

The main ruins were concentrated in a deep bowl between two hills. Clearly visible, the remnants were smothered under a grim mantle of slime.

On one side of the city there stood what looked like a ruined temple – great stone pillars tumbled by earthquakes in antiquity. Opposite was a collapsed palace – a homage to power and greed.

Will navigated up to a vantage point, from which the three of them peered down in awe.

'Are you getting a signal?'

'A faint one, sir.'

'Which direction?'

'South-south-west.'

Jerking the yoke to the left, Will jammed the accelerator down. Listing sharply, the hover-car surged forwards through the ruins.

'Getting stronger,' said Chaudhury.

Emma pointed straight up.

'Look at that!'

Towering above the vehicle was a cenotaph. It was topped by a magnificent bird, its wings outstretched, a human prey clutched in its talons.

'The Garuda!' cried Will.

'A touch to the west, sir.'

'Are we on track?'

Chaudhury nodded.

'Think so.'

As the Rolls-Royce hovercraft faltered over a pool of sea water, Chaudhury pressed his ear to the Location Unit, motioning for Will to slow down. The instrument was clicking like a Geiger counter picking up radiation.

The Rolls slip-slided to a halt.

'Must be in those ruins over there,' said Emma.

'The one with the staircase?'

'Yes.'

Will leapt down.

'Bring her around to the other side,' he shouted, scurrying over the blocks of stone.

As quickly as he could, he climbed up to the highest point.

Even if he had been able to dislodge the blocks, there was so much seaweed and mud that spotting the mask would be all but impossible.

Chaudhury took in the timer: 11 minutes 23 seconds.

He scanned the controls.

To the right of the yoke was a row of miniature brass levers. They were protected by a cover that prevented them from being accidentally knocked.

The personification of caution, Chaudhury would not normally have gambled. But he knew Hannibal would have planned meticulously, having realized full well the difficulty of the mission.

'There must be some way we can help Will,' Emma said.

It was the prompt Chaudhury needed.

Flipping up the protective cover, he jerked down the first lever.

A hydraulic lance shot out from the Rolls-Royce's left side. But the ruins were on the right. By gently manipulating the lever, Chaudhury found he could retract the lance and deploy it on the other side.

Calling out to Will, he urged him to make use of the hydraulic lance. Grabbing it, Will found the device was designed to lever away the blocks of stone – providing him entry into the building.

Chaudhury tugged down the second lever.

As soon as he did so, a stream of detergent blasted through the lance, transforming it into a high-pressure hose. Down below, Will used the fluid to wash away the mud.

He scanned right and left.

The chamber's stone walls were adorned with hieroglyphs featuring a great mythical bird. As Will searched desperately for the mask, Chaudhury nudged the third lever down.

The FMMLU clicked out of its holder.

Snatching it, Chaudhury scrambled out of the hover-car, up over the rocks and into the chamber where Will was searching.

The Location Unit clicked wildly.

'Quick! Over here!'

Chaudhury threw the unit to Will.

Guided by the sound, Will ran through into a passage, diving down into the sludge.

He was gone a full minute.

In an explosion of breathlessness, his head emerged.

Covered in seaweed and mud, an object was clutched in his hands:

The Garuda Mask.

By the time they were back at the vehicle, the timer read 5 minutes 31 seconds.

'There should be enough time,' said Will, pressing the ignition button.

The hover-car's cushion inflated, mud splashing out from under it. Will yanked the steering yoke round to the right. A second later the vehicle turned.

'All we have to do now is to get out of the…'

His words were cut short by the roar of another engine.

'Over there!' shouted Emma.

They all lurched round to look.

Heading straight for them from across the ruined city, was a state-of-the-art military hovercraft.

'What the devil?!' shouted Chaudhury.

'Must be the Magi,' responded Will, wrenching the yoke round and slamming his foot down. 'They were waiting till we got the last component.'

'Don't understand how they found us,' said Emma.

'Just like Hannibal said, they're everywhere. They never tried to get us while there were still components to find. They wanted all the work done for them.'

Gritting his teeth, Will heaved the yoke to the left. The rudder kicked in, fishtailing the vehicle round.

But, as it swerved in an arc, the engine went dead.

'Oh my God.'

'Hope this contraption's armoured!' grunted Will.

Chaudhury leapt out, unbuckled the cowling and loosened the carburettor springs.

'Try again now.'

'No joy.'

'What about now?'

'Nothing…'

Will looked straight ahead. The jet-black hovercraft was racing towards them at top speed. It was so close they could see the soldier piloting it, a reflective visor drawn down over his face.

As if the hovercraft were not danger enough, the Rolls shuddered.

'The tsunami… it's coming!' cried Will.

On the other side of the engine, Chaudhury was fumbling frantically with a dozen strands of multi-coloured wire.

'Shall I try it again?'

'Not quite, sir… a moment longer.'

'I hate to rush you, but even a moment's a luxury right now.'

'Three minutes,' said Emma. 'Make that two-fifty-eight.'

The jet-black hovercraft slalomed past the Garuda cenotaph and was seventy yards away. The pilot was firing an Uzi SMG mounted on the front.

'Try it now!' called Chaudhury.

Will jammed a hand on the ignition.

The engine came alive with smoke and noise, the hover-cushion ballooning out.

'Waoooo!'

Ripping ahead through a gap between the ruins, the Rolls narrowly missed the Uzi's spray.

'That way, sir!' snapped Chaudhury. 'We can lose him.'

'No time for a car chase,' said Will, swerving the yoke back to the left.

The black hovercraft was gaining on them.

Its air cushion sprayed with incoming fire, the Rolls automatically compensated, powering up all the more.

Will glanced at the last lever.

'I'm feeling lucky,' Will said, a touch of Clint Eastwood in his voice.

He flicked it down.

An RPG launched, twisted through the air above the ruined city, and made brutal and immediate contact with the enemy hovercraft.

'No time to gloat!' snapped Emma. 'Thirty seconds and we'll be washed away!'

Will thrust his foot down hard.

The tsunami's giant wave was thundering forwards.

They could feel the wind preceding it. Their ears were filled with the roar of water as it rolled towards the shore.

'We're not gonna make it!' said Emma, her voice cold.

'Fifteen seconds,' added Chaudhury.

'Ten… nine…'

They were out of the city, but there was still half a mile to go. And, in any case, the shoreline would provide no security.

Will scanned the controls.

Eight…

'C'mon Hannibal, you knew this was going to happen!'

Seven…

At that moment, a foghorn sounded and a mechanical hand telescoped out from the dash. Held between thumb and forefinger was a switch.

Six…

'What the hell?' spluttered Will.

'Push it!' shrieked Emma.

Five...

Will pushed the switch.

An explosion was triggered, like the noise of a cannon firing.

Four...

A colossal hot air balloon was deployed above the Rolls.

Helium pumped in from pressurized tanks stowed inside the hover cushion, the canopy billowing outwards.

Three...

Steel cords straining, the scarlet balloon tightened, its vast surface ornamented with the distinctive monogram of Hannibal Fogg.

Two...

With Herculean force the tsunami ripped through the ancient ruins.

One...

A second before the waters engulfed it, the Rolls-Royce hover-car lifted gently into the air.

Climbing onto the back seat, Will opened the helium valves fully.

But the gas wasn't filling the canopy fast enough.

The vehicle was descending.

Thinking fast, Will climbed over the windscreen and onto the bonnet. Jamming his feet into a pair of holes positioned perfectly, he opened up the cowling.

He knew next to nothing about vintage aircraft engines – but Will wasn't concerned with the engine itself.

As Chaudhury and Emma watched in alarm – and as the water came closer and closer – Will grabbed a lever on the right of the housing.

Wrenching it back, he braced himself.

In the nick of time, the Falcon engine fell away, like a spent booster rocket jettisoned in outer space.

Instantly, the Rolls-Royce rose into the clear blue sky, as the full force of the tsunami reached the lost city below.

Striking the shore, the water made landfall, surging up through the jungle.

High up on a plateau, the Garuda tribe were safe. Their awe at surviving the catastrophe was made more poignant by the sight of the scarlet helium balloon... emblazoned as it was with the symbol of the Great Being – Hannibal Fogg.

From: *Hannibal Fogg and the Supreme Secret of Man*

La Psycho Thriller

ON THE WAY to the embassy, Miki came to a public telephone. Remarkably, it hadn't been vandalized like all the others. Suddenly, she had an idea – she would call her parents and ask them to send her a little money. It was an emergency after all.

Giving the number to the international operator, Miki waited for her mother to accept the call. But instead of a woman's voice, she heard an old man on the line. He seemed bewildered and fussed.

'Ojiichan!' she cried out. 'Dear Ojiichan, it's Miki!'

The frail voice seemed to strengthen a little, as though buoyed by good news.

'Miki-chan!' he said, wheezing. 'How is your journey? How is my beloved Paris?'

Miki's eyes were streaming with tears, her face muscles exhausted from weeping.

'Paris,' she said. 'It is... it is... it is *wonderful!*'

The *ojiichan* let out a muffled laugh as though he knew it was wonderful and had no need to ask.

'I told you,' he said. 'I told you that it was Paradise on Earth!'

The line went dead, and Miki stood there, the receiver in her hand, her cheeks lined with fresh tears.

407

Calmly, she bowed to the receiver and, with both hands, placed it back on the telephone.

Gripping the handle of the suitcase, she was about to wheel it forward, when half a dozen girls approached her. They were in their early teens and were far less prim than other Parisian children she had seen.

The oldest girl held up a paper.

She asked Miki if she would sign her petition. Miki didn't really understand but, before she could refuse, a pen was in her hand, and her hand was on the paper.

The girl asked where Miki was from.

'From Japan,' she said, adding: 'I have been robbed and so I am going to my embassy.'

'There are a lot of thieves in Paris,' said the girl. 'They look for tourists like you and then they attack them.'

'They are not good people,' Miki replied. 'A man gave me a gold ring and then he chased me, demanding money. And the ring was not gold, and it got stuck on my finger.'

The oldest girl turned to her friends and said something fast. It didn't sound like French.

'Are you from Paris?' Miki asked.

'No, no, from Bucharest – from Romania.'

Miki put her head on the side and sucked in air through her back teeth.

'Oh,' she said. 'Romania.'

'We are Romany,' the girl explained. 'We came to Paris to make money.'

'You do not go to school?'

The girl shook her head.

'We have to earn money because our families are poor,' she said.

Miki thanked the girls for their conversation and wished them luck with their petition.

Then, bowing, she reached out to grasp the handle of the wheelie case.

But the case was gone.

At the Japanese Embassy, a security officer waved his hand forcefully through the air above his head.

A great brute of a man from Brittany, he disliked the Japanese very much indeed. Having taken the job because nothing else had been on offer, he took delight in doing all in his power to bring misery to the people he was supposed to be assisting. And the easiest way to bring misery was to be of no help at all.

'The embassy is closed for the weekend,' he said curtly.

Miki looked at her wristwatch.

'But it is one minute past five,' she replied.

The guard shrugged.

'I am following orders from the Japanese staff inside,' he explained.

'But I have been robbed,' Miki said. 'My passport has been stolen, and my money, too, and all my clothes as well. And the heel has come off my shoe...'

Stepping back, the guard looked at Miki's feet. He sniffed.

'The embassy will open on Monday morning, at nine a.m.,' he said.

'Is there an emergency number I can call?'

'No.'

'Are you sure?'

'Yes. Quite sure.'

Miki closed her eyes.

She made out the silhouette of a man walking towards her through blinding light. Long before she had seen his face, she had smelled his cologne. It was gentle on the nose, like Provençal lavender. She smiled and, as she did so, Comte Hugo de Montfried took her hand and pressed his lips to its knuckles. 'I will never leave you,' he said.

The security guard coughed hard and the daydream vanished.

Opening her eyes, Miki walked over to the grand wrought iron gates that led into Parc Monceau.

She sat down on the first bench she could find, and thought of all the gift packs she had distributed for Angel Flower, in frozen Shiba Park. Then she thought of the kind young sales clerk at the Kinokuniya bookshop, and her best friend, Ichiko, and of her parents. And, lastly, she thought of her *ojiichan*.

Miki had been attacked and robbed, but she never wanted her beloved grandfather to know of her distress. It was the rose-tinted memories of Paris that were keeping him alive.

As she sat there, reflecting on the trials and tribulations of the day, Miki spotted a group of girls prancing boisterously through the park. At least two of them were wearing pretty floral sundresses, dresses that were overly familiar to her eyes.

Her blood suddenly fortified with adrenalin, Miki leapt up and ran over to confront the girls.

'Give me back my luggage!' she cried out.

Whooping and whistling, the girls surrounded Miki and started pushing her back and forth. They taunted her, pulling at her hair. Then they got her on the ground and began to kick her. Her arms thrashing, she tried to fight back, but she was no match for a Romanian girl gang.

Eventually tiring of the attack, the teenagers drifted away, leaving Miki covered in dirt, her dress shredded from the brawl. She lay there for a long while, passersby avoiding eye contact, assuming that she was a drug addict who had strayed in from the suburbs.

Picking herself up, Miki staggered back to the slatted wooden bench. Her mind was so befuddled that she was unable to process a single memory or thought.

While she sat there quietly and blank-faced, a man approached her.

In his hand was a gold ring.

'I think you dropped this,' he said.

Miki looked up and found herself staring into the eyes of a face she had recently known. Without thinking, she pulled off her shoe, the one missing its heel, and she battered the man in a whirlwind of screaming and rage.

Pleading with her to stop, he fled, the gold ring gripped tight in his fist.

*

WHEN THE MAN was gone, Miki stood there, shoe in hand, a look of utter indignation on her face. To the joggers, and the young mothers out with their pushchairs and their prams, she must have seemed no different than a few moments before – before the man with the gold ring had appeared.

But something deep down in Miki's psyche had changed.

Gone was the feeble, stooping, apologetic, self-excusing young woman – replaced in an instant by a dark, wrathful alter ego.

The pupils of her eyes were dilated, the muscles around her mouth taut. Her fingers were gnarled and ferocious, and her back was craned forward like a bird of prey preparing to strike.

With one shoe on, and the other still clutched in her hand, Miki roamed through Parc Monceau. She was to report much later that she had no memory of her actions after attacking the conman with the ring.

Weaving a haphazard path through the park, she came to a homeless man standing on a flowerbed. His trousers and underwear were down around his ankles, and he was peeing.

Horrified and angry, Miki jerked forward.

A moment later, she was attacking him, striking him again and again with her shoe. After that, she moved on to a nanny out with a toddler. First, she reprimanded the woman for dropping a piece of litter little bigger than a snowflake. And then, in an act that was to horrify the nation, she took the child's ice cream and stuffed it into her mouth.

As if suddenly aware of geography, Miki strolled down to the Champs-Elysées. Picking the left shoe from her foot, she tossed it away, along with the other. And, taking a deep breath, she stuck her hands up above her head and ran in a crazed zigzag along the wide pavement, screaming at everyone she passed.

Parisians are not unused to acts of insanity.

Most of them simply walked on, or pretended that Miki wasn't there. One or two elderly tourists barked back at her. But by the time they could do anything, she was long gone, her bare feet tramping fast over the smooth flagstones.

Eventually, after zigzagging back and forth through the crowds – screaming, ranting, bawling – Miki reached an imposing building, fashioned from light grey stone. Way up on the roof was a flagpole and, below it, a great golden monogram set against a background of burnished bronze.

The legend of LV.

Her arms flailing and her mouth yapping insults and vitriol, Miki ran straight in through the main door.

Once inside, she jumped from one display to the next, shouting ferocious exclamations and expletives.

The immaculate customers and the legions of prim serving staff stopped and watched.

Running through the body of the shop, Miki began howling like a wolf. Then, as the security guards closed in, she lowered her hands and, very calmly, went up to the nearest sales counter and said:

'I would like to see your coin pouches, please.'

Flustered, the sales clerk pulled out a display drawer. Across from him, a pair of burly security guards were moving forward, as if in slow motion.

As the first coin pouch was removed and held up, Miki turned around. Lifting up the hem of her dress, she pulled down her knickers, bent down, and mooned at the sales clerk.

*

THE EVENING NEWS featured a reconstruction of Miki's outburst, using a Chinese actress and indistinct video footage taken from security cameras on the Champs-Elysées.

Outside the flagship Louis Vuitton store, six satellite trucks were positioned at the kerb. Nearby, a clutch of reporters with microphones in hand were doing their best to describe what had taken place.

By late evening, at least two channels had put investigative reporters on the case. They hoped to draw in extraneous elements, and thereby satiate the public demand for more information on what had become known as '*l'attaque LV*'.

The great interest led to the reporters tracking down the homeless man from Parc Monceau. He was interviewed, and given a hot meal and bones for his dogs. Realizing that he might do well from the attention, the man with the gold ring, also battered by Miki's shoe, came forward and got his fifteen minutes of fame.

That evening, a late-night news programme assembled a panel of experts who discussed the state of tourism, and what it meant for France. Another channel debated the philosophy of anger. A third devoted a full hour of prime time to examining the cultural significance of mooning.

Meanwhile, there was still very little information about the attacker herself. Undeterred by the lack of details, most of the news channels simply made it all up.

One station went so far as to hire an artist to draw the assailant from eyewitness statements. Curiously, it showed a woman six foot two, with huge powerful hands, a thick neck, and a lantern jaw.

All through the night, scant fragments of information were released by the police. And, next morning, Louis Vuitton's security unit released CCTV footage of the moment the attacker ran in through the doors. Within minutes, Miki's face had been captured from the video and beamed all across the world.

Sitting in a hotel room in the shadows of Mont St. Michel, the chairman of Angel Flower was clipping his toenails, wishing he were back in Japan. Brushing the clippings onto the floor, he picked up the remote control and flicked on the TV, in the hope of tracking down a little free porn.

To his astonishment, the face of his former employee filled the screen. It was rather blurred, but there was no doubt that it was Miki Suzuki – the woman who had become synonymous with offering gift packs for free in Shiba Park.

Pulling on his trousers, the chairman knocked at the next room. Once he had pushed Noemi into the bathroom, Pun-Pun opened the door.

'The television,' the chairman said.

'Yes.'

'You must look!'

'Yes.'

'Miki Suzuki. She is on television!'

*

IN A DANK police cell two floors underground, Miki sat motionless on a cheap plastic chair. She was wizened and limp, her long, black hair matted with dirt, her eyes ringed in dark circles.

Closing them once again, she pictured a river wending its way through a meadow, its banks shaded by weeping willows, its waters glistening lightly in the late summer sun. Her mind's eye caught sight of two hands holding each other tight. The first was small and delicate, the second strong and powerful, with perfectly manicured nails.

Her imagination panning backwards, Miki saw herself with the Comte de Montfried. She was dressed in a pretty taffeta frock, and he was in a suit cut from starched navy-blue linen. Pausing, he looked into her eyes, then picked away a strand of stray hair hanging over her face.

Miki smiled, her lips parting, as they readied themselves for his.

There was the *clunk* of steel on steel, and the cell door opened.

A gendarme entered.

He had a cold expression and a brusque manner, as though his time would be better used catching dangerous criminals.

But Miki didn't notice the officer.

She was still in the meadow with the count.

'Put your hands in front of you,' the gendarme ordered, as he swung handcuffs into place. In all his years at the Commissariat Central on rue Bonaparte, he had never encountered such bird-like wrists.

Miki did as she was told.

A moment later, she was shuffling forwards in advance of the gendarme. They went up two flights of stairs, the walls scuffed and unpainted, the neon strip-light giving an unearthly quality to the lines of cells they passed.

Up on ground level, the officer opened the door to an interrogation room and Miki's bare feet shuffled in. It was small, square and painted slate grey. There was a table, a couple of plastic garden chairs, and a faint stench of excrement. Miki might have been concerned about the surroundings, but she was past caring about anything.

Sitting down, she rested her cuffed wrists on her lap and put her ankles together. The soles of her bare feet could feel the raised pattern of the linoleum floor tiles. Again, Miki's mind slipped back to the riverbank.

There were swallows in the air.

She leaned back a fraction, breathed in deep, and smelled the scent of nature. Her ears were filled with the sound of water trickling gently over pebbles, her spine warmed by the balmy sense of sunlight filtered through the bows of a majestic willow tree.

The gendarme sat down on the other side of the table.

'Which part of China are you from?' he asked angrily.

Miki didn't look at her questioner. Her eyes were fixed on the middle distance, for it was there that she could see the meadow and the riverbank.

'I am from outside Sendai, in Miyagi Prefecture,' she replied in a rather absent voice.

'Is that near Beijing?'

'No. Sendai is *not* near Beijing.'

'Why were you attacking people in Parc Monceau?'

'Because the ring got stuck on my finger,' Miki said.

'*The ring*?'

'The gold ring… I mean the gold ring which was not gold.'

The officer frowned. He lit a cigarette and placed it on the edge of the table, with the burning end poking over the side.

'Why did you attack Louis Vuitton?'

Miki smoothed a fingertip to her left eyebrow. She smiled, her smile erupting into a giggle, the giggle into a laugh.

'Because I wanted to buy a coin pouch for my *ojiichan*,' she said.

'But you didn't have any money.'

'Yes. No money.'

'And your passport?'

'Gone,' said Miki, almost without caring. 'All is gone.'

*

THREE HOURS OF interrogation followed, in which the officer extracted a few basic details from the detainee, but no more than that.

He managed to establish certain key facts – that she was not Chinese but Japanese, that she was called Miki Suzuki, and that she had been staying at the George V Hotel.

After being photographed against a blank wall, holding a number, her wrists still cuffed, Miki was sent back to the cell to wait while the duty officer tried to make contact with the Japanese Embassy. Unfortunately for her, the number on file at the Commissariat Central was missing a digit, and so it didn't work.

The detainee's mugshot was leaked to the press, who were desperate for any information about the woman it had nicknamed 'La Psycho Thriller'.

Within minutes, the picture had been broadcast all over the world and had graced every news site on the web.

By mid-morning all the surveillance footage from the store had been leaked as well.

Instantly, it went viral on YouTube, with a local French rap star using it to launch his latest hit. As for the mugshot, it was doctored by a prominent internet artist, who added Marilyn Monroe's hair and lips, vampire fangs, and a tiara made from crushed emeralds.

Within a day of her arrest, Miki was regarded as one of the most recognizable people on the planet, although no one really knew anything about her – anywhere, that is, except in Japan.

From: *Paris Syndrome*

The Qemqems

AT THREE MINUTES past four, the doors to the great Cadenta Hall swung inwards and a pair of primitive-looking creatures scurried in, the second close on the heels of the first.

In a certain way they resembled armadillos.

They had long snouts, even longer tails, and armoured shells ribbed in deep, undulating grooves. But that was where the armadillo likeness ceased, and where raw oddity began.

Known as 'qemqems', the creatures were a peculiar shade of fluorescent green. They had five legs, each of which was a different length and ended in an almost human-like hand. They enjoyed gorging themselves on figglewist fruit, of dreaming of the sound of falling rain and – most curiously of all – were always born at 3.13 a.m. on a Sunday. They had more obsessions than any other life form and were especially obsessed with pondering why they were so obsessed.

Among the oldest creatures in the Realm, qemqems were not jinn nor, despite their appearance, had they anything to do with armadillos, nor anything else from the mortal world. Against remarkably slim odds, they'd developed from the sap of a palm tree.

The xistic palm.

A tree so rare that anyone claiming to have ever seen one was almost certainly telling falsehoods.

Packed with extraordinary qualities, xistic palm sap was the only known cure for the dreaded ra-mû-clam cough, and was the best liquid in which to cook the lesser green mzofoo fish. It was used as a currency in the Kingdom of Sligg, whose ill-advised monarch once swapped his entire wealth for a half-filled mug of the prized sap.

Across the Realm, the search for the xistic palm had driven the sane mad and led to some of the greatest discoveries in exploration.

Discoveries such as that of Jetsula – a kingdom in which the inhabitants were hollowed-out forms of themselves.

The oddest thing about the sap of the xistic palm was that it could become almost anything at all that was needed desperately at a particular time.

That was how the qemqem came into being.

For all their obsessions and idiosyncrasy, the creatures had an attribute that was greatly prized:

An aptitude for absolute precision.

A skill seldom required, it was often overlooked. Except, that is, when the slightest error would lead to disaster.

Or death.

Or both.

Once inside the Cadenta Hall, the qemqems scurried into the middle of the room. Neither showed any surprise that the vast chamber was devoid of trainee Jinn Hunters, and filled instead with a hundred thousand identical numbered desks.

On each desk sat a simian monkey.

A simian monkey hunched over a battered old typewriter.

Against the din of a million nimble monkey fingers touch-typing, the qemqems weaved their way between the desks. As they scurried ahead, the first got a stray thought of a succulent figglewist fruit.

The second thought of falling rain.

Suddenly, both at once, they stopped – in the narrow aisle between desk number 49,998 and desk number 49,999.

'Crick-crick?' the first qemqem questioned, in their language.

'Crick-crick!' the second replied firmly.

The first peered upwards, his miniature eyes blinded by the candlelight.

'Crick-crick! Crick-crick!' He paused, and peered up again. 'Crick-crick!'

The second qemqem flicked the end of his elongated snout.

'Crick-crick?'

'Crick-crick!' the first shrilled.

With tremendous care, he positioned a tiny glass bottle on the floor between the desks. All around it, the monkeys continued to type as though their lives depended on it.

No larger than an upturned thimble, the bottle was plugged by a minuscule cork.

The second qemqem removed its stopper, and the first pushed the bottle a fraction of an inch to the left.

'Crick-crick!'

Gazing up into the darkness above the chandeliers, the creatures blinked knowingly in time with one another.

As they held their breath in anticipation, minds flashing with the thought of figglewist fruit, a strand of fibrous ribbon lowered itself.

Down through the blackness.

Into the dim, yellowed glow of candlelight.

Until it was six and a quarter feet from the floor.

Placed perfectly below it was the tiny glass bottle.

At their faultless precision, the qemqems grunted in unison.

A few moments passed in which the simian monkeys clattered away at the typewriters, even more stridently than before.

Then, very slowly, a droplet of pink, waxy liquid slipped down the length of the ribbon and dripped silently into the bottle.

*

DESPITE PERMUTATIONS OF infinite possibility, no lemon-yellow jinn had ever fallen into a drunilia flower before, for reasons the Advanced Calculation Committee had never quite understood.

So, when Borbor tumbled from the heavens and into the kaleidoscopic flower, he was in uncharted territory.

When the petals had closed up, a pungent scent was emitted – not by the flower – but by the Gröl Swamp. The effect was to send Borbor into infantile sleep. A curious thing was that the trees were actually a central part of the bog, as were the slimy rocks, the fissures, and even the damp air hanging listlessly above the ground.

As the odour dissipated, the swamp exuded a great deal of qluzy, a substance welling up from clefts in the marsh. Oily, and maroon in colour, it poured out, as though an unending vein had been tapped.

Having been triggered to activate by Borbor's sudden arrival, the swamp did something that surprised even itself.

Streaming out from the fissures, qluzy covered the rocks and inched up the tree trunks, until the marsh had all but vanished.

The qluzy dried and hardened.

When the maroon ground was firm, with no rocks left in sight, shoots began to sprout.

Not the shoots of flowering plants or trees.

But the shoots of buildings.

Pushing out, they soared up into the boundless sky through which, only minutes earlier, the lemon-yellow traveller – still trapped in the drunilia flower – had been tumbling.

Within ten minutes, more than thirty buildings were dotted over what had so recently been Gröl Swamp.

An hour after, thousands more high-rises had appeared – encasing the entire expanse of three and a half horizons.

All the while, Borbor dozed in the flower, stomach rumbling and grumbling, his dreams devoted to food.

By the next morning, a metropolis had grown up – bustling with traffic. Like any great city, there were plush areas with mansions and parks, and ghettos where have-nots eked out a miserable existence.

By the end of a day, the city had risen and matured, as though it had endured for centuries. There were libraries filled with communal knowledge, statues celebrating leaders, schools and universities, skyscrapers, factories, and even a velodrome.

In a landscape altered beyond all recognition, the only object carried over from the former incarnation was the single drunilia tree.

The tree in whose kaleidoscopic flower its captive lay asleep.

As if cued to do so by the fact the city was in some way complete, the petals opened slowly. Dreams deluged with light, Borbor woke, stretched, scratched his head, blinked, and took in his surroundings...

The fragrant scent of a flower in which he was cupped, its petals a flamboyant display of colour.

All he could remember was a wizened old hand pushing him, tumbling from the glass sheet, and falling fast through nothingness. The point of impact had come so fast, the memory was a blur.

Borbor peered out from the flower.

The drunilia tree now found itself in a walled garden, the commotion of a vast city in the distance. All around, there were beds of aromatic shrubs, and row upon row of medicinal plants, each of them labelled by a precise hand.

Climbing down, Borbor strolled through the garden. Feet padding over the dew-covered lawn, he breathed in the scent from the miscellany of flora.

Before he knew it, his stomach was rumbling, reminding him it hadn't been fed in what seemed like an eternity.

Goaded on by hunger, he made his way through the garden, and up to the front door of a little cottage. Basking in shade, it was all covered in ivy, as if straight out of a child's fairytale.

Above the door a sign hung from slender chains.

It read: *Hope is a waking dream.*

Borbor screwed up his face.

He was sitting on his mother's knee eating feeloop porridge from a ladle, the Tale of Bastulap conveyed line by line from an elderly pair of lips to a young oroking's ear.

Turning, Borbor looked at the garden and the wall, with the city beyond, then back at the cottage shrouded in ivy and shadow.

He heard his mother's voice, as clear as it had been when he was young:

'Hope is a waking dream,' she said. 'Those are the words suspended above the ivy-covered door at the home of Leila, magician princess of Bastulap.'

Just then, against the sound of unoiled hinges rasping, the door opened inwards.

Without thinking, Borbor stepped inside.

*

A DROPLET AT a time, the pink waxy liquid slipped down the length of the ribbon.

Gradually, it massed in the bottle, the qemqems watching with keen attention, and the monkeys typing frantically all around.

After no more than a handful of drops, the bottle was filled.

But rather than overflowing, it expanded, stretching itself so as to accommodate more liquid. Each time it was full, the bottle swelled a little more, until it was just over sixteen and three-quarter gallons.

Curiously though, the vessel's neck was not enlarged.

When the flow of waxy pink liquid had ceased slipping down the ribbon, the first qemqem fitted the stopper.

'Crick-crick!' snapped the second.

More normally, the qemqems would have hurried directly to their masters at the Department of Perfectly Precise Calculation. But, on this occasion, they'd been given strict instructions to return to the Cadenta Hall.

Not the permutation with the typing monkeys – in which they'd collected the pink waxy liquid – but the one at which Annis was waiting for them.

Through crunching infinite permutations of possibility, a helter-skelter egg had correctly predicted in which permutation the pink waxy liquid that had been Oliver, or rather a version of Oliver, would arrive. Locating the right version of the hall by itself would have been impressive.

But the calculation was made all the more notable when taking into account it had to be one in which the tapeworm, from the belly of a green sloth jinn, was positioned at the exact spot in which the waxy liquid would fall.

Of course there were an infinite number of other places throughout the Realm in which the wax had fallen – and not fallen – but Annis had stipulated it had to be in the Cadenta Hall.

The reason was risk.

Reconstituting a victim melted through form reversal was only remotely possible when the chance of failure was less than fifty-five billion, six hundred and twelve to one.

In the circumstances, the odds were not quite as favourable as they might have been. The most enthusiastic calculation put Oliver's chance of being brought back to something that resembled normality, at just less than forty-nine billion, nine hundred and thirty-six million, three thousand five hundred and six to one.

Struggling to lift the bottle, the qemqems staggered between the desks, spry monkey fingers typing all around, until they were halfway down row number 5952.

Once there, they laid the vessel down.

With three of its five feet, the first qemqem fumbled for an invisible handle.

An invisible handle to a door.

An invisible door to the conduit.

The conduit leading to the permutation where the chief instructor was waiting.

*

FEW THINGS IN the Realm were quite so baffling as conduits, and the way they worked.

So convoluted, so utterly unlikely, and so perplexing were they, that entire civilizations had devoted every waking moment in trying to understand them. The study was typically thwarted by the fact that the more you tried to appreciate how conduits linked one thing with another, the less you understood. The only way to make any progress at all was thought to be the use of a little-known scientific off-shoot which went by the acronym 'DNKLESWIT'.

For all the study, theories, elongated acronyms, and mind-numbing treatises, the most celebrated and original piece of scholarship on the subject had been penned by a six-year-old child, who went by the nickname 'Little Mo'.

The son of an outcast family, he lived in the Kingdom of Marsalus at the edge of the Great Slime Forest, in a house made from waxed avocado seeds.

Dispensing with big-headed pomposity that tended to fill reports on the subject, Little Mo got down to the nitty-gritty and thought in a new way.

A way that was as stripped down as it was profound.

Written in large block letters lengthways down the page, his thesis was refreshing and succinct to the point of genius.

It read:

DON'T THINK
...DO

The paper appeared in the right place, and at the right time.

So fatigued with his own search for understanding, the paramount thinker of Marsalus championed Little Mo.

Within a matter of hours, the boy had been catapulted into the limelight. Regarded as the one person alive who could explain the unexplainable, he was showered with attention and accolades. Everything he said was written down by special scribes and bound in ornate volumes in aged yolok hide.

Many of them contained no more than a handful of words.

A few of them were entirely blank.

The less writing they contained, the more valuable they were deemed to be.

Travellers came from far away to touch the feet of Little Mo, and to be in the presence of his masterworks.

The more he himself begged the people of Marsalus to forget about him and get on with their lives, the more they acclaimed him as a prophet.

Until, one day, unable to take the adulation any longer, Little Mo climbed to the top of the palace that had been built for him.

Having let out a shrill giggle, he jumped.

The end was as immediate as it was messy.

His mangled remains were paraded through the streets of the capital, as the inhabitants of Marsalus beat themselves with poisonous nettles. They mourned the loss of Little Mo, the most original thinker in their history. Having interred his body in a vast marble tomb, replete with fire dragons and sacred flames, they crawled around it, prostrating themselves in awe.

Over time, a new religion developed.

A faith known simply as 'MO'.

Through centuries, it spread like wildfire, bringing extraordinary wealth and recognition to the small Kingdom of Marsalus.

The tomb became a place of pilgrimage.

The leatherbound volumes containing the *Teachings of Little Mo* were guarded, studied, and were worshipped by every man, woman, and child.

Word of the faith spread far and wide.

With time, the neighbouring powers became so envious, they declared war simultaneously.

Carnage followed.

The Kingdom of Marsalus was destroyed, and its inhabitants enslaved.

But, still, MO thrived like never before.

Set free on the ghost wind.

*

A LATE SUMMER'S day beside the river.

Sunshine streaming through weeping willow.

Pools of light and shade dancing over reeds.

At the water's edge, a man's bare feet ambling through lush grass.

A woman unpacking a picnic nearby.

Ripples in the water.

The sound of splashing.

The man crying out, his finger pointing.

A little boy rushing forward.

A dolphin sashaying through crystal water.

A crown of mistletoe on its head.

But this time there was a difference...

Instead of visiting the scene in memory, Oliver was actually there.

*

EVEN BEFORE HIS feet had crossed the threshold, Borbor knew exactly what his eyes were about to witness.

Like all lemon-yellow jinn mothers, his own was an extraordinary storyteller. A storyteller who painted effervescent tales with words. Omitting no detail, she had described the cottage so vividly that it existed in Borbor's mind long before he ever set eyes upon it.

In the hallway, a sideboard on which pirate buttons were arranged.

Coloured glass bottles filled with the pickled teeth of hanged ghouls.

A dining table set for thirteen, overlaid with a cloth woven from goro-goro hair.

Straggly plants growing on octagonal aspidistra stands.

An ornate frame fashioned from carved jinn bones.

Six fingerless hands made from wax.

A cupboard adorned with bracelets cut from mermaids' wrists.

Then, a door.

Beyond it, another – half the size of the first.

Squeezing through, Borbor made his way on tiptoes over floorboards into the salon. The curtains were sewn shut, an iron candelabrum doing little to illuminate the dark. Pacing in, the traveller knew Leila, the magician princess, would be waiting there, as she had been in the Tale of Bastulap.

As his eyes adjusted, he heard his mother.

'If the password isn't spoken just right,' she said, 'the floor will shake and open and…'

A woman's voice interrupted the stream of memory.

Borbor squinted.

Furled head to toe in black, a figure was sitting at the far end of the room on a nursing chair. She was knitting a cloak from strands of fear.

'*Sarulam*,' she whispered.

Without thinking, the lemon-yellow jinn replied:

'*Mysteriass*.'

Delighted at having remembered the password, he paced forward onto a carpet of damp woven seaweed.

The floor began to tremble, then shake.

Suddenly, the boards beneath the carpet disappeared.

An instant after, the woven seaweed rectangle plunged down into the mineshaft.

Resorting to instinct, Borbor threw both paws above his head, as he leapt upwards.

In a feat worthy of an eclypsian acrobat from the Kingdom of Muxak, he grabbed hold of the candelabrum, his mind fumbling for the word…

The word that had slipped from his mother's mouth so long before.

A word which, until that moment, had never had any need to be afforded perfect pronunciation.

Face flushed, fur spattered with melting wax, Borbor let out a series of frantic cries:

'*Mysteriass! Mee-ster-eee-ass! Mest-e-assss! Mest-er-eeee-a-ss!*'

At the far end of the room, the woman's figure didn't flinch – her fingers knitting the final stitches of the cloak.

Swaying from the candelabrum, wailing, whimpering, Borbor heard something.

It wasn't a sound in the princess's salon.

But, rather, a memory.

A memory with no visual image attached.

The sound of his mother sneezing, over and over, as she told the tale.

She had a cold, Borbor said urgently to himself. *So her pronunciation wasn't quite right.*

Thinking fast, arms throbbing from the great weight suspended below them, he cried out:

'*Nysteriass!*'

Leila, the magician princess, peered up from her knitting.

'*Zarularfong,*' she replied in a kindly tone.

No sooner had the word left her lips than the room was reset.

The mineshaft vanished beneath floorboards, overlaid once again by the seaweed carpet.

An instant after, the traveller was lying in a heap on the rug, paws rubbing the patches of wax.

'The cloak is almost ready,' said the princess, knitting a last stitch or two. 'Was beginning to wonder whether you would ever arrive.'

Getting up, Borbor introduced himself, bowed reverently, and declared:

'All hail the Kingdom of Bastulap!'

*

OBSERVED IN MEMORY, the riverbank was a mosaic of imagery, perfectly conceived.

When giving seed to dreams, the late summer day's sequence of events was equally enchanted – yet similarly incomplete.

As if guided by an invisible director, it showed no more than was required.

This time it was different.

The scene was not dreamt, or perceived as a past occurrence.

Watching in real time, Oliver was actually in its presence.

Any detail he wished for was available.

Taking in the precious view – the rainbow dolphin, his parents, and himself – Oliver understood something.

Something that had always escaped him.

The sequence of the dolphin with the mistletoe crown – which came to Oliver in both waking hours and sleep – wasn't about a fragile connection to his parents.

Nor was it about magic in the mortal world.

It was a tether.

The point at which his soul was rooted.

Not to himself – but to the sinews of existence.

*

THE GHOST WIND raged through one kingdom after the next, leaving death and destruction in its wake.

Entire cities were ground into dust, their inhabitants slaughtered. Without a grain of mercy, the wind continued to advance, bringing terror on a scale unknown since the Time of Black Fear.

Nothing was safe from its wrath.

Not even those who'd taken sanctuary in the rusted iron fortress of Drestulam.

An entire population was hiding there.

Thousands of them.

Terrified, they huddled low in the underground passages snaking deep under the citadel. Some prayed. Others were doing what they could to comfort their children and the elderly.

In a darkened corner, far beneath the south tower, a mother was clutching her little daughter. Born six summers before, the child had been named Mortica. She looked like any girl her age but was different from the other children, and from everyone else seeking shelter in the iron fortress.

The reason was that Mortica was really the daughter of a frost jinn, delivered at birth to the family who were raising her as their own. As with all infants from the bloodline of frost jinn, she could perceive things hidden to others.

While the people of Drestulam regarded the advancing ghost wind as a threat about to destroy their kingdom, Mortica saw it differently.

She saw it as a blessing.

A blessing in disguise.

*

HEAVING WITH ALL their might, the pair of qemqems forced the unwieldy glass bottle through the conduit and into the Cadenta Hall.

Although they were in exactly the same position in which they'd been only moments before, the new permutation of their surroundings was quite different.

Gone were the simian monkeys and their battered typewriters, and the sloth jinn's foetid tapeworm – replaced by emptiness.

Candles flickering in chandeliers above.

The labyrinthine floor below.

There wasn't a soul, except for the short, stout figure of Annis.

Pacing up and down, he was agitated beyond belief.

'What took you so long?!' he spat, as the qemqems scurried through the conduit and out from the shadow thrown by the bottle containing the pink liquid remains.

The remains of Oliver Quinn.

'Crick-crick!' the creatures chirruped defensively at once.

'That's no excuse!'

Again, the qemqems twittered.

Rummaging in his carapace, the first produced a thick fibrous document, which he held out to the chief instructor with his longest leg.

Annis scowled.

'You qemqems are all the same! All you think about is damned paperwork! Can I remind you there's no time at all to waste?!'

Courageously, the second creature positioned himself in front of the bottle. He wouldn't budge until the contract had been signed in triplicate.

'Happy now?!' Annis scowled.

As the qemqems hurried away to blow their payment on figglewist fruit, the instructor clapped his hands together.

Three and a quarter seconds of silence passed.

At the end of it, a hard and brown object slalomed across the labyrinthine floor. Spiralling round and around to where Annis was standing, it came to rest at his feet.

An antique mahogany box.

The lid sprung back, revealing a pair of cloth gloves.

The left one was white. The right was black.

Hurrying to put them on, Annis buttoned them at the wrist.

Once his eyes were closed, he used all ten fingers to sketch out a design in mid-air.

Like an orchestral conductor crossed with a stage magician conjuring a spell, he mapped out the intricate details of a mechanism.

The gloved hands racing, a design materialized, made up of multi-coloured lines. Varying in texture, they appeared to take on a life of their own. Twisting around one another, intersecting, they lurched in all directions, forming an immense and elaborate blueprint.

The blueprint of a machine.

Moving faster and faster, the gloves dampened with perspiration – not that of the instructor – but of the jinns shaped into glove-like form.

All of a sudden, Annis stopped stock-still.

Opening his eyes slowly, he breathed in, then out, and watched – as the mechanism turned from a fantastic diagram into reality.

There were alembics, retorts, and elongated condensing tubes, conical flasks, burners, distillation dishes, magnets, and hydration chambers, vats with reinforced glass walls, high-powered engines, pistons, and interlocking clockwork gears.

The size of a three-storey family house, the mechanism was an advanced study in inexplicability. Most curious of all was that it wasn't simply an inanimate mechanical machine.

But, rather, it was alive.

The multiple constituent parts were all fused together, like individual organs in the abdomen of an organic, breathing creature.

A full minute after slipping on the gloves, Annis found himself inspecting the apparatus. Had there been time, he might have marvelled at its outlandish beauty.

Alas, time was the one thing against him.

With every passing second and a third, the chances of reconstituting Oliver Quinn into something resembling human form decreased by a million and one.

When it was ready, the mechanism let out a grunt, blushed poppy red, and eased into a uniform shade of cloisonné blue.

Having paced over to the flask, the chief instructor jerked out the stopper. Grimacing from the stench, and from worry, he yelled an order in the language of bottle-nosed jinn:

'*Karatulamasticualak*!'

The last syllable had not left his mouth when the mechanism sprang into action.

Instantly, fifteen arms grew from its side, leading to as many hands, each of them muscular, intricately wrinkled, and cloisonné blue.

Snatching the great flask as though it weighed less than a feather, they poured the precious pink contents into a funnel which had appeared on the right side of the machine.

As soon as the last drop of liquid had entered, the hands and arms withered like dead vines. With nothing holding it, the flask fell, smashing onto the labyrinthine floor.

The waxy liquid moved slowly through a series of transparent valves, towards the body of the mechanism.

A stone's throw from where Oliver's mortal remains were being reconstituted and processed, Annis grasped his hands together at his chest. Mouth dry from angst, his eyes were dim, having lost their characteristic glow.

As he stood there, deafened by the tremendous grinding noise emitted from the machinery, the doors to the Cadenta Hall were flung open.

A pair of feet sprinted across the threshold, then over the vast expanse of the Cadenta Hall's floor, ceasing only when they had reached the spot where Annis was standing.

Panting from the run, face flushed through anticipation, Amarath paused.

Her gaze having taken in Annis, and his own pained expression, it panned fast up onto the mechanism.

'*Whhhhhat's...* happening?' she exclaimed, the question drowned out by the machine's raucous strains.

Annis didn't turn.

Amarath stepped closer.

'He's dead, isn't he?!'

The instructor didn't reply. His mind was elsewhere, divided between two concerns of equal consequence:

1. Whether the only student he had ever encountered with a chance of reversing history would survive.

2. Whether there was a hope of staving off catastrophe – the one certain to result from the very same student's failure.

The waxy pink liquid surged through the valves and into a series of alchemical apparatus, then to a condensation tube before entering an accumulation tank. Unlike the first stage of the mechanism, which had been transparent, the next part was hidden behind a mottled cloisonné-blue skin.

Again, Amarath pleaded for information.

Annis said nothing.

Instead, he shuffled forward a pace or two until he was up close to the machine. As if sensing his presence, the mechanism grew a single arm, then a hand – both far more whimsical than those which had grabbed the flask.

Clenched into a fist, the hand tumbled in circles, before presenting itself an inch or two in front of the instructor's face. In its own time, the fingers drew themselves back, like the petals of a flower warmed by sunlight.

In the middle of the palm was a delicate glass bottle.

A bottle half-filled with a concoction stained cloisonné blue.

Reaching out, Annis unscrewed the lid and used the in-built pipette to drip a single bead of the liquid into each of his eyes.

Dark blue vapour streamed from his ocular sockets.

As it did so, Amarath covered the last few feet between herself and the instructor.

Her face close to Annis's, no farther than the width of an open hand, she watched as the vapour melted away, leaving his eye sockets empty.

'What've you done?' she said incredulously, her voice little more than a whisper.

'To see we must be blind,' Annis replied glumly.

'*We?*'

He held the bottle out.

'Take no more than a drop.'

'What… what… what does it…?'

'Cease your questions!'

Amarath's eyes scanned the instructor's face.

Up.

Down.

Left.

Right.

Brow to chin.

Ear to ear and cheek to cheek.

Lips.

Nose.

Eyes.

But there were no eyes – just sockets.

As though acid had burned them out. But instead of emptiness, there was a glow, like the ethereal radiance of the Northern Lights.

Without thinking, Amarath took the bottle and squeezed a single droplet into either eye.

A pace or two in front, the apparatus was churning, grinding, wailing, and swelling in size.

But Amarath's concentration had blocked out everything.

Everything except for the slipstream of her immediate consciousness.

She thought of a mountain, all snow-covered and bleak.

Of a cavern in the belly of the mountain, lined with crystalline rocks.

Of a stream of purest water coursing towards a tunnel at one end.

And she thought of a single ant clinging to the cavern's jagged roof.

As the cloisonné-blue concoction burnt out her eyes, Amarath found the images were replaced by something far more obvious, yet with the supremacy to show her what was really going on.

Blinded, her sight was replaced by a galaxy of other senses.

She could feel how it was to be the stream, the great crystal rocks, or even the mountain itself – not from the outside in, rather from the inside out.

So honed was the new palette of senses that she was the stream, and the rocks, and the cavern, and even the ant clinging to the ceiling.

Her mind straying, Amarath found she could imagine anything at all – but in a new way, as observed from its very essence.

A field of flowers in early spring.

A jinn born from an inferno's flames.

The silence of a desert's dusk.

The senses were no longer those of sound and sight, taste, smell and touch. Rather, they were others, made possible by blocking all that was obvious and plain.

Amarath heard a voice.

A voice not spoken, but felt.

'Come with me.'

'*Annis*? Where are you? Where am I? Come…? Come where?'

'No more questions!'

The exclamation emanated from a blurred image of raw energy.

An energy which was the instructor, in a form constituting his actual essence.

Suppressing questions, Amarath followed in silence.

Roaming through textures and senses she had never imagined could have existed, she found herself inside the mechanism.

A waxy pink liquid was running through the machinery. Although Amarath didn't see the colour or the consistency, she felt it, as she did everything else.

All of a sudden, the liquid changed form.

First, it turned into ball bearings – millions of them.

Ball bearings became gas.

Gas turned to numbers.

Numbers morphed into a churning, riotous wave on an ocean.

Suddenly, the wave was a little black fish with a pearl in its lips.

Then, the fish became a rusted iron key.

As in a dream, the succession of objects and the details were abstract and unimportant. It wasn't about what was perceived, so much as what was not shown.

Eyes burning once again, Amarath was knocked down by a wall of energy. More powerful than anything she'd ever imagined, let alone experienced, she felt as though her entire body had been reconfigured.

A voice was speaking.

Distorted. Faded. Grim.

Rubbing her eyes, Amarath strained to stand.

She collapsed.

Ears working to decode the sound.

Eyes desperately trying to make sense of the blur.

Gradually, her senses edged into focus.

The mechanism was gone – replaced by a wooden box.

A coffin.

A coffin crafted from Japanese oak, its grain stained drab grey.

Face sapped of colour, the instructor stood beside it.

'The moment of truth,' he said, unsure quite whether the remark was spoken.

Fingertips pressed together, he mumbled a prayer. An act as unlikely as it was desperate. For Annis was not a man who clung to faith or superstition.

He prayed to the Noxika Stone in the Kingdom of Blind Xilid Frogs.

He prayed to the single sheaf of wheat left in a dominion ravaged by famine and war.

He prayed to the jinn of Forgotten Hope.

Last of all, he prayed to the Blue Wind.

For only it could transmute improbability.

Then, with Amarath's shadow traced over him, Annis pulled open the casket's lid.

*

KNITTED FROM STRANDS of fear, the cloak had enabled the hero of the tale to cover a vast distance without a single footstep.

Holding it out to Borbor, the magician princess reminded him to keep faith during the journey.

'You will encounter terrible distress,' she said. 'And…'

'…And my skin will come loose from my bones.'

Leila nodded.

'Before you go, d'you wish to ask me anything?'

Borbor thought for a moment, his eyes wide and trusting.

'Will you tell me something?'

'What is it you wish to know?'

'Have I been summoned by the Order of Councilus to be praised, or to be punished?'

The magician princess glanced at the back of her hand.

'Neither,' she said quietly.

'But then... why have they summoned me?'

Cocking her head at the cloak, Leila smiled.

'Put it on, and you will find out,' she said.

*

ADVANCING AT TREMENDOUS speed, the ghost wind reached the ice-capped mountains sheltering Drestulam from the outside world, pulverizing them into dust finer than talc.

Within minutes, the entire city had been levelled, except for the iron fortress in which the population were hiding. Howling with glee, the wind swirled into an immense tornado, sucking up air from beyond ten horizons.

The sky went ink black.

Bearing down with all its might, the ghost wind lurched at the citadel's bulwark. As the tempestuous churning mass touched the grey stone walls, it heard a voice.

Not the voice of a ruler begging for compassion.

Nor the sound of screaming.

But, rather, the voice of a little girl guffawing with scorn.

A little girl called Mortica.

Pricking up its ears, the ghost wind hesitated, for no one had ever laughed at it before.

'Who dares mock *me*, the mighty ghost wind?' it bellowed. 'The wind that's cleaved a path across the Realm?'

Mortica was too busy laughing to reply.

She laughed and laughed, and laughed and laughed, until her cheeks were numb.

Enraged beyond description, the ghost wind swelled a thousand times, the black plume of its gigantic expanse reaching the heavens.

Again, it bellowed, its voice far stronger than before:

'Show yourself, whoever you are, and feel the power pitted against you!'

Her laughter ceasing, Mortica slipped on her shoes and made her way up through the tunnels, until she reached the battlements. So miniature was she that no one noticed her climb deftly through an arrow slit and down to the ground.

Waiting there, in a veil of ultimate destruction, was the ghost wind.

'Here I am,' said the little girl, in a plain and fearless voice.

Peering down, the ghost wind's single eye widened with amazement.

'The smallest puff from my lungs and you'd be hurled into the farthest reaches of eternity!' it bellowed.

'I don't doubt it,' said Mortica.

'So take your last breath, and prepare to die!'

'Very well,' the little girl replied.

Again, the tornado sucked up air for a thousand miles and, again, it bore down.

As the ghost wind lurched forward, spinning like a harbinger from hell, Mortica held up a finger.

'Just one thing,' she said.

The single eye balking at yet another interruption, the tempest stopped in its tracks.

'*What*?!'

'Well, I was wondering something.'

Swelling to a magnitude far beyond immensity, the ghost wind juddered with rage.

'And what, pray tell, might that be?'

The daughter of the frost jinn picked up a smooth-sided stone and weighed it in her pint-sized palm.

'Was just wondering whether you could turn this pebble into a little perfume bottle.'

Again, the ghost wind balked, its colossal form darkening.

'I am the ghost wind!' it cried. 'I don't make frivolous knick-knacks. I destroy!'

Mortica nodded.

'Just as I thought,' she said.

'Are you content?' cried the wind, preparing to bear down on the fortress and cleave a path on to the next horizon.

'Oh, yes. It's just what I wanted to hear,' said Mortica casually. 'Because it means I have won my bet with another little girl, who's hiding in there with everyone else.'

Curiosity piqued, the ghost wind let out a grunt.

'What bet?' it asked.

The daughter of the frost jinn blushed.

'A silly little bet,' she replied. 'The kind little girls make with each other when they're hiding in rusted iron fortresses like the one behind me, waiting for ghost winds like you to grind them into dust.'

'Tell it to me,' quipped the wind, 'and I'll decide whether it is silly or not.'

Blushing once again, Mortica replied:

'I bet my friend you couldn't make a perfume bottle from a simple pebble, and then squeeze all of yourself into it.'

Its single eye flashing with ire, the ghost wind sucked the little pebble from the girl's hand. Having bored it out until it was hollow, the wind etched a pleasing motif over the outer surface.

Then, folding in on itself, the wind descended.

Mile upon mile it plunged down from the heavens, like a mushroom cloud being sucked back into an atomic bomb.

Very soon, the ghost wind's entire form had disappeared into the pretty little bottle.

In her own time, Mortica leant down, picked it up, and plugged the end with a button pulled from her dress.

Shaking with fury, its voice no more than the faintest whisper, the ghost wind pledged retribution on a wicked scale.

Indifferent to the threats, the daughter of the frost jinn nudged the perfume bottle into the pocket of her dress. Scaling the fortress wall, she went to tell her adopted mother what had taken place.

Within an hour, all the inhabitants were standing on the pebbled plain lying between the citadel and the remnants of their capital. The King of Drestulam led the cheers in honour of little Mortica, and then led his people in a fiesta which continued through days and nights.

Every pair of feet in the kingdom danced until it was sore.

Every mouth laughed, and gave thanks for salvation.

When the festivities were at an end, the people of Drestulam began picking through what was left of their beloved city. Facing grim reality, they resigned themselves to poverty.

In the following days, some of the people rose up against their king, who was now just as destitute as everyone else. Tying him to a post, they hurled stones at him and blamed him for the misfortune which had befallen them all.

The leader of the uprising waved a fist at their bloodied ruler.

'Once our meagre supplies of food are finished,' he cried, 'we'll starve to death! Our destitution is your doing!'

As the king passed out from his wounds, the dissenters waved their fists and taunted all the more.

None of them noticed an upturned packing crate meandering out from the citadel and onto the plain. It came to a halt near to where the disgraced monarch was slumped, still tied to the post.

With calls for revolution in the air, Mortica clambered out of the crate and up on top.

Clapping her hands, she waved, and clapped her hands some more.

Having gained the attention of all the people, she yelled:

'There's nothing our beloved king could have done to save the city!'

Baying for blood, the dissenters protested.

The daughter of the frost jinn clapped again.

When silence prevailed, she addressed them:

'Let him go and I will make you a promise!'

'Go back to your mother!' called a man at the back.

'Leave us alone!' cried another.

'The king must die!' bawled a third.

The daughter of the frost jinn clapped her hands more urgently than before.

'Your memories are as short as you are foolish,' she remarked coldly, staring out at her detractors. 'And if you kill the king you'll remain as you are now. But, do as I say and, in less than a year, you will be wealthier than in your wildest dreams!'

From: *Jinn Hunter: Book Three – The Perplexity*

A Trifling Achievement

SIR GEOFFREY CALDECOTT took a pinch of macouba and followed it with a glass of Madeira.

He had chilled the bottle out on the window ledge overnight and took great satisfaction in the fact that there was a touch of frost on the sides. Sipping the drink, he leaned back in his favourite chair. It had just been returned by the upholsterer in cloisonné-blue silk.

William DeWitt knocked, then entered.

'The narration will recommence in thirty minutes,' he said.

'Bloody Cochran,' grunted Sir Geoffrey quickly. 'Go and tell Falkirk to fetch Jenkins. We have no choice but to avail ourselves of his services. No choice at all.'

DeWitt went back to the door. As his fingers touched the brass knob he remembered that Falkirk had given him a letter on the way up, declaring that it had just arrived by private messenger. He pulled the letter from his inside pocket. It was small, smudged with dirt.

'I believe this came for you, Sir Geoffrey,' he said. Caldecott took the letter and stared at the front of the envelope. It was addressed to him. He broke the seal and scanned the short text. DeWitt said something, but he didn't hear.

'Is it from the expedition, Sir Geoffrey?' said DeWitt a second time.

'Major Peddie...'

'Has he reached the golden city?'

'Major Peddie...'

'Yes?'

'Major Peddie and his entire party have been slaughtered by savages.'

Half an hour later, Adams was standing before the audience in the library once again. He didn't enjoy narrating his tale, or having to endure the inane comments of London society. But then, as he continually reminded himself, every word spoken brought him a little closer to Hudson.

He waited for Cochran's signal.

When it came, he stood up, thanked the audience for their attendance, and began.

'We had reached a dry waterhole,' he said. 'The Moorish commander wept like a child. Until that moment he had been a man of considerable ability, a tower of strength to his party. But the dry hole destroyed his will to continue. He fell onto the baked ground and tore out his hair, jerking his body back and forth like a madman.

'"We will die now," he said despondently in his tongue. "Our death is certain."

'I spoke up, declaring that we could kill one of the camels, drain its paunch and drink it. The leader abhorred being advised by anyone, especially a Christian.

"'You did not hear me, slave!" he shouted. "Death! He rides with us; his shape forms the shadow of every man."

'There may have been no hope, and I may have been a Christian, but the commander did as I had suggested. A male camel was slaughtered and its paunch was drained. The foul liquid was poured into the skins, the blood drunk, and the meat packed up. A little time later we moved on, our footsteps far slower than before, as if each man could sense the spectre of Death beside him.

'After three days of marching we spied an encampment.

'The Moors were greatly excited by the sight. Their step quickened and we were soon being welcomed by the leader of the place. He was an old man called Touliq, whose face had been severely burned at one time. The right side of his face was missing its ear, its eye, and part of the nose. When he saw me though, his good eye seemed to light up. Pointing in my direction, he said something to the commander.

'The two men shook hands, and I found myself the possession of Touliq.

'A week after our arrival, the Moors who had taken me from Timbuctoo departed. None of them, not even the commander, looked at me or said farewell. As far as they were concerned, I was a chattel, an object without value, especially as we were so far from anyone prepared to pay for my redemption.

'My new master, Touliq, eked out an existence with his family on the margin of the desert. His sheep spent their lives searching the baked earth, hunting for roots or whatever they could find. He had three wives. The older two were haggard and both blind. They had no respect for their husband and regarded each other with contempt. Yet, the person they loathed more than any other on earth was their husband's third wife. She was a girl of about twenty years named Aisha.

'Unlike them, she was agile, soft-skinned and was extremely gentle in the face. When she saw me, she sent her servant to feed me porridge. It was mouth-watering. Each night a bowl would be brought to me, and I lapped it up like a dog that had been starved.

'Two weeks after my arrival there, Aisha asked if I would attend to her small flock of goats, as she feared they might be eaten by wolves. She promised to pay me, and pointed to an empty bowl, indicating that more of the porridge would be served. I watched over the animals willingly, but she did not pay me. I may have been a slave in their eyes, but I felt that I ought to be paid as promised. So, that afternoon, I remonstrated, to which she promised again, declaring that payment would come that very night.

'When my master and his other wives were asleep, Aisha sent her servant to me. I asked her for my bowl of porridge. She said that her mistress would give it to me herself. So I went to her tent. She fed me a large bowl of the food and, when I had finished, she gave me even more.

'I was very content and I thanked her greatly. She smiled, approached me, and pushed the garment off her shoulders. It fell to the floor, leaving her entirely naked. Then she forced herself upon me, declaring that her husband did not satisfy her. I pushed her away, exclaiming stridently that I was spoken for and that, in any case, such a liaison would be a death knell.

'Aisha stood to her feet and she screamed.

'"We will both be killed!" I shouted.

'"Only you will die," she replied.

'An instant passed, then my master, Touliq, arrived at the door of the tent. As soon as his good eye spied me there, he called his sons to catch me. They held me down on the ground and their father came over to execute me. The blade was about to strike my neck, when a voice told him to stop. It was another old man who had been staying with Touliq as a guest.

'Raising his hands in the air, he declared that execution by the blade was too good for me, that it would be death for a man with honour. He promised his friend that, the next day, he would take me into the desert and leave me for the wolves. The sword was thrown to the ground and I was guarded for the remainder of the night, lest I run into the desert alone.'

Hearing a commotion at the back of the library, Adams stopped mid-flow. The audience began mumbling and, as the mumbling grew louder, they stood up and looked to the door.

Suddenly Cochran gasped, stood up too, and bowed his head.

Adams was unsure what was happening. He looked around and spotted an immensely fat figure looking at him. It was the prince regent, who had come from the portrait sitting, and was still wearing his new field marshal's uniform. Standing on his right was Lord Alvanley.

'That is the American, Your Highness, the one who claims to have set eyes on Timbuctoo.'

The prince held up a hand, commanding the audience to be seated.

'Carry on!' he cried out in Cochran's direction. 'You may pretend that I am not here!'

Caldecott charged over and attended to his royal guest, who had taken a seat on a low chair at the back of the room. The doyens of high society were buzzing around the prince like bees before a hive.

Cochran signalled to Adams to continue.

'At dawn, I was tied to the back of a camel and taken into the desert once again,' he said. 'That beast walked until the sun was high above us. It was so hot that I could smell my naked back roasting. Touliq had sent his oldest son to make certain his friend kept his promise to execute me.

'I passed out and, when I regained consciousness, the camel had stopped. Its master ordered me to climb down. Touliq's son watched as I was pegged out on the sand. My wrists and ankles were bound so tightly that the blood ceased flowing. I passed out again. Touliq's son must have then left, because when I came to once more he was not there. But his father's friend was still standing over me.

'He had waited for the boy to leave, then he unfastened the bindings and forced me to follow him. He had never intended to dispatch me, for as I was a Christian slave he knew that, somewhere, there would be a consul ready to pay a ransom for my life.'

Adams finished speaking, and waited for Cochran to catch up with the transcription. At the back of the room, the prince regent was struggling to avoid Caldecott's fawning advances.

'Your Highness, it is a pleasure beyond our most distant expectations to have you within our humble company,' said Sir Geoffrey, wincing.

The prince had only just met the chairman, but was bored to death by him.

'How could I remain isolated from this distinguished gathering?' he asked. 'After all, it is the talk of London.'

'How very kind, Highness.'

'To think of it...' said the regent, lumbering to his feet, 'that an American has beaten you all to Timbuctoo. How perfectly delicious!'

Caldecott's face turned lilac with ire.

'It is a trifling achievement,' he replied, 'but America is after all a land of scant success.'

'If it be so trifling an achievement, sir, then why have our most celebrated pioneers been eluded by the feat?'

Sir Geoffrey felt his scalp overheating. With gritted teeth, he said:

'Your Highness, it appears that the brawny American constitution is well suited to the rigours of the African continent.'

'I should like to make the acquaintance of the American,' replied the prince, walking in the direction of the lectern where Adams was still standing.

'At once, Your Pre-eminence, at once.'

Caldecott waved a hand to Cochran, scowled, and waved again. A moment later, Adams was face to face with the regent.

'If Your Royal Highness would permit me to introduce to you the individual in question.'

'Charmed, sir, I am quite charmed,' said the prince.

'I am pleased to meet you,' replied Adams.

The regent raised his quizzing glass and inspected the American.

'How were you amused by Africa, Mr. Adams?'

'*Amused*?'

'Indeed, how were you touched by its raw appeal?'

Uncertain how to reply, Adams just smiled.

'Did you see any fauna?'

'Fauna?'

'Any animals?'

'Yes, plenty.'

'Excellent! How did you like them?'

Again, Adams remained silent, unsure of what to say.

He cocked his head in a nod.

'Excellent,' said the prince regent again, 'then you must come and see my collection. For I would value your opinion on the new acquisition prowling my African savannah.'

'What creature is it?'

'A polar bear!'

From: *Timbuctoo*

The Story's Seed

By FIRST LIGHT, the oasis was a distant memory.

Moving forward, the heat rising by the minute, the travellers moaned and groaned, and the pack camels did the same.

From time to time, Baibar would untie his turban and wring it out, unleashing a great pool of saltwater, which drained into the sand.

Always at the front, Scheherazade led the way over towering dunes and down through valleys between them, as though leading an army into war. Her pace didn't let up, not for an instant. Whenever the others cried out for her to slow, she would turn momentarily, and wave them forward.

Sindbad the Sailor only managed to keep going by pretending he was sailing a dhow across an open sea. But, as soon as he remembered where he was, he'd collapse onto the dunes and beg to be transported to anywhere but where he was.

Behind him, her strides becoming shorter and shorter, was Aladdin. A thousand times she'd imagined the others learning of her identity, and what they might have made of it. And a thousand times she thanked all she held sacred for freeing her from the savage binds of injustice.

As for Ali Baba, he had a secret of his own, one that kept his feet moving despite his body aching as though it had been torn to shreds and stuck together again. He may have been older and more corpulent than the others, but nothing could stop him.

Nothing, that is, other than what was to come.

Day and night they journeyed, halting no more than a few minutes each dawn, and the same again each dusk. The beasts of burden lurched from side to side with exhaustion, grunting and snorting as though the end of their lives had come.

Six days and six nights beyond the oasis, Baibar thrust all four arms into the air in jubilation.

'I see the city!' he boomed. 'I see the City of Brass!'

The words fortifying them like sustenance from heaven, the travellers hastened forwards.

Three hours later each one of them caught their first sight of it – the outline of a city capped with magnificent gilded domes.

Soon after that, they were crossing the flood plain of a mighty river, glimpsing the first greenery they'd seen since the desert paradise.

Drawing closer, they spied flocks of fat-tailed sheep grazing in meadows of knee-high grass, and cows striding majestically towards the water's edge.

There were egrets, too, hundreds of them, their long bills rooting for worms in the soft soil. Most importantly though, there were people – milling about in the distance on donkeys, horses, or simply ambling through the lush landscape plucked from every desert traveller's imagination.

As they approached the last span of the flood plain, a deafening noise drowned out the sounds of nature, and the sky darkened.

Something was hurtling down from the sky – what looked like a colossal, square-edged meteorite. Peering up into the heavens, the travellers watched as another massive stone shot down, fixing itself to the first.

Then another, and another.

'They're linking up!' Sindbad shouted.

They all watched in stupefaction, the ground shaking as one block joined up with the last.

'Baibar, strike them away!' Scheherazade yelled.

Following orders, the Black Jinn bounded forwards, all four arms swiping left and right, as though trying to swat a plague of flies.

Every time he tried to hit one of the blocks, it simply jerked out of the way, and came to a rest beside the others.

'A wall!' Aladdin bawled. 'It's building a wall!'

Scheherazade's face turned cherry-red with rage.

'The work of the sorcerer, Yunan!'

'We can climb it!' Aladdin said enthusiastically.

As the short sentence was spoken, the wall began growing from the ground. Within a single minute, it was so high that the sun had been blocked out.

Sindbad was the next to speak:

'Baibar, take off your shirt!'

The others looked round in puzzlement.

As requested, the Black Jinn removed his shirt.

Working double-speed, Sindbad tore the garment down the main seam, and curled the cloth around the tent poles. Soon, he'd fashioned a kind of canopy, attaching four lengths of cord to it.

'This is where we leave the camels and attendants,' he explained.

Ali Baba screwed up his face.

'Are we going to magically lift into the air and float down the other side?' he asked.

'No magic!' Scheherazade barked.

'No, no,' the sailor confirmed. 'No magic! We'll tie ourselves on, and ask our dear friend Baibar to throw us over. There's no magic in that.'

'And let us plunge to our deaths?' Aladdin whined.

'No we won't. We'll float down.'

The queen stepped away from the others, cursing her husband, then his sorcerer. She was about to suggest they give the matter more thought, even though time was against them, when Baibar yelled out again.

'I think Sindbad's idea is a good one,' he said.

'And I think it could get us all killed,' Ali Baba replied.

'An imperfect plan today is better than a perfect plan tomorrow,' Baibar responded.

'Are you a philosopher all of a sudden?'

The Black Jinn shook his head.

'No,' he answered. 'I'm just pointing out the obvious.'

With that, he jerked a paw behind him.

The travellers turned.

Ranging over the horizon in the desert's darkness was an army.

'They look like snake ghouls to me,' the jinn said.

'What the hell are snake ghouls?!' Sindbad cried.

'A pain in the backside,' Baibar groaned.

'Can't say I'd know, because I've never encountered them before.'

'That's obvious,' the Black Jinn shot back.

'Why?'

'Because if you'd ever met a snake ghoul before, you wouldn't be standing there looking at them coming towards you.'

Scheherazade stared at the approaching army, their fusillades of arrows getting closer and closer through the shadows. Then, turning one-eighty, she looked out at the great wall.

'Certain death,' she said, the word expressed without emotion.

Sindbad clapped his hands.

'Come on! Let's tie ourselves onto the sail and get thrown up over the wall! We'll be eating kebabs in no time!'

All eyes turned to the queen.

'All right,' she said, frostily. 'But only because we're out of choices.'

As quickly as he could, Sindbad knotted the others in place, and then himself.

'Sorry to be leaving you, Baibar,' he said.

'Don't worry about me,' the Black Jinn said with a grin, 'I'll get over there somehow and we'll have kebabs together.'

The snake ghouls were close now, their arrows and spears striking the ground all around the travellers.

'Hurry!' Sindbad cried. 'Cup us in your fist and throw us up with all your might!'

Baibar did as the sailor had asked him.

Scooping the others up in one of his four paws, he tilted back, and launched them full force into the air.

As though shot from a catapult, they climbed up into the sky.

But, rather than clearing the top of the wall, they slammed into it.

Shrieking in pain, they screamed as they fell.

The Black Jinn dived towards the wall, and managed to catch them just before they hit the ground.

Sindbad snarled:

'Try again, and put your back into it this time!'

The arrows were falling like rain now.

Grasping the travellers tight in his fist, his back covered in arrows, Baibar hurled the sail and its passengers up into the sky a second time.

Yet again, they slammed into the wall, and fell.

'Can't do it,' the Black Jinn groaned as he caught his companions. 'I don't have the strength.'

'How d'you get strength?' asked Ali Baba.

'By flattening kingdoms,' the jinn replied.

'Isn't there any other way?' asked Scheherazade, focusing on the army of snake ghouls, which was closing in.

'Causing terror and misery,' he said bashfully.

466

'Well, why don't you cause *them* a little terror and misery?!' Aladdin cried.

'Won't work.'

Aladdin balked.

'Why not?'

'Because they're magical beings, and magical beings don't count.'

Sindbad raised a forefinger.

'Do the jinn rules say what kind of kingdom it has to be?'

'No,' Baibar answered. 'Only that it must be "obliteration on a gigantic scale".'

The sailor's face seemed to brighten.

He pointed to a termite mound.

'Flatten that!' he yelled.

In one stride, Baibar had reached it, and crushed it.

'Ooooh,' he said contentedly, as a fusillade of spears hurtled down. 'Think that did it. I'm feeling revived.'

'*Strong* and revived?' Scheherazade asked.

'Very much so.'

'So throw us with all your might!'

Doing as the queen had bid him, the Black Jinn tossed the travellers up into the air – so high that they were covered in icicles. Peering down, they saw the wall far behind in the distance.

Then they fell. Or, rather they floated down in the canopy made from Baibar's shirt.

As they neared the city's outline, they called to one another, jubilantly.

'I can smell the kebabs roasting!' Aladdin wailed.

TAHIR SHAH

'And I can see the palace!' Ali Baba added.

'I'm going to take a bath!' Sindbad howled.

'And I'm going to find the story seed!' Scheherazade yelled.

Whether it was a case of the Black Jinn having aimed well, or plain good fortune, the canopy drifted down through the cloudless sky right above the city, its passengers blinded by dazzling light.

The streets so close below them, they could hear voices of the stall-keepers in the market touting vegetables, and could smell the delicious scent of chickens roasting on open spits.

As they descended, Sindbad heaved the great canopy to the left, steering it towards a patch of soft grass below the palace walls.

Just before they touched down, however, a ferocious wind hurled them up into the air once again. It didn't seem to affect any other object, as though it had been aimed at them, and them alone.

Wailing with terror as they were thrust up into the sky, the four travellers clung hold of the ropes with all their might, trailing against the headwind.

At what seemed like lightning speed, they flew for hours, until their limbs were blue and numb with cold.

Clutching hold for dear life, all Scheherazade could think of was the story's seed, and how she'd been so close, but was suddenly so far. In a single fleeting fragment of time, she and Aladdin caught eye contact. Against the hurly-burly of the pulverizing wind, Aladdin seemed to smile reassuringly at the queen.

Through days and nights they flew, stars glinting in the heavens like jewels, and the sun blazing down with all its might. They crossed oceans and landmasses, immeasurable and bleak.

Then, all of a sudden, the wind ceased, and they floated down towards the radiant waters of a sea.

Sindbad was the only one enlivened at the sight of waves.

'Breakers!' he cried out in delight.

'We'll drown!' Aladdin gasped in horror.

Once again, the sailor steered the canopy, heaving it to the side with all his strength, guiding it towards a smattering of russet-brown islands, a little archipelago.

This time, there was no sudden wind. And, to their delight, they came to rest on a beach.

One by one, they gave thanks, and congratulated Sindbad.

He stepped forward to the queen, his expression sombre.

'We will get to the City of Brass, and will find the seed,' he said. 'I promise you.'

Scheherazade managed the faintest smile, as though not to grace her lips with it would have been heartless.

'On behalf of all the women whose lives you are saving by helping me, I thank you,' she said.

Apparently unfazed by the setback, Sindbad marched into the forest bordering the beach, and set to work chopping down a copse of balsa trees.

Ali Baba did what he could to assist, even though he had no experience in building rafts.

'How will we ever find out where we are?' he whined.

'Irrelevant!' the sailor responded.

'Is it?'

'Yes! What matters is where our destination lies.'

'But how will we find it? How will we find the City of Brass?'

Sindbad paused from hacking with his sword.

'The same way any sailor ever reaches where they want to go.'

'How?'

'By asking the wind to take us,' he said.

At that moment, the queen approached.

'I am going into the forest to search for fruit,' she explained.

The sailor frowned.

'Better for me to go with you,' he retorted. 'It's not safe for a woman.'

Pacing forward to where Sindbad was standing, sword in his fist, Scheherazade raised her hand and slapped him across his cheek.

'Never again doubt the ability of a woman,' she snapped. 'Especially one who's a queen.'

Calling Aladdin to join her, the two of them set off into the hinterland.

At the western edge of the archipelago, the island was rimmed with beaches that gave way to forest, and the forest to crumbling outcrops of rock at its core.

With no signs of human life whatsoever, nature had taken an unyielding hold, or at least something had, whether it was natural or not.

As they picked their way through the undergrowth, climbing over roots and pushing away vines, Scheherazade and Aladdin noticed the lack of birds and other creatures. It was as if every possible form of life had been scared away.

'D'you feel it?' Aladdin asked, as they tramped ahead.

'Yes I do,' Scheherazade answered right away, even before hearing what 'it' was. 'But we can't set sail on Sindbad's craft until we've gathered a good supply of food.'

Just then, they spotted a magnificent dragonfly coursing through the forest, a kaleidoscope of light playing over its rainbow wings. Without thinking, both women hurried after it, as though hoping it might lead them to a secret.

And that's exactly what it did.

Pausing to drink from the sap of a towering tree, the creature shot upwards into the boughs.

'Look! There!' cried Scheherazade, pointing.

'Breadfruit!'

Aladdin scaled the tree, and started throwing down the enormous prickly fruits.

Taking shelter from the bombardment, Scheherazade stepped back into the surrounding undergrowth. To her surprise, she spotted another rainbow dragonfly skimming through the leaves. Again, she felt drawn to it, and took chase before realizing what she was doing.

A short distance from the breadfruit tree, into the boughs of which Aladdin had climbed, Scheherazade came to a tree covered in perfectly ripe plums. Plucking one, she bit into it, and was overwhelmed at the delicious taste.

Reaching up for another, she was caught off-balance.

She lurched backwards, arms flailing left and right.

As she tumbled to the ground, her sandal slipped from her foot. She peered around to see where it had gone, and realized it had fallen down a hole.

On hands and knees, she looked down into it.

What had at first appeared to be no more than a little pit was in actual fact a shaft, the width of a barrel.

Straining to focus in the darkness, she saw something glinting and gleaming far below. Overcome with curiosity, Scheherazade was unable to help herself. Taking hold of a good-sized vine from a nearby tree, she unfurled it, and used it to climb down.

Within a few minutes she was standing on the shaft's floor, and saw her sandal had become lodged in the branches of a tree that grew from its base. As she reached up to retrieve her shoe, her gaze was diverted to something extraordinary.

In the lower branches, an oval mirror was hanging, as though positioned with care to provide illumination. But it wasn't the mirror that amazed the queen. Rather, it was the fact that among the branches was a kingdom of miniature people, none of them taller than a man's thumb.

Their skin was painted in vivid colours, and they were dressed in costumes fabricated from the bark of the tree. They appeared to live in little houses fixed to the branches, and were climbing up and down tiny ladders as they went about their lives.

Remarkably, none of the little people had noticed Scheherazade. Watching them for a good long while, she took in the details of the civilization, marvelling at it.

All of a sudden she heard a squeaking, and saw an especially small figure, a little boy, pointing up at her. He was screaming out, warning all the others that an attack was about to take place.

Instantly, the tiny people hurried into their houses, leaving the tree silent.

'I'm not going to harm you,' Scheherazade said.

Still silence.

'Please don't be afraid,' the queen whispered gently. 'I merely climbed down to get my sandal, which had tumbled down into this hole.'

A little time passed, and the child who'd spotted the visitor in the first place appeared on a slender branch. He'd slunk out of his family's house, and didn't seem to have any fear at all.

'If you try and kill us, we'll gobble you up!' he yelled.

A high-pitched squeal followed, as the boy's mother tore out of a house, grabbed him by the scruff of the neck, and dragged him back inside.

Again, Scheherazade spoke:

'I'm not here to harm you,' she said. 'Please come out and let me see you all.'

A few minutes slipped by, then an elderly man stuck his head out from a treehouse.

'Where are you from?' he enquired.

'From beyond the oceans and the mountains,' the queen replied.

Another head appeared – that of a young woman. She asked:

'Did you see the gollop?'

'What's that?'

Pressing her ear close to the tree so she could hear the voices, Scheherazade heard expressions of fear. All of a sudden, everyone was out of their homes, waving their fists.

'The gollop wants to eat us!' yelled the woman.

'If he gets us, he'll chew us up!' exclaimed another.

'We live in terror of him!' howled an old lady, no taller than a toothpick.

'I felt a coldness up in the forest,' Scheherazade answered. 'As though there was something lurking there, something keeping creatures away.'

'The gollop!' the miniature people cried, their voice as one.

'Who are you?' the queen asked.

'We're Grilliax.'

'Are there more of you?'

'There used to be,' a young man said. 'But one by one all the villages like ours were devoured by the gollop. So we're the last one.'

Scheherazade scratched a fingertip to her cheek.

'Is there any way of stopping the gollop?' she asked.

The villagers all spoke at once.

'I can't understand you! You'll have to speak one at a time.'

The young man pushed to the front.

'There's only one way to stop the gollop,' he cried.

'What's that?'

'By catching him in a net, and throwing him into the sea.'

'I wish I could help you,' Scheherazade replied, 'but as soon as we've built a raft, we will leave the island.'

The voices all cried out again:

'Before you go, please catch the gollop for us!'

'But I don't even know what the gollop looks like,' the queen said. 'And I don't have a net.'

'We can help,' said the little boy, shimmying up a branch no thicker than a twig. Fumbling, he pulled out a tiny scroll, and unfurled it.

Scheherazade took in a neat drawing of a creature with whiskers, pointed ears, arched back, and long tail.

'That's a cat,' she said with certainty.

'It's a *gollop*!' the tiny people replied.

'It may be a gollop to you, but to me it's a cat, and I know how to catch cats.'

'With a net!' the people yelled. 'You'll need a net!'

'No need for a net.'

'What will you use if not a net?'

'A fish,' said Scheherazade.

Climbing back out of the hole, the queen promised to return once the gollop had been caught.

Then, heaving the breadfruits back to the beach with Aladdin, she found the raft almost complete. Sindbad had stripped a dozen balsa trees of their bark, and bolted the trunks together with nails fashioned from palm wood. As for a sail, he'd made it from Baibar's shirt.

The breadfruits were loaded aboard, along with a supply of coconuts filled with water.

'Sindbad,' Scheherazade said, 'can you catch me a fish?'

Before she knew it, the sailor had caught a huge tuna, and had roasted it on the beach. Cutting off the tail, she disappeared into the forest once again.

An hour later, she emerged with an exceedingly affectionate tabby cat, purring in her arms.

'Where did that come from?' Ali Baba asked.

'From the forest. Apparently she's the only cat on the island.'

Handing the animal to Ali Baba, she headed into the forest again.

'I'll be back soon,' she said.

Retracing her steps to where the breadfruit tree stood, Scheherazade climbed down into the shaft, and addressed the Grilliax.

'Did you see the gollop?' they asked fretfully, their tiny faces gripped with fear.

'Yes.'

'Did you manage to catch it?'

The queen nodded.

'Yes I did. And, there's no need to throw it into the sea.'

'Then what will you do with the terrible gollop?' yelled the little boy.

'I'll take her with us and release her on an island much larger than this.'

The villagers cooed with delight.

'How can we ever thank you?'

'No thanks are needed,' replied Scheherazade.

A round of applause went up.

'Now, I must leave,' said the queen.

'Wait!' yelled one of the women.

'We have something for you!' a second cried out.

'A sacred relic!' called a third.

All together, they dragged a circular object over, which was hanging on the end of a branch.

'It fell from the sky!' the first woman hollered.

'From the home of the gods!' bawled the second.

'It'll make your wishes come true!' the third shouted.

Taking the object with thanks, Scheherazade recognized it as a twist of wire, dropped perhaps by a passing bird.

'I'll wear it always,' she said, slipping it onto her finger as a ring.

The raft set sail at first light, laden with coconuts, breadfruit, and with the tabby cat as an extra passenger.

Although uncertain of which direction to take, Sindbad the Sailor followed his nose, and asked the wind to guide the way. At times he may have been self-important and haughty, but the others marvelled at him. As incompetent as he'd been riding a horse, he was in his element before the mast.

Tilting out of the water, the raft skimmed along at a tearing pace. All day it kept on a heading due west. As night cloaked the waves and revealed heavens glinting above, Sindbad lowered the sail fashioned from the Black Jinn's shirt.

Through the light of six days they sailed, catching fish when they could, to the delight of the gollop, which made a change from the diet of breadfruit. And through the darkness of six nights, the vast nocturnal firmament above awed each one of the travellers, reminding them of their insignificance.

Each evening, one of them would tell a tale for the amusement of the others.

One night, the gollop cradled in her arms, Aladdin offered to recount an adventure.

'Each one of you has lived far more interesting lives than me,' she said. 'So forgive me if what I say is not worthy of your ears. This is what I have to tell...'

Casting her head back, drinking in a hundred billion stars, she stroked a hand tenderly over the tabby's back, and began:

> Once upon a time, in the distant reaches of Hind, there lived a king who had everything a man could ever wish for. His stables were filled with the finest horses, his treasure vaults piled with gold and jewels, and in his apartments there were the most lovely women ever to have graced the earth.
>
> But, as is the way of men, the ruler – whom we shall call King Shalimar – was not content. Rather, the more material wealth he gained, and the more radiant the women who attended him, the less content he became. Through long days and nights, he called for larger and larger platters of food to be brought

so that sweetmeats could take his mind off his state of melancholy.

There were platters of shish kebabs laid out on beds of rice, entire roast sheep, sides of beef, and melons the size of cannonballs. Day and night the king gorged himself, until he was the size of an ox. Eventually, he became so fat that he could hardly get out of bed.

Moaning and groaning, he promised to bury in a heap of gold anyone who could cure his sorrowful state. As you can imagine, everyone in the kingdom grew very excited.

Queuing up in a zigzagging line that snaked through the capital's streets, they tried to cure the king's state of melancholy one by one. Some people told jokes. Others jumped up and down and spun around. One or two inflated camels' bladders and popped them.

But nothing worked. The king was more despondent than ever. The chief vizier was about to dispatch a messenger to the neighbouring kingdom to plead for help when he heard a disturbance at the palace gates. A young boy was being scolded by the royal guard. The vizier came to learn that the boy wanted to make the king happy again, as was his right.

'Everyone else who's tried has failed,' the vizier said sternly. 'What makes you think you're any different?'

'I'm different because I don't think like the adults,' the boy answered. 'I think like a child.'

'And is that good?' asked the vizier.

A sparkle in his eye, the little boy broke into a grin.

'Of course it is,' he answered, 'because it's how people are supposed to think!'

The boy was cleaned up, instructed in how to behave in front of the monarch, and led into the royal chamber. Making his way to the bed, he bowed, then said:

'Your Majesty, I haven't come to cure you so much as to tell you something. I'm afraid to say that you'll drop dead within a month, because an assassin has been sent to kill you.'

The ruler, who was lying back on a pile of pillows, munching at a platter of kebabs, looked up in horror.

'How do you know this?!' he exclaimed.

'I know it because my father works in a distant kingdom, and he overheard the assassin telling another that he's coming for you.'

The king was about to call the guards when the boy stopped him.

'There's nothing you can do to halt the assassin,' he said.

'Of course I can, because I have a thousand guards protecting me!'

'No, no, no,' the boy replied. 'You see, the assassin that's coming for you is wearing a magic cloak which makes him invisible.'

The king's forehead furrowed like a farmer's field. Pushing away the kebabs, he clambered out of bed and started pacing up and down.

'Your Majesty,' said the boy, 'I have to leave now, but if you are still alive in a month, I shall return.'

The boy left the palace. With him gone, the king paced up and down day and night, ceasing only to sleep a few minutes from time to time, or to answer the call of nature.

All he could think about was the assassin in the cloak of invisibility, and how he might gain entrance into the royal apartment.

Unable to eat even a single grape through worry, the king paced on and on, his mind racing. On strict orders, no one was admitted into the royal bedchamber, for fear the assassin would slip in at the same time.

Precisely a month after his first visit, the boy returned to the palace. Given the king's panicky state, even he wasn't permitted entrance. Eventually, he managed to climb in through the window.

The king screamed.

'You've come to kill me!' he roared.

'No I have not,' the boy replied. 'If you remember, it was me who told you about the assassin. And, if you look at me, you'll see that I'm not wearing a cloak of invisibility.'

'Well,' the ruler stammered, 'if you look at me, you will see I'm still very much alive!'

'Yes,' the boy replied, 'and if you walk to the mirror over there, you will see that you are half the weight you were a month ago.'

'I didn't eat,' the king moaned. 'I was too fearful.'

The boy grinned from ear to ear.

'Now that I've cured your case of overeating,' he said, 'I shall take you into the mountains with me.'

'Why would I ever agree to that?' the king demanded petulantly.

'Because, you may think you have absolutely everything, but there's one thing you don't have,' he said.

'And what might that be?'

'A friend,' said the boy.

And so, the king and the boy went into the mountains together and became firm friends. The king offered to have the child buried in gold pieces, but the boy asked for the reward to be given to the poor.

When asked why, he answered:

'Because I've seen the sadness of money, and the joy of freedom.'

And, I am pleased to say that the king was never sorrowful again, and the little boy always had a sparkle in his eye, even when he grew into a man.

From: *The Arabian Nights Adventures*

Nasrudin's Vicissitudes

Shiraz, Iran

Return to Sender

Having toured Iran for many weeks, Nasrudin had almost run out of funds, and didn't have any money for a flight home.

Fearful that he would overstay his visa, he went to the post office.

'How much would it cost to send a parcel weighing sixty-two kilogrammes to this address abroad?'

'Airmail or by sea?' the clerk asked.

'By air.'

'One thousand, four hundred and five rials.'

The wise fool counted his money.

'That's fine,' he said. 'I'll pay you now, and will leave the parcel outside the post office in an hour.'

Paying the money, Nasrudin hurried to the market, bought a crate large enough to fit into, and took it back to the post office.

In the shade of the building, he punctured some holes in the crate's sides, and slapped 'fragile' stickers on them.

Then he wrote his home details on the lid.

The pen, which had been lying in the sun, was leaking, and ink splattered all over the address.

With time against him, Nasrudin clambered into the crate, and pleaded with a passer-by to nail down the lid.

'Are you sure?' the man asked.

The wise fool nodded.

Thinking he was doing a good deed, the passer-by did as he had been asked.

At that moment the post office porter heaved the crate onto his cart and, within the hour, it was in a van heading to their airport.

Inside the crate, Nasrudin beamed at having cheated the system yet again.

After one flight, and then another, the crate was off-loaded at a depot, and loaded onto another van.

Having reached the province to which the crate was supposed to be delivered, the driver tried to read the name of the town – which was hidden under the ink-splatter.

'Looks like *Dalohan*…?' he muttered. 'Where on earth could that be?'

'*Taloqan*, you stupid fool!' Nasrudin yelled from the crate.

The driver began shaking.

'What kind of phantom are you?!'

'I'm not a phantom, you idiot! I'm simply a parcel that wants to get home to his family!'

Assuming he was hearing things as a result of working too hard, the driver took out a rubber stamp, spat on it, and slapped it down on the crate:

RETURN TO SENDER

ADDRESS UNKNOWN

TAHIR SHAH

Tallahassee, Florida
Boxed Experience
As a young man, Nasrudin had no experience, which meant he couldn't get a job – because employers would only take on staff with experience.

The wise fool had all but given up hope when, on his travels through the Deep South, he spied a little advertisement in a local newspaper.

The advert claimed to be selling 'boxes of experience'. As the price was reasonable, Nasrudin sent off his money and waited impatiently for the package to arrive.

Weeks passed. Then, one spring morning, a large box was delivered.

Overwhelmed with glee, the wise fool opened it.

Instead of the mass of papers and manuals he'd expected, he found a scrap of paper on which was written:

You have paid a fortune for this which proves you're desperate.

No, we didn't leave anything out, so there's no reason to complain.

When you ordered the box, you were raw and now you are ripe.

Next time you are asked for an example of your experience, explain about buying this box, and the lesson it taught you – and watch with wonder as the doors to your life open wide.

Feeling rather gypped at having spent so much money on such a small piece of advice, Nasrudin put it to the back of his mind and got on with his journey.

A few days passed. Then, one afternoon, he spotted another little advertisement in a newspaper. This time, it was searching for an intern to work for next to nothing in return for experience.

The advert didn't say what the job was. Intrigued, Nasrudin applied and was called for an interview. When asked for his experience, he explained about the box he had bought, the one containing the message.

'You've got the job,' the interviewer said firmly.

'Really?! Thank you!'

'Now, I'm sure you're wondering what the job is,' the manager said.

The wise fool nodded.

'We place adverts in newspapers offering boxes of experience at sky-high prices,' the interviewer told him. 'Your job will be making the boxes, putting the experience message inside, and shipping them out to people stupid enough to buy them.'

Kolkata, India
Desperate Times

Having shunned all material possessions but not having received the largesse from a benefactor as he'd hoped, Nasrudin had no other choice but to take work as a *rickshawalla*.

He rented the ancient contraption and stood near the Oberoi Grand Hotel, waiting for a customer to hail him.

TAHIR SHAH

It wasn't long before a very large lady with a mountain of shopping called out.

When she had climbed aboard, the bags and parcels were heaved up into place on the passenger's lap.

Gritting his teeth, the wise fool grasped the handles and struggled to pull the rickshaw into the fray.

But he couldn't move it, not even a single inch.

Perched up on the seat, the customer offered a stream of insults.

'Even my husband's stronger than you,' she yelled, 'and he can't lift a feather!'

'Believe me, madam,' Nasrudin responded, 'I am pulling with all my strength.'

'Well, why can't you move it, then?!'

'Because "it" consists of the rickshaw, the shopping, and *you!*'

'If you knew yourself to be so scrawny, you shouldn't have taken a job as a *rickshawalla!*'

'Unfortunately, luck has been against me,' Nasrudin countered. 'And desperate times call for desperate measures, which is why I find myself standing here talking to you!'

El-Fayoum, Egypt
Fault of the Student
While searching for good camels for a journey across the desert, Nasrudin was directed to El-Fayoum, where the very best camels were said to be bought and sold.

It soon became clear that all the finest animals were owned by a miserly one-eyed dealer named Habib.

Despite bargaining hour after hour, the prices never went down.

In a bid to try a new tack, the wise fool tried to impress the merchant with stories of his adventures.

'One time I was stranded in the Thar Desert, and the local chief said he'd have me beheaded if I couldn't make him laugh. So, I did something no other man alive can do... I made my camels dance!'

Habib the camel dealer looked unimpressed.

'Don't believe it,' he grunted.

'But why not? It's absolutely true!'

Regarding the traveller with his single eye, Habib declared:

'If you can get any of my camels to dance, I'll give you whichever one you want for free.'

Next morning, Nasrudin picked a camel out from the herd, approached it slowly, and whispered in its ear. Then, staring deep into the animal's eye, he held up a forefinger and wagged it about.

An hour passed, but still the camel did not dance.

A second hour slipped by, in which Nasrudin grunted and groaned, and exchanged camels no less than five times.

Then, a third hour passed, with no sign of any dancing.

The only thing that happened, other than a crowd gathering as word of the dancing camels spread, was that a large male camel bit him on the ankle.

Infuriated, his pride severely dented, Nasrudin shook his fists in rage.

'What's the problem with your Egyptian camels?' he wailed. 'Camels in other countries are far better students than these!'

Agra, India
B-Movie

Nasrudin had managed to get a well-paid job for himself at the Taj Mahal, leading guided tours to American visitors.

One morning, while taking an especially large group of Californians to the mausoleum, he was overheard informing the visitors that the Taj Mahal had once been a pleasure palace to an ancient Aztec emperor.

'Picture the scene,' the wise fool said, 'jugglers, dancing girls, and courtesans, all of them here, and all of them from distant Mexico!'

The American visitors seemed confused.

'But everyone knows that the Taj was built as a burial place by the Mughal Emperor Shah Jehan for his beloved queen, Mumtaz Mahal,' one of them cried out.

Nasrudin winced, his eyes widening.

'You are Californians, are you not?'

Every head nodded.

'Well,' Nasrudin replied, 'as such, I assumed you'd want the B-movie version of history.'

Kathmandu, Nepal
It Is What It Is

Although a celebrated traveller, Nasrudin had a pitiable grasp of geography – a point which he tried to keep to himself as much as possible.

On a journey through Nepal, it came to the attention of a secondary school in the capital that the wise fool was visiting. The headteacher asked if he would take a break from his travels and teach geography for a term.

Flattered in a way he hadn't been flattered in a long time, the wise fool agreed, and was led to the class of teenagers awaiting him.

In the first lesson, he pointed to the large map of the world on the back wall of the classroom.

'Who can tell me what this place is?' he asked, pointing his baton at Australia.

'That's Australia, sir,' said a bright student at the front.

'Wrong!' he replied sternly. 'That is North America.'

Then, he pointed to North America and asked for its name.

A girl at the back put up her hand.

'North America, sir.'

'Wrong again!' Nasrudin called out. 'It's Africa!'

The process went on all afternoon, with the children calling out the right names, and their teacher insisting they were wrong.

Next day, the headteacher called the wise fool into his study.

'We have had complaints,' he said in a gruff voice. 'Some of your class complained to their parents, and they have complained to me.'

Fearful his lack of knowledge had been exposed, Nasrudin winced awkwardly.

'Who's to say what one place is and another is not?' he answered brightly.

The headteacher sighed.

'You were hired to teach geography,' he barked, 'not philosophy!'

Macau, China
Yamazamadooo!
An avid gambler, Nasrudin had been banned from all the casinos in Europe and the United States.

Fearing he would never be able to get to a gaming table again, he heard that Macau was so in need of gamblers that the territory never barred anyone.

Boarding a flight, he touched down at the airport and, within the hour, had taken his place at a splendid roulette wheel.

At first, all was well.

The wise fool handed over his money and was presented with a big stack of chips.

Then, placing them with care on the grid of numbers, he listened as the ball began to bounce around on the spinning roulette wheel.

As it slowed and clicked about, he thrust both arms above his head and yelled:

'Yamazamadooo! Yamazamadooo! Yamazamadooo!'

As if by magic, a butch-looking security guard appeared, and ordered the gambler to cease his disturbance.

Nasrudin seemed glum.

'But without my little rituals,' he moaned, 'how am I ever expected to win?'

Paracas, Peru
The Great White Shark

From the moment he'd swallowed the Komodo dragon, Nasrudin felt queasy and weak.

Indeed, the biliousness was unlike anything he had ever experienced. Even though he'd not experienced intestinal equilibrium since swallowing a bluebottle, the Komodo dragon had been the final straw.

And so, after consulting a backstreet oracle in the Indonesian capital, the wise fool travelled to the Peruvian coast and waited for a great white shark to put an end to all his problems.

As any scrawny example of humanity that's waited for a great white to find them knows, great whites are notoriously eager to feast on them.

Exactly a minute and a half after stepping into the water at Paracas, Nasrudin spied the dorsal fin of a great white zigzagging through the water towards him.

Ten seconds of silent trepidation followed.

Then, the moment of impact.

Now skilled in directing an advancing predator to his throat, Nasrudin swished to the side in the nick of time...

The great white shark hurtled into his mouth and was soon in his stomach.

Whooping with joy, the wise fool paddled out of the water. Once he was on the sand, he gave thanks to Providence, for ending the run of misfortune that had begun when he'd swallowed a bluebottle long, long before.

Ashkhabad, Turkmenistan
Same Imagination

Since early childhood, Nasrudin had possessed an over-developed sense of imagination.

While the other children were playing out in the fields, he was sitting in his room, sketching intricate patterns. His parents feared their son would never make anything of himself, because all he could do was draw patterns.

Time passed.

One day, Nasrudin found a workshop in which Oriental carpets were being woven by a master craftsman. The expert showed off his stock to Nasrudin and demonstrated the way he took patterns from a sketchbook and conjured them into carpets.

Day after day, the wise fool would visit the master.

A little at a time, he learned the secret techniques of weaving the most intricate carpets ever made.

The years slipped by, and Nasrudin became a celebrated carpet-maker in his own right. Kings, queens, and presidents sought him out. However famous he became, the wise fool retained his sense of modesty, a point that went down well with the well-born and the rich.

Every year, Nasrudin's carpets became all the more intricate, while he himself appeared to be even more modest than before.

One day, he received a commission from the President of Turkmenistan. A fan of all things Turkmen, he completed the carpet, and travelled with it to the palace.

Unrolled in the throne room, Nasrudin's creation was admired by the president.

'I've never seen such astounding work!' he declared. 'Your imagination is really a thing of wonder.'

Bowing modestly, the wise fool blushed.

'It's really nothing,' he replied in little more than a whisper. 'In fact, it's less than nothing. I am ashamed to say that it's not my best work. Indeed, it's an utter abhorrence. If I were you, Mr. President, I would give the order for me to be clapped in irons, dragged to the dungeons, and tortured on a special machine used only to punish wayward carpet-makers like myself. Then, I'd have me flayed with canes made from the roots of monkey puzzle trees, and after that have me plunged into a vat of boiling bat vomit!'

The president looked at the carpet-maker in horror.

'Forgive me, sir,' whimpered Nasrudin. 'It's the same imagination that created the carpet getting the better of me again.'

Riyadh, Saudi Arabia
Selfish Courage

Nasrudin's life of adventure had seen him lauded as one of the most decorated military officials of his generation.

Having survived more campaigns than anyone could remember, he was frequently asked to speak to students all over the world. His lectures covered the subjects of war, peace and, most of all, courage.

At one event, a thousand school children packed into a large, air-conditioned auditorium. With rapt attention, they listened to the wise fool's address.

After much applause, a boy at the front raised his hand.

'Commander Nasrudin, I'd like to ask you what courage is.'

'I will tell you,' the soldier replied in a flash. 'Courage is selfishness.'

'What do you mean, sir?' the child called back.

'Well, if I was to die in battle,' Nasrudin elucidated, 'the man next to me would get my rations. That is a state of affairs I would not wish to happen. Rather, I want him to get killed so I can get my hands on *his* rations.'

'So, the courage that's been responsible for making you a war hero was all down to hoping for extra rations of food?'

Nasrudin frowned awkwardly.

'Some things in life are wonderful when considered from close up,' he said, 'but far less attractive when viewed at a distance.'

Nyaung Ohak, Myanmar
Honest Bait

Nasrudin had been exploring the ancient temple structures at Nyaung Ohak, overgrown as they were with foliage, creepers and vines.

Just as he was about to make his way back to the path, he spotted the most beautiful butterfly with iridescent wings soaking up the sun on the branch of a tree.

With great care, he approached.

'Stay there so I can catch you,' he whispered.

To his surprise, the insect answered back:

'So you can stick a pin through me, fix me to a board, put me in a frame, and hang me on a wall?'

'No, no, no,' Nasrudin stammered. 'I promise it wouldn't be like that!'

The butterfly let out a grunt.

'Then what would you do with me?'

'I'd take you back to my country and…'

'*And*…?'

'And keep you as a pet.'

'That's a lie!'

'No it's not.'

'Yes, it is, and we both know it!'

'OK OK! You're right! It's a lie!' Nasrudin admitted. 'But how am I expected to catch anything with the truth?'

Damascus, Syria
Knowing Your Ways

Nasrudin flew into Damascus in the middle of the night and was horrified to find that his suitcase was not waiting for him at the carousel.

Undeterred, he simply grabbed someone else's luggage, making sure that it bore the same general look. The way he figured it, anyone with a suitcase like his would have the same clothes.

From the airport, the wise fool took a taxi to Bab Tooma and made his way to the guesthouse he had booked. Once in his room, he put the case on the bed and opened it up.

To his surprise, the luggage was filled with terribly inferior clothes, none of which fitted him. Incensed that he had been put out so badly, Nasrudin fumbled for the luggage label, and saw there was a phone number given.

He dialled the number.

'How dare you have such terrible taste!' he yelled.

'Who is this?' said a concerned voice on the other end.

'I'm the person who took your suitcase. *Why?* Well, it's obvious... I couldn't see my case, so I took yours. After all, it's just about the same size and colour as mine.'

The owner of the case was about to launch into an attack and demand his luggage back, when Nasrudin cut him off:

'I can't believe you expected me to deal with such rotten clothing as yours! It's a disgrace!'

There was silence for a moment, while the man at the other end registered what was happening.

'How the hell can you be complaining?!' he screamed. 'After all, you're the thief who stole my case!'

'I have every right to complain,' bellowed Nasrudin.

'No you don't!'

'Yes I do!'

'How on earth could you reason that?' the owner of the suitcase yelled.

'Because if the tables were turned... and it was you who stole my case... I'd expect you to complain to me.'

'Wait a minute... You're complaining because you think I would have complained?'

'Yes,' sniffed Nasrudin.

The rightful owner of the case could hardly speak, such was his rage.

'How the hell d'you know what I would do in the circumstances?! You don't even know me!'

Nasrudin cast an eye over the belongings that were not his.

'Maybe I didn't know you at the start of the call,' he answered icily, 'but I've got a pretty firm idea now of what you're like!'

Doha, Qatar
Different Luck

Nasrudin had learned from a local magazine that a fortune could be made in the oil fields of Qatar.

A prospector at heart, he dropped everything, flew to the desert emirate, and arrived at the Oil Ministry.

TAHIR SHAH

The official in charge took his paperwork, then asked how much land he intended to acquire for the search for oil.

'Three square feet should do me,' Nasrudin replied brightly.

The clerk balked.

'Are you out of your mind?'

'Perhaps,' the wise wool responded, 'but I hardly think it has a bearing on my current activity.'

'How do you expect to have any luck in discovering natural reserves in such a tiny plot of land?'

Nasrudin shrugged.

'It may be a small area to you,' he responded snootily, 'but in my family we're blessed with a different kind of luck.'

From: *The Voyages and Vicissitudes of Nasrudin*

Finis